JOURNAL-LETTERS FROM THE ORIENT

JOURNAL-LETTERS
FROM THE ORIENT

BY

CLARA KATHLEEN ROGERS
(CLARA DORIA)

Edited, with Introductory Letters
and Supplementary Notes, by
HENRY MUNROE ROGERS

WITH ILLUSTRATIONS

PRIVATELY PRINTED AT THE
PLIMPTON PRESS · MCMXXXIV

PRINTED IN THE UNITED STATES OF AMERICA

FOREWORD

IN " The Story of Two Lives " privately printed and issued from the press in 1933, Clara Kathleen Rogers, my beloved wife, alluded to the fact that she had, during our journeyings in the Orient, written letters either to her sister in London or to my sister in Boston of our daily happenings. From time to time she read these letters to friends who expressed their interest at the vivid descriptions of persons, places, incidents of travel, and other things seen through the eyes of one who was viewing eastern countries for the first time.

It has been a desire on my part that these letters should be preserved in print. They are now privately printed as a part of " The Story of Two Lives."

H. M. R.

INTRODUCTORY

I T WAS in the summer of 1903 that we — my husband and I — accepted an invitation from our old friend, Mrs. Phoebe A. Hearst, of California, to spend the summer with her at her beautiful Hacienda, situated at Pleasanton, somewhat over thirty miles from San Francisco. I happened, one day, to tell her that the first thing Harry did, on arriving at San Francisco, was to make inquiries about the sailings of the different steamers for Japan in October; upon hearing which, Mrs. Hearst exclaimed: " Are you really thinking of going to Japan? "

" Yes," replied Harry, " to Japan, China, India, and as much more of the Orient as we can take in."

" How strange! " she exclaimed. " It is the very thing I have been longing to do, but never was there such a propitious moment for starting on such a journey as now; this happens to be the one time when I could see my way to absenting myself from home for a prolonged trip. Will you let me go with you? "

Of course, the prospect of her company was only too delightful to us, so we arranged then and there to start in October as soon as possible after the wedding of her niece, Anne Apperson, which was to be celebrated at the Hacienda.

C. K. R.

LIST OF ILLUSTRATIONS

INTRODUCTORY LETTERS

BY HENRY MUNROE ROGERS

explaining how a trip to California
became an Odyssey of the Orient

we pushed to this point and spent the night, though we had not a tooth brush or a " nighty " between us.

You ought to have come up the zigzag on a mule, the road only wide enough for a mule to walk and our party in single file, and the precipices and abysses thousands of feet below us, and not a foot from the mule's hind legs! As you looked down the chasm, and then at the mule's feet, you came to the conclusion that it was a tight fit for room, but not at all! Plenty of room and to spare, said the mule! And there was. Well, if our hair had not been glued on pretty tight we might have been bald this A.M.

Hacienda del Pozo de Verona, Pleasanton, Cal.
[*July 9th*, 1903

It is a month today since we left Boston, and we certainly have crowded our days since then with everything possible and within the reach of our minds, hearts, and understandings. I telegraphed to you from Raymond on Thursday P.M. the 2nd of July, as we reached that place in our exit from the Yosemite trip, and as we came to the railroad once more. We had ridden that day forty-five miles by stage or mountain wagon from Wawona, where we had spent a part of two days, visiting the Big Trees and otherwise disporting ourselves. Our ride had been somewhat hot and dusty, — the thermometer at Raymond stood 115° in the shade that day, — yet we had not suffered especially; some discomfort, of course, but nothing worth mentioning in a trip which had been so full of interest and of wonders.

Let me say that our whole experience in the Yosemite was almost beyond description or expression. You cannot exaggerate either the wonder or the beauty of the Valley and its environment. The individual view may be equalled, possibly, of some waterfall, dome, peak, or

what not, but the ensemble is simply beyond comparison. In this the Valley differs in essentials from all my
other experiences. You cannot look anywhere in that
broad valley without exclaiming aloud at the beauty of
it all, and when you get to mountain tops and see the
reaches and miles of other mountains and snow caps,
you realize anew the wonderful beauty, as well as grandeur of it all. Beauty and grandeur together are a rare
combination. you are apt to get the awesome in Nature
without at the same time having the impression of
beauty. But in the broad sweep you have the exquisite
waterfalls — poems and dreams of beauty — with rich
verdure and wondrous domes; cathedral spires and pin-
nacles rising to the Heaven of Heaven and reflecting the
light of sun or moon, at rise or set, as if somehow there
was a joy in it; and, way in the beyond, the cold, silent
snow peaks and miles of snow, proclaiming such an in-
finitude of quiet and repose, that it is not so much awe
as love that sweeps over you, and the tears come to your
eyes, and you get a lump in your throat, and you think
of the Psalms and " how wonderful are Thy works."
One cannot come out of that valley of the clay he goes
into it! For all time, consciously or unconsciously, he
must be a different human being!

On Friday A.M. we were at San Francisco once more,
and after a day there with Mrs. Hearst we all came to
the Hacienda in the afternoon.

Let me say a word that I omitted to say above. We
left the Valley on Tuesday, June 30, and spent that night
at Wawona, twenty-six miles off, and the next day gave
to the Big Trees. No tongue can tell the spell that comes
over one in the presence of these wonders, in their quiet
woods and forests, some six hundred of them, with great
white pines and other trees, as their companions. You

get the overwhelming conviction of a past that belongs
to nothing else I have yet seen. It has taken thousands
of years for these trees to grow, and your mind gets into
the consideration of the thought, *these* were centuries
before Christ walked the earth; before Rome and Greece
had their maturity: when Egypt and Assyria held sway,
and by the time you have walked or driven inside some
of these silent giants, you begin to wonder why some
poet has not made them talk, if they themselves were
condemned to silence. I say to you unreservedly that
to take lunch among these gentlemen — named after
states, generals, scientists, etc. — seemed very mun-
dane, though their grateful shade and an *appetite* convinced you that was just the thing to be done at the
moment!

Think of sardines and boiled eggs, sandwiches and
fruit pie *and* the Big Trees, on the same day! As Mr.
Dickens remarks, " Here's Richness! "

On the Fourth of July we had a great gathering here
and a barbecue. Mrs. Hearst had chartered a special
train from San Francisco or Oakland, and her guests began to assemble at about eleven o'clock at the Hacienda,
when carriages took the whole party to her live-oak
grove, on the hill, perhaps half a mile from the house.
Here, since three A.M., the fires in a pit, twenty-five feet
long, five or six feet deep and four or five feet wide, had
been settling live-oak coals as a basic fire, which had
heated the bottom stones and sides of the stones lining
the pit. A bed of live coals, over which, as we got there,
the barbecue cooks had great spits across the top of the
pit and resting on stones, rounds of beef, halves of sheep,
or legs and shoulders of lamb; and the men, on each side
walked along and turned over the spits, walking the
length of the pit and then returned to repeat the process,

a little gravy and fat dripping into the coals meanwhile. By this process the outside of beef or lamb is *coated,* and then all the juices go into the beef and mutton, making the cooking the very best I have ever known anywhere. Such beef and mutton, chickens, roast corn, roast potatoes, I never tasted. It was like eating poetized beef and mutton. I had supposed a barbecue meant in effect a lot of underdone or raw meat or overdone and burnt meat, but these experts were " past masters " in the art.

The oak grove, with four-hundred-years-old trees and two great tables beneath them, and the servants already spreading the edibles, and the great bowls of lemonade or hock cup, with tents and hammocks and seats built in the trees, and the children wild with delight on one donkey here and drawn in the donkey cart there, and the young fellows and girls in a match game of baseball, and old and young, rich and poor, gentle and simple, wandering around, with the sweetest and dearest hostess the mind of man could conceive beaming on everybody, seeing to everybody, thinking of everybody — made such a scene as you read about and seldom see. Learned professors and their wives in the very heart of everything, their children about them, and people not professors, all on the same pleasure intent.

You must always bear in mind that the weather is perfect. Bright sun, cool breezes. Like the ideal days of June. Today, for example, the weather is exquisite, thermometer at half past eight (breakfast hour here) 64° in the shade of the piazza. You take long walks in the sun with the thermometer at 80° and you come back refreshed, get into your tub, get into fresh clothes, and you are game for anything. No exhaustion. We have not had a shower since we left, I believe. We lost our umbrella in the Yosemite, forgetting we had one!

THE HACIENDA DEL POSO DE VERONA

Mrs. Phoebe A. Hearst's home in Pleasanton County, California

Then came the dinner and such fun! I made the only speech of the day, in toasting our elected Queen to whom we pledged our love and loyalty and crowned Phoebe the First, the Last, the Only! She gave me the seat of honor by her side on her right, and opposite me and on her left was a Captain Bradford, of San Francisco, formerly in the Confederate Navy. He and I, at a certain stage of the dinner, escorted each other to the band (I forgot to tell you we had a band from San Francisco) and requested the leader to play " The Star Spangled Banner." By Jove, how they did play it, and how we all sang and cheered!

Towards four o'clock back to the Hacienda and more music and out-of-door lemonade, and a Virginia reel which I led with the Dear Queen, and when I suggested she might be tired, after the first figure, " Not at all," she said, and on we went to the end. God bless her sweet heart and soul! As I proposed her health and our love and loyalty, she standing there meanwhile like a surprised child, people mopped their eyes, for many there knew things in their own lives which she had never told, where she had been the God-given, loving heart that had been their strength and support. Whole families which owed their present happiness and possibilities of self support and of growth to her bounty and thoughtfulness.

Well, after the lunch, the special took some ninety of the guests away, leaving only the house party here over Sunday, and we separated for a little rest and to dress for dinner. There must have been one hundred and twenty people or more at the dinner, and many a family in the neighborhood not only partook of the dinner but also of the barbecue joints in their own homes. She never forgets anything or anybody. The last message I heard her give was to see to it that the conductor of the special

train, the brakeman, the fireman, and engineer were
" remembered."

In this Aladdin's Lamp of a place we are to remain at
present until Tuesday next, the 14th, when the Queen
sends us as her guests to the Del Monte at Monterey,
there to await her coming on the 23rd for a brief stay
with us there. She has to go on the 13th to Wyntoon,
near Shasta, about the Castle, which is delayed in the
decorating and furnishing, and where they say she is
needed. She will spend about a week on her journey.
After that, to Monterey first and afterwards to the Hacienda again. You can imagine nothing more beautiful
than the Hacienda these moonlight nights.

Pleasanton, Cal., July 12th, 1903
I WRITE this letter especially to say that we have under
consideration the extension of our travels to Japan,
China, India and Egypt, leaving Vancouver on October
5 for Japan on " The Empress of India." The reason especially for choosing this year is that Mrs. Hearst wants
to go *now,* this year, that is, and she has written to Clara
Anthony [3] to accompany her and she wishes us to join
the party. We have been talking this over for a week or
two, and last evening she came to her decision.

Pleasanton, Cal., July 24th, 1903
ON Tuesday A.M. last, the 21st, while we were break-
fasting at Del Monte, we received word that somebody
wished us at the telephone, and on going there I found
that Miss Egan, Mrs. Hearst's secretary, and a lady
whom we have grown very much attached to, wanted to
say that Mrs. Hearst was then at Hearst Building, having arrived from Wyntoon that A.M.; that she wished us
to come up from Del Monte, if we would like to, and go

[3] Mrs. Nathan Anthony, of Boston.

to the Hacienda the next day, on her special train, with the Italian ambassador, Signor Des Planches, and others who were to be her guests at lunch at the Hacienda. That Mrs. Hearst would like to have us come if we had finished our visit at Del Monte, and if not to come any-way, and perhaps we would all return to Del Monte for a week or so together there when we could find the time to do it.

We could not catch the A.M. train for San Francisco, so we took one at 6.40 P.M. and at 10.40 were in San Francisco, where a carriage was in waiting for us, and we went to the Hearst Building for the night. Mrs. Hearst had preceded us to the Hacienda.

The next morning we dressed and joined the party at the ferry (you know you have to land at Oakland when you come to S. F. from the East, and take the ferry to S. F. and take the ferry out of S. F. when you want to go northward; this is our route always to Verona, — near Pleasanton), and then there occurred a very interesting meeting. While crossing, a gentleman looked at me very hard, and then came to me and said, "This *is* Mr. Rogers. I saw the back of your head in the glass and knew it was you, but thought I would better see your face to make sure! " It was Mr. Thomas Bridgewater, a barrister of London, who, with his brother and whole family, were always most polite to us in London, and he and his brother are very intimate with Frank and Belle Macomber who always stay with them in London. We had parted in London and he had come to San Francisco by way of India and Japan with his bride, who was then with him on the boat, and to whom we were at once intro-duced. I was so glad to see him. Of course we wanted him to join us, but he had a lunch party to attend. He and his wife are going to visit Frank and Belle, and Mrs.

Hearst is going to invite them to the Hacienda tomorrow.

We continued our journey, and soon the Italian ambassador and Count Grimain and Mr. and Mrs. Clark and Miss Wheeler (a dear girl who is now staying at the Hacienda) and Prof. Gayley and his wife and others, were all very busy chattering in various languages. When we arrived, the carriages met us, and we went to the Hacienda and took the guests around and into the music room, where we had a little music and then a very jolly lunch; then rides to the stables and the live-oak grove, and the guests were sent off to San Francisco in a special at about $4\frac{1}{2}$ o'clock. They had a wonderful time, and could not say enough of the charm of the hostess and the royal reception given them.

It is exquisitely beautiful here, and we return to it with joy and ever-increasing pleasure. The climate is so delicious and so smiling, with cool breezes, and the flowers and trees are always so wonderful. We walked today down to the kennels to see Admiral and Heather Mint and their four puppies. The Admiral and his wife are superb collies, both prize winners and of high pedigree. Then there are other dogs, but not many as the kennel is dispersed. Mrs. Hearst used to have eighty-five dogs in her kennels, all of superb breeding and pedigree!

Pleasanton, Cal., July 27th, 1903
MY LETTER of the 12th inst. informing you of our contemplated visit to the Orient was naturally a surprise to you. It was a surprise to us to go and to me to write it. On the day I reached San Francisco, and before I had been on the streets *alone* for an hour, I had already investigated the subject of Japan, China, and India; had interviewed steamship companies; had obtained dates

of sailing, etc., etc. of various lines, and was reasonably fixed in my determination to go to the East if I could get Kathleen's [4] assent. When we talked over the matter together there seemed to be so many " lions in the path," at least to her, that I simply let matters drop and drift, relying upon my belief, too deeply rooted to be easily overcome, that if we were to go it would be made clear in good time. Soon after, Mrs. Hearst began to talk about the East, and her desire to go and *to go now,* and I then told her what had happened, and what I had done. I confided to her that as Anno Domini was running rapidly against me, and as for thirty-five years it had been my dream to go to the East and my determination to do it sometime, that *now* was my time. She said, " I will send for Clara Anthony, and we will all go together, if you are agreed." She at once began to clear her path of the million lions in her way, and I began to give notice to those interested of our intention to sail in October — for I soon made the day and date fixed so far as possible. *Now,* it is " The Doric " from San Francisco, and not Vancouver, October 7th, please God! By Honolulu to Japan and not by Vancouver and the northern route.

We are all of us working quietly in the direction of going some two months hence. Meanwhile, we will see what comes up!

Pleasanton, Cal., July 29th, 1903

MRS. HEARST told us yesterday a funny thing which I repeat. The newsboys had a meeting of their club to elect a treasurer. They did not have absolute confidence in each other, and after a debate one of the little fellows piped up: " Say, what's the matter with that Phoebe

[4] Mrs. Henry M. Rogers.

Hearst? " " Holy Gee! " cried another, " If we make her treasurer we won't have to pay no dues! " " Oh, shoot it! " said a third. " We can't have no women! " Mrs. Hearst was delighted to learn that she was at least considered trustworthy and that she had " honorable mention."

Pleasanton, Cal., Aug. 3rd, 1903

ON SATURDAY our friends Mr. and Mrs. Bridgewater, of London, fresh from India, China, and Japan, and their friend, Mrs. Probert, whom they are visiting in San Francisco, came to us here to stay until Monday afternoon, and we have had a most charming visit from them. We have, as it were, already travelled to India, to Java, to China, and to Japan; have met their friends; have interviewed the servant who had them in his keeping in India, and with note book and maps have done what we could to get a distinct itinerary in our minds — at least *I* have; for as this is to be " a personally conducted party," and as I am " the only gent," I am taking it upon myself to see to things myself.

My general plan is to go with reasonable speed only; to see what we can see of the best pretty thoroughly, and leave what cannot be seen till *next time;* to avoid fatigue and worry for all concerned; not to overdo anywhere, and especially, in hot countries, and to use all reasonable precautions to keep rested, well, and capable of enjoyment wherever we may go. This going travelling to make it " lightning express," to hurry everywhere and to bring back only hurried impressions, does not appeal to us.

We have already changed entirely the basis of our objective point and the length of our absence, to make other and better plans, perhaps. For the moment it is agreed, first, to leave here October 7, reaching Honolulu about the 12th, and Yokohama about October 26th. To visit principally northern Japan in the chrysanthemum and maple season, and to shorten our stay there somewhat, leaving Nagasaki for Shanghai about November 10th; visit Hongkong and Canton by the 17th, and then push for Colombo (Island of Ceylon) *via* Singapore, reaching Colombo say December 3rd or 4th. Then cross to India, engaging " Daniel " and another Indian servant in advance to meet us at Colombo, to look after us and our luggage while we are in India. To give, say, two weeks to country south of Madras and to Madras itself; thence to Bombay and the places *en route* about three weeks; thence to Agra and Delhi and Lahore, and, if we conclude to go to Peshawar and Khyber Pass and Cashmere and the north, to stay up there till March first; thence to Calcutta and Darjeeling, where we inspect the Himalayas; thence to Rangoon in Burmah; thence to Penang, Singapore, Hongkong, and back to Shanghai; and then visit Pekin *via* Tientsin; thence to Japan again for the cherry blossoms in April, and back to San Francisco by May, and home.

This leaves out our Egyptian pilgrimage, and about this we can speak later. Mrs. Hearst would like to be back here in May, and we shall be ready to do as she says for many reasons — some of which are, that by this course we shall have an extra time in India and Japan, getting good views of these countries under most favorable conditions of season, and particularly getting Japan in chrysanthemum and *also* in cherry-blossom season. Mrs. Hearst feels that Egypt should be reserved to a time when certain things are farther advanced there than they can be by next February, and by hurrying from India for Egypt we should lose much there in India

and yet not get in Egypt all we might get at a later period. Again, the length of absence will be much less, and
her affairs here, her building of the great Mine Building
for the University of California, the memorial to Mr.
Hearst, and other things may need a glance of her eye,
etc., etc. For me, of course, to take a shorter journey and
have another at some other time, God willing, will suit
me. Well, the Bridgewaters and we have gone over our
general plan, and it meets the approval of all concerned.
So you can all of you now get down your maps and begin
to study your geography lesson. That's what I am doing, among other things.

On Sunday evening, as we were about to retire, and
while we were all bidding each other good night, we had
a distinct shock of an earthquake. It felt, as Dorie describes it, as if we were on a ferry boat, and it had suddenly gone against the pier and was rocking. The hanging lamps swung, and there was a shaking of things,
without any damage, though some plaster was shaken
out in one of the upper rooms. It was rather uncomfortable withal! The books say that in Japan these things
are of frequent occurrence.

Bohemia, Cal., Aug. 8th, 1903

HERE I am, having passed my first night in the Grove!
That I still live to tell the tale is due to the fact that I
have *not* accepted all the invitations and courtesies that
have been extended to me. Mr. Deering and his chum,
Mr. Stowe, and Mr. Stowe's brother and I have the
superb and prized tent upon the hill, to which we can
retire when the mood comes over us to sleep, and where
we are reasonably far from " the madding crowd," but
not too far to get the sounds of revelry by day and night.
There is no possibility of exaggerating the wondrous

beauty, the hearty good fellowship and the joyousness of the outing of the Bohemian Club, and I wish to record for you some of my first impressions while they are first.

I left the ferry at eight yesterday A.M. and took the train for Guerneville (I believe that is the name of the place), and, arriving there at about eleven-fifteen, took train that runs directly to Bohemia and the Grove. On the train I met Mr. Marsh, and a Mr. Jenks introduced himself to me, having been told by Mr. Deering that I was to be on the train. I was introduced also to others, and I shall have to recall names later and after conference with Mr. Deering. He met me at the train, and we went to the tent together, walking through the Grove.

It is positively impossible to describe this Grove, of great redwood trees — only second in size and beauty to the Wawona trees. The natural grove has been preserved, and tree after tree rises above you from one hundred and seventy-five to three hundred feet and upwards, with diameters of fifteen or twenty or thirty feet, and with all the glory of light and shade, of grandeur and mystery and undisclosed wisdom that you feel at Wawona. Every minute of the day one gets new vistas, for the hills — not quite mountains — rise up in gradual slopes all around the Grove, wooded to the extreme tops, so that the vistas of trees from every coign of vantage are of bewildering frequency and beauty.

Around the Grove of the immediate headquarters, so to speak, tree after tree and group after group of trees stand like sentinels everywhere, and in the midst is an enormous circle of seats, ten in number and twenty feet long, hewn with an axe by a single woodman from a single fallen tree, and the first seat made about fifty feet from the roots. The axe that did the business is fastened into one of the seats, in a groove made for it, and sunk so as to show axe and handle and all complete.

These seats are, as I have said, ranged in an enormous circle, over which, seventy-five or one hundred feet up, the spreading branches of great trees act as shade, and through which at night, here and there, you catch glimpses of the stars, and of the moonlight piercing the gloom, and making effects that are simply indescribable.

In the middle of this circle is built the enormous camp fire — logs of redwood, eight feet long, piled up and kept going all night, or at any rate until I left last night. The stage of the High Jinks is a little way off, and the stage of the Low Jinks not a great way farther, and on the opposite side of the main avenue.

There are now upwards of two hundred men here, and the next train and later trains will bring nearly two hundred more, the largest attendance ever known.

As you enter the Grove from the train, a great flag hangs across the way with the Owl — the emblem of the Club — to greet you. An Indian, cast by Aiken, the sculptor, stands against another tree, with the deep background of a burnt-out redwood and the effect is wonderful. Here and there are streets on which are signs with absolutely unintelligible names — this High Jinks being Aztec the streets have already become mysteriously obscure. The tents, the homes, are variously named: " Home of the Feeble-Minded," for example or Dr. Cook's tent (tepee) " Xops & Scotxs. or " Chops and Scotches," as X = ch, and many others. At the barber's shop is the sign, " Hair cut and shave while you wait! "

Yesterday I arrived in time for lunch. The tables were spread in great circles, under the trees, one circle within another, so as to make room. An awning covers part of this. The lunch was from the *chef* of the Club and waiters from the Club and assistants. Everything was good, and service sufficient for the purpose. I got a seat with Stowe and Deering, had my napkin and ring given me, and was then one of them. I was introduced right and left, and at lunch and afterward had some delightful hours with Mr. Charles Field, Mr. Lesser, the musician, Prof. Stephens or Stevens of the University of California, Ben Greet of London (" Everyman " manager), Dr. Rosenstern (I think), a charming man, Mayor Phelan, Capt. Fletcher, Mr. Barbour, Nat Goodwin, the actor, and lots of others.

In the P.M. I put myself under the direction of Dr. Rosenstern and Mr. Field (a cousin of Eugene Field), who reminds me curiously of Appleton Brown, and we went in swimming in the river pool. The river near the camp has been dammed, and the water flows through the swimming pool, which is hundreds and hundreds of feet long and too long a swim across for me to try. Such fun and such antics in the water! A professional was there to look after things, and the " stunts " in swimming and the fun of the bathers was most contagious. We got home to the tent and fixed up by brushing our hair, and got ready for dinner at 6 P.M., and here I must stop and go to lunch.

I came back from lunch with " Uncle George " Bromley. He is only eighty-six. He confided to me that night before last he did not retire till three-twenty A.M. Friday, and last night he did not retire till three-thirty of Saturday A.M. He is a lively young fellow to try to keep up with.

Along the street to lunch tables — Montezuma Street — are various artistic designs of great merit. At one place, on a tree, the figure of one of the Club at a table on which is a large pitcher marked " fresh water." The club figure represents this gentleman warning a crowd with glasses in their hands to *abstain*. Nearby is a package marked W.C.T.U. (Women's Christian Temperance Union). On another tree is a well known member of the Club throwing out his chest with the word " Ma-tzuma," the title of the Low Jinks play.

Well, last evening was wonderful. The piano is on a platform within the circle, but on the edge of it, within plain sight of everybody, and here, with the glare of the campfire on the faces of the spectators and the nearly full moon glimpsing here and there through the foliage, we sat till nearly midnight. Mr. Lesser played Chopin's " Nocturne " exquisitely and another piece, familiar, but name not recalled; then quartettes, recitations, songs and dances followed as man after man appeared in answer to summons. Nat Goodwin gave a splendid imitation of Billy Crane, Stuart Robson, Sir Henry Irving, Joseph Jefferson, in the Leblanc song, from the extravaganza of " Evangeline," music of which was written by Ned Rice of the Papyrus Club, and libretto by J. Cheever Goodwin, also of the Papyrus, when we were all young together and knew things — among other things Leblanc's song. It was a great delight to me.

The table of the artists, covered with all kinds of painters' supplies, is on Montezuma Street, or near it. Canvases are hung, and artists are at work day and night, making pictures of all sorts and kinds, burlesque, portraits, scenes for the theatre, etc. And some of the work is *fine:* imaginative and full of suggestion. It is the real essence of Bohemia. Meanwhile, day and night, at any old time, a few fellows will get at the piano and give songs and dances and choruses just for fun, while a crowd of fellows are sitting around in the circle listening and

applauding. Everybody follows his own sweet will and
goes and comes as he pleases. It is an outdoor and enlarged Tavern Club spirit.

Well, I went to bed, the last man of our tent, or of our
two tents, for the parts of the tent have a space for two
cots each, with flaps separate and a table between; and
as I am told I did not wake anybody up, I suppose I was
in my right mind. Some of " the boys " did not have
time to go to bed last night, and held a meeting at four-
thirty this A.M. to decide whether it was worth while to
go to bed at that hour anyway!

It was such goodfellowship and fun all the time that
you could not help feeling the joy of it. The man who is
too old for this kind of a time, either because of his years,
or because his heart is dry as summer's dust, would better stay away! But to one to whom the wondrous mystery of the trees is enough of inspiration for all the rest,
this is an occasion to which his memory will come back
lovingly to the very end of time.

These trees, and the marvellous beauty of them! As
I look out now from the writing-room tent, and see the
light of the sun brightening the carpet of fallen brown
leaves and spears and needles from the trees themselves,
and hear the orchestra, just arrived from San Francisco,
rehearsing the overture to the High Jinks, it is a sight
never to be forgotten.

Pleasanton, Cal., Sept. 14th, 1903

Here we are in the throes of preparation for the wedding tomorrow. Carpenters, decorators, florists, and a
host of others, male and female, are working day and
night and Sundays to get all things ready. Will Hearst
and his bride are to arrive this A.M. with Mrs. Hearst,
who went to San Francisco to see them and to welcome

them yesterday. They are putting up an altar in the music room and enclosed is a bit of the carpet of the flooring of the altar.

Pleasanton, Cal., Sept. 16*th,* 1903

THERE were, I think, twenty-three at dinner, and for the night at the Hacienda, William Hearst and his bride; Orrin Peck, their friend and almost brother, for Will and Orrin were brought up together and slept together as boys and all that; the bride elect and Dr. Flint, the groom; Mr. Balfour, the best man; Miss Woolworth, " the best woman," or whatever else she may be called; and lots of others. I believe the mother and sister and brother and others of Dr. Flint's relatives were at lunch only, and went home and came up on the " special " for the wedding yesterday.

We were all up bright and early for the wedding yesterday (the 15th), and such a radiant day, so bright and joyous and beautiful you can hardly imagine. Of course I was bathed and shaved and shirted and cravatted and made to look as much like " the best man " very early, and Alice and Robert and Charles and Louise, and all the servants around laughed to see me in my white vest and tie proclaiming my entire fitness to be married or anything! Dorie and I got ourselves ready so as to leave our rooms for the coming guests to prink in. Dorie looked like a darling. She had on a new dress, which was a foulard satin of golden brown on a ground of white, with a little touch of black in the pattern, trimmed with medallions of black lace let in. I have just asked her and she has given me the correct description — whatever it may mean. But she looked like a love, and was so helpful and interested that I was quite ready to go to the altar or elsewhere with her.

By the way, I had presented to her her own brooch the day of my arrival, a fleur de lis of pearls with amethyst pendant, and she had worn it at dinner where it had been entirely approved. Then I had my brooch for Lilias, and Dorie thought that very sweet and appropriate, and I wrote a little note to Lilias (Wheeler), telling her that I didn't see why, just because people were getting married, her Uncle Harry couldn't give her a little brooch, with forget-me-nots, that he had bought for her in Boston one day when he had been thinking of her, and brought to her with his love and greetings, and the hope that this day and every other day would be the happiest day of her life. Then Dorie put the brooch in a pretty box, and so when the guests arrived I waited for Lilias, who came on the " special," and when she saw me, she came running toward me, a perfect painting in pink, dress and hat and all, and in the face of the assembled thousands put her arms around my neck and kissed me, her dear Uncle Harry. She was so glad to see me again. Then I found a chance to give her the brooch and the letter. She left and soon returned, with the brooch pinned over her heart, and saying how she appreciated it and my letter. Well, she is a darling, and her sisters, younger than she, are fascinating in their perfect simplicity and naturalness.

The beauty of the music room, with the altar cloth of golden embroidery upon an altar a step above the level of the floor, surmounted by a superb Spanish painting of the Madonna from an old monastery, and, at the back, flowers, lilies, and white stock in great profusion, and at the sides of the painting two Della Robbias, encased, as it were, in a panelling of flowers (white stock) as if upon a wall of flowers. The approaches to the altar an aisle of standards, between which the bridal procession marched, and these standards each bearing the most exquisitely colored lilies, and everywhere flowers and hanging baskets and festoons to the roof. When the sun shone into the room it seemed like a poetized chapel, with the tapestries and paintings and works of art all around. A band of music behind the palms introduced to the guests assembled by the march from " Lohengrin," the advance guard of the bridal party, and this guard brought tears to your eyes: four children, each bearing a long staff trimmed with flowers at the top, came slowly down the steps from the main entrance, and down the stairs and between the standards toward the altar. It was really very beautiful, and " the tots " enjoyed it so. They were " it," and as they separated to let the minister and Dr. Flint and the best man, followed by Mrs. Hearst and Ann, pass to the altar, it was very, very lovely. For the description of things generally I shall abridge my writing by taking the cutting from the newspaper which has come today (as soon as I can get a copy). But it was all bewilderingly beautiful, and only too beautiful to be enjoyed and seen by so few people.

The Episcopal service was beautifully performed, and then, after congratulations to the bride and groom in the other room, — for the bridal party left when " Joseph and Ann " had been made one and received in the large room adjoining the dining room, — the guests were able to examine the beautiful altar and decorations, and then all went to lunch in the great tent built within and covering the patio, where large tables had been built to seat nearly one hundred guests — an outer and an inner table; the outer for Mrs. Hearst and the guests; the inner table for the bridal party proper. There were a few toasts drunk: " Dr. and Mrs. Flint "; " Wil-

liam Hearst and his bride." William made a short and
very excellent response, and Dr. Flint himself in a short
speech spoke with great feeling of all that had been
planned and done by Mrs. Hearst, whose whole life was
devoted to making others happy, and we all stood up and
drank to the dear Queen. The children sang an appropriate song which gave the necessary lightness to the
occasion, and the bride and groom on leaving for their
home journey, to be followed by their trip to Wyntoon,
were duly showered with rose leaves and rice, and then
the guests went off in the carriages to take the " special "
for San Francisco.

It was certainly an occasion of most unusual character, and perhaps nowhere in the world could there be a
duplicate of it, but I was constantly thinking that if
these things had been a necessary part of getting married
to Dorie and me, we should probably be single up to
this day of our Lord.

I tell you, people have to be pretty fine themselves to
make an occasion such as this was in perfect balance —
harmonious, symmetrical, and in keeping. Clothes and
externals cannot make people, that's certain, and I could
not help feeling, as I looked around, that greater simplicity and less elaboration would have fitted us " common niggers " just as well. But the dear Ladye wished
to do everything for one who had been almost like a
daughter, and it was she and not we who would have it
so. I was glad when it was over for the sake of the Ladye,
and was glad when, at about five, she went to her room,
and did not appear again till noon the next day.

My dear Lilias and her sisters were like sunbeams all
day, and were a perennial joy to Kathleen and myself.
Their father, Mr. Charles Wheeler, a fine fellow and a
distinguished lawyer, I now met for the first time, and

we came together all right. Kathleen had met him, and had seen a good deal of him at Wyntoon. Mrs. Wheeler is a sweet, Madonna-faced woman, and a delight to look at and to be with. It is lovely to see the father, mother, and children together; they are all such friends.

I must tell you that the little Wheeler, who was a maid of honor, and of whom the young lad said, " The girl I took in had no front teeth " (she is of the toothless period), always carries with her a china poodle dog in her hand, and on this occasion it was still her companion, with a white ribbon around his neck, and turned to see everything. It is too funny to see her, and she is such a darling!

September 17th, 1903

KATHLEEN and I have been to the vineyard this A.M. The grapes are ripening, and we can gather enough for our needs at any time. We are now packing, intending to leave for San Francisco in a day or two; to the Palace Hotel and stay there and get ready for our journey.

The next " event " is on Thursday, the 24th, — the dedication of the Amphitheatre given by William Hearst, and we are invited to lunch with President Wheeler and wife.

Pleasanton, Cal., Sept. 20th, 1903

IT IS three months today since we first came to the Hacienda — which is, on the whole, the most beautiful place I have ever seen.

Today we are in the throes of packing, for we intend to leave for San Francisco tomorrow, there to abide until we start on the 7th of October. We shall have certain things to do ourselves, and we know that Mrs. Hearst will be very much occupied. It seemed to us best to leave

her a free course, and not let her have us on her mind
for a minute.

Mrs. Hearst and William and his wife have been away
since Friday, and so Miss Hooper, the dear, quaint, and
most attractive lady from Marblehead, and who has
been with Mrs. Hearst all summer, and who, you will
remember, is in charge of certain beneficent schemes of
Mrs. Hearst in Washington, is looking after us. Kathleen
and I are keeping house, and enjoying the quiet and the
simplicity of our living. William Hearst's little wife is a
sweet, affectionate, and amiable child, of about twenty
years of age. William goes his own way and pays no
attention to what people say or think, so far as I can
judge him, but a sweeter attitude towards his wife, or a
more loving one of hers to him you will not find. He is
fond and proud of her and of his mother, though not a
demonstrative man in any sense. He is simple, abste-
mious as an Arab, gentle in his ways and speech, direct,
and a pleasant, if not exciting companion. Everyone at
the wedding was drawn towards his little wife, who
passed through the trying ordeal of meeting so many
strangers all at once, simply and naturally, without em-
barrassment and without forwardness.

Palace Hotel, San Francisco, Cal., Sept. 23rd, 1903
WE ARE settled at the Palace Hotel until our departure.
We came to this city on the 22nd. Already I have been
getting the trunk man to overhaul trunks and bags and
things, and we have our goods and chattels about us in
our bright, sunny room here, and we are much as we
are when together in Europe. Mrs. Hearst is at the
Hearst Building with William and his wife, busy as a
" wood sawyer," and we keep out of the way as much
as possible to give her a free field.

We all met at the Symphony concert yesterday afternoon, and Mrs. William Hearst and all of us had time
for a little chat. Mrs. William is a sweet little woman,
and I am sure Mrs. Hearst Senior loves her as a daughter already. I shall be greatly disappointed if Mrs. William does not take the place of all the others in her
affections.

Palace Hotel, San Francisco, Cal., Sept. 27th, 1903
KATHLEEN and I are having a very " homey " time in
S. F. just now, for everybody but ourselves has gone to
the Hacienda to spend Sunday, and we are glad to have
the quiet and rest of our life here. We are preparing for
our journey, quietly and not hurriedly, and in the evening we go out to some restaurant for dinner, as we
used to do in Paris, and afterwards we stroll about
the streets for a while and then come home to bed
early.

Clara Anthony is due tomorrow evening. Mrs. Hearst
has a letter saying she would start on the 24th. That
makes her due here the 28th. We sincerely hope she is
well and strong again, and ready for what must at best
be a hard and exacting journey. We shall try to go to
the train to welcome her on her arrival.

We dined on Friday evening at the Sanborns'. Mr.
and Mrs. Sanborn are dear people, and have been very
kind to us. She is a sister of Orrin Peck. I had a severe
influenza that evening, and Mrs. William Hearst was
under the weather, too, so I don't think either of us was
at his or her best. However, we did as well as we could:
angels can do no more!

As William Hearst on the same evening was not feeling well enough to go to the dinner at all, we could not
help laughing! The dinner originally was for us and

two or four more; it gradually increased to a dinner of fourteen or sixteen. They are so hospitable here.

Willard opened in " The Cardinal " in London, as announced, and Rosie [5] wrote us a glowing account of his success. He too has written us, and he seems to be pleased with what he has done so far. The King and Queen and others attended the other evening, and King Edward sent a cordial message of thanks for the play and the acting.

Palace Hotel, San Francisco, Cal., Sept. 29th, 1903
I WENT over to Oakland to receive Cousin Clara and Reed last evening. The train was two hours late; it always *is late;* but they did not seem either especially fatigued or troubled about anything and they seemed rejoiced to see me. I had engaged their rooms at this hotel for them, at the request of Mrs. Hearst, and Mrs. Hearst had her Mr. Scott go over to attend to baggage, etc., and there was a carriage in waiting for them. All we had to do was to get into the carriage, come here, where Kathleen met them at the door, and soon we were all in the dining room, taking supper, and talking nine-teen to the dozen.

Mrs. Hearst is coming from the Hacienda today, and I understand we are all to dine with her at the Hearst Building tonight. Then we may be able to talk over what we are going to do, for thus far Mrs. Hearst has not been able to devote a minute and a half to me. *Damn* this being a slave either to one's possessions or to the parasites and strikers and crimmers who hang upon to make slaves of the rich! I would rather be in Hell without a fan than live a life of such slavery. Mind you, it is not necessary! It is all a gratuitous and unnecessary

[5] Mrs. Rogers' sister, Mrs. Robert Francillon, of London.

waste of energy to allow one's self to be so badgered, and then it makes life so confusing and restless, without time for reflection, for recovery of one's equipoise. Not any of it for me!

I do not find a soul around Mrs. Hearst except the servants who does not want something, sooner or later. They do not seem to want to find out what they can do for her, but what they can *get*. Curiously enough, I think Mrs. Hearst likes it, in a way. I think she is accustomed to be in the midst of a whirl, and between not having it at all and having it as it is, there being no happy medium apparently, she would prefer the whirl and take her chances.

Kathleen and Clara Anthony have been doing shopping together, and so, as we all breakfasted together, I can only say that Clara seems fairly strong, and I think the sea journey will be a fine thing for her.

The " Doric " arrived from Yokohama yesterday, sixteen days, sixteen hours, a good passage. We have been down to the Pacific S.S. Company this A.M. to arrange about paying for our passage, etc.

Palace Hotel, San Francisco, Cal., Sept. 29th, 1903
Two ladies came running towards me this afternoon and one offered her hand, — which I promptly took — exclaiming, " This *is* the Earl of Lonsdale, is it not? " To which I replied, " N-o-o-o, Madam, I *look* like the Earl, but I am not he! " Apologies made and accepted! No cards! I wonder if I would better pose as the Earl!

Palace Hotel, San Francisco, Cal., Oct. 4th, 1903
I HAVE just come back to the hotel after an inspection of the " Doric." I wanted to examine certain things myself and also take a good look at our accommodations to see if we needed anything in particular.

Clara Anthony and Mrs. Hearst are at the Hacienda today. From all we hear Clara continues well and in good condition, and I do not know any reason for apprehension in her case any more than in the rest of us. She will get stronger during the voyage, I believe, and then when we get to Japan I do not intend to *drive* things as if there never were to be another day or another opportunity. My general idea is to take it as easy as circumstances will allow and let those *go,* or *rest,* who prefer the one thing or the other at any particular moment.

Yesterday we went up Mt. Tamalpais (Tam-ál-pis', the country of the *Tamals,* an Indian tribe), and got some superb views. The railroad is the crookedest in the world — eight and a fourth miles long in ascending a mountain not quite half a mile high (2592 feet). The fog shut down upon us at the top, so we could not see much from up there.

The most interesting thing about the trip was meeting a gentleman, eighty-eight years of age, Mr. John Perry, Jr., formerly (until 1851) of Boston, a broker there, who knew Father. Mr. Perry has been in business in San Francisco since 1851, and he was most interesting in his conversation. He knew all of the B. C. merchants of Boston, and told me many things about them. He gave Kathleen a large photograph of Mt. Tamalpais.

Palace Hotel, San Francisco, Cal., Oct. 5th, 1903
KATHLEEN is delivering her essay this A.M. I looked into the hall while she was speaking, but did not dare go in lest I should throw her off her subject or embarrass her. She looked very lovely, and had an excellent and attentive audience of ladies of the Century Club. Gentlemen not admitted, though I did see one or two gentlemen in the audience.

Her subject is " The Ideal and the Technical in Art," and she has written a most interesting paper. I have read it, and it treats of what she is always saying, that the ideal and the technical are to be reconciled; for the rock on which most artists split is the misunderstanding of the two; and they think or act as if they thought the technical — skill in finger exercises — the knowing how the larynx is constructed — makes the player or the singer.

It is a lofty and yet very direct and simple exposition she is delivering today, full of the fruit of her experience and I think it will make an impression. I wanted to hear it very much, but I had to peep into a doorway at the back of the hall, and I was so afraid even then that I might cause her to slip that I came away.

Steamship " Doric," San Francisco, Cal., Oct. 7th, 1903
HERE we are, our luggage all on board. Our stateroom steward is a nice little Chinaman named Ah Foo! I speak to him in pigeon English, just as he speaks to me.

Everything looks all right. We shall soon be off. Kathleen is storing our goods and chattels in stateroom 23, where we live. Clara Anthony and Mrs. Hearst and the maid Marie have 21-19.

JOURNAL–LETTERS FROM
THE ORIENT

by Clara Kathleen Rogers

with supplementary Notes
by Henry Munroe Rogers

Journal-Letters from the Orient

Steamship " Doric," Oct. 7th, 1903

WE LEFT San Francisco today at one o'clock on the
steamship " Doric." Such a crowd was there to see us
off, " us " meaning principally Mrs. Hearst — friends,
retainers, servants, and hangers-on of all sorts. There
were many wet eyes glistening through the smiles, there
were many shouts of " Bon voyage! " and oh! the flowers! There were dozens and dozens of enormous boxes
of the choicest blossoms of every description. It really
grieved me to the heart to see this wealth of beauteous
blossoms, knowing as I did, what their imminent fate
would be. In California the floral expressions of good
will seem to be even more rampant than in New York
and Boston! Even *we* had seven or eight boxes of
American beauties, or large white and pink roses, and
box upon box of wonderful violets with stems eight
inches long, buried in maiden-hair fern. But what I was
most pleased with were some branches of the madroña
tree, which grows so profusely on Mount Tamalpais,
with its gorgeous clusters of crimson berries, to put in
our stateroom behind the racks, for they have no odour.
They keep beautiful for a long time and are wonderfully decorative.

The " Doric " seems to be a fairly comfortable ship,
and one might well imagine oneself on an Atlantic liner
were it not for the presence of the Chinese sailors and
stewards, instead of the motley group of different nationalities that one always finds on the former. Here
everyone is Chinese, interspersed with an occasional

37

Japanese, except the chief steward, the stewardess, and the ship's officers. It took me quite by surprise, when we went into lunch, to see the Chinese waiters gliding about in long, blue robes of linen. Such a picturesque sight! They are really beautiful, some of these Orientals! You get quite a different impression of them from that received from the Chinamen you see in the laundries. Not that these Chinamen are handsome according to our taste, but they are most interesting as individuals. Their imperturbable dignity commands one's respect, and there is a certain mystery about these Cantonese which one cannot fathom. When one gives them an order, no change of expression, nor the slightest look of intelligence, indicates that they have understood or even heard what you said, but in a flash the order is executed, and a mistake is never made.

Our room steward, Ah Foo, is a perfect treasure. When we arrived on board he not only settled all our small baggage in our room, but, quite unbidden, he unpacked our things, hung up our shoe bags, etc., and, in fact, performed the services of a private valet. I have always heard that Chinamen are the best servants in the world, and I can well believe it! At dinner they wear long white robes, similar to the bright blue ones at lunch, but I think that their long, black queues show up better on the blue, and the effect is more picturesque.

The scenery, as one approached and passed through the Golden Gate, was very fine. The mountains and islands are so varied in form and colour. We ran right into a heavy sea, with the result that every one promptly disappeared from the deck, and no one saw the Farallone Islands, the last of the land between us and Honolulu — rocks which stand up straight out of the water, and are inhabited principally by wild birds.

October 8th
A ROUGH night, and the heavy sea continues, though this morning it was a trifle quieter. Harry and I were among the very few at breakfast. Mrs. Hearst, who slept fourteen hours at a stretch, is looking somewhat better today, though she is still very 'white. We have persuaded her to remain in her room for several days — until she is quite rested. Cousin Clara was a bit qualmish this morning, but I think she is going to be a good sailor. I am tremendously fit, and Harry also.

October 9th
A VERY rough night and today the ship is still rolling terribly. I have been solacing myself by reading " Kotto," by Lafcadio Hearn, which I find very suggestive and also very poetic. His account of the Japanese superstitions, their myths and traditions, gives me a fine insight into the way the Japanese mind works. I shall read all his books. I am fairly steeping myself in Japanese lore, in fact we all are. It is a queer sensation to hear the Chinese sailors' songs while they are setting sail. There seem to be no musical intervals, and consequently no tune as we conceive it. It is more like a pattern which repeats itself as on a stenciled paper. And the voices! Well there!

October 10th
WE ARE still rolling like everything, but the weather overhead remains persistently fine, and the water is of a wonderful blue. It grows warmer and warmer. We are reducing our clothing daily. Mrs. Hearst comes to table now and she really begins to look rested and like her own sweet self. Our fellow passengers seem to be a

good sort. There are some missionaries with their families who are going to convert the heathen or be converted, I don't know which. Then there are families who live in Shanghai and other parts of China, who are going back after a holiday. And there are globe trotters, principally English people, who like ourselves, just want to see things.

October 11th

WE ARE at last in smooth waters again and it is oh, so restful after being banged about. The events of the day, besides an Episcopal service in the morning and a sermon from a missionary in the afternoon, were the construction of a large tank, of sail cloth about 12 by 18, into a swimming bath into which they pumped about 12 feet or more of sea water, an exhibition of swimming and diving on the part of some of the passengers followed. The ladies are to have a chance tomorrow in the afternoon, for the tank is to be a permanent thing for the rest of the trip.

October 12th

TODAY everybody is writing letters to send home from Honolulu, where we are to arrive early the day after tomorrow. The little deck library is crowded, and one has to watch one's opportunity to get a vacant writing table. This evening we had a fine specimen of a Pacific sunset, the kind they have at Honolulu. It was wondrous!

October 13th

ALL IS excitement today in anticipation of landing tomorrow. All the officers and some of the passengers are dressed in white duck, and look very festive. We shall

HAWAII: "Plumy palms drowsing by the sea"

all of us have to get into the thinnest of thin clothes, as the heat will be great when we land. Some white flying fish have been disporting themselves this morning. They look almost like birds. The air is wonderful here, so soft! We have not become intimately acquainted with any of our fellow passengers, so far. The fact is, we prefer reading to clay-pigeon shooting, gambling, ping-pong, and all the other games which are rampant on deck. The pidgin English of our Chinese servants is a source of perpetual delight to me. Somebody at our table just asked a second time for an orange, and Ah Foo answered, in an injured tone, " Boy go *ketch* one." Harry and I are on the broad grin most of the time!

October 14*th*

THIS morning I jumped out of my berth before sunrise, and, throwing a wrap over me, went on deck, so anxious was I not to miss the first glimpse of land. Our ship had been at anchor outside the harbour all night, and had just got up steam again. It was nearly an hour, however, before we sighted the various pyramidal rocks which preface " Diamond Head " and the outlying cliffs and mountains of Honolulu. My first view of these was through the port of the bathroom, where I was attempting to " cool off " in a sea bath, and what I beheld so excited me that I could hardly proceed with my ablutions. No doubt there are some who would say that the scenery is not unlike some parts of the coast of Ireland or Scotland, but I stoutly maintain that the approach to Honolulu is unlike anything I have ever seen, if only on account of the strange colouring of some of the cliffs and mountains, many of which have had their heads blown off by volcanic eruptions. Some of these are literally mere shells of mountains; they look fair and solid outside, but they are hollow inside. One, in particular, aptly named " The Punch Bowl," has nothing but an outer rim to stand on, from which one looks into the extinct crater below, now overgrown with rich tropical verdure.

When we were quite a little distance from the wharf some of the natives, who are positively amphibious, swam out in groups and jabbered to us in their soft and musical language of vowels, what was recognised by the initiated as a request for us to throw coins overboard that they might dive for them. It was really very amusing to see these shapely, brown-bodied youths, with their large, woolly heads, disappear under water for a second or two, and invariably come up triumphant with the coin in their mouths.

By the time we landed it had alas! begun to rain vigorously. It was the first rain we had seen on land for over three months. I had taken the precaution to array myself in a nice cool, pongee silk suit in consideration of the tropical heat, against which I had been warned; but indeed I had reason to regret that I had not donned a short cloth skirt, for I had to cover up my delicate finery with a waterproof cloak. As we watched the clouds emptying themselves into the Punch Bowl the fond hope of taking the famous drive to the " Pali " dwindled, until finally we had to give it up altogether. We tried to comfort ourselves, however, with the thought that there was the Bishop Museum, of which Harry's old classmate, William T. Brigham, is at the head — with its famous Polynesian and other collections, well worth a journey to the Hawaiian Islands to see, and that if we could not drive about and enjoy all the wonders of tropical nature, we could, at least, study the history of the Islands, and see within these four walls all their products from the beginning of their history.

Harry had written to Mr. Brigham that we were coming on the " Doric," and, sure enough, there he was on the wharf to welcome us, fairly trembling with excitement. He had his carriage there for us, but as we were five of us, including Mrs. Hearst's maid, we hired another to take us to the Museum, which is situated about two miles from the town.

[*Note by* H. M. R. " As we approached the wharf there was dear old Billy Brigham, waving his hand and shouting his welcome to me, and I shouting mine to him, oblivious of everything but the fact that two of " Sixty-two " were coming together upwards of five thousand miles from Harvard, but with all the old-time affection still there as it was, when we were school boys together, way back in 1854 or 1855. Two venerable looking, gray-bearded men, both of some dignity of carriage and behavior under ordinary circumstances, shouting and calling and waving to each other like mad, oblivious of everything but the fact that one was on the deck of a ship and the other on the dock, and that for a few moments they were apart by the logic of the situation! I can't help laughing when I think of it! Soon Billy was aboard, and we had grasped hands, and he was presented to Mrs. Hearst and to Clara Anthony, and to Dorie he renewed the greetings of an old acquaintance."]

Just as we were leaving the wharf in our chariots an old friend of Mrs. Hearst's, who lives in Honolulu — a Mrs. Wheaton, drove up to welcome us, laden with the remarkable chains of flowers called " leis," which it is the custom at Honolulu to present to arriving and departing friends. These chains, are some of them quite long, are made of blossoms threaded closely, one inside the other, on a string. Many of them look almost like feather boas of brilliant colours, so large and so closely packed are the blossoms. The one Clara Anthony had was made of the butter-coloured Frangipani blossoms, which are of a wonderful fragrance as well as great beauty.

As we drove through the town we saw children with numbers of these leis for sale, of great variety and most brilliant colours, made of flowers which were for the most part strange to us. Here and there we would meet one of the natives with a leis round his hat or neck — for men and women alike wear them, and you see some with as many as seven or eight leis, one outside the other, which makes them look like ambulating flower beds, standing on end. This is such an individual note that it stamps Hawaii at once as something apart from any other place. It gives one a strong impression of fragrance, gaiety, and festivity; at the same time, of a sweet primitive simplicity.

There is a great deal of quaintness about the town, with its little, low-roofed provision stores. The first things one notices at these are bundles of tall sugar cane outside the door, and sundry unusual vegetables and fruits — as, for instance, the bread fruit, the alligator pear, and the taro, from which they make " poi," besides native oranges, limes, pineapples, grapes, etc. One sees many Japanese about the streets, as well as Chinese and natives. The Jap women nearly always have babies on their backs, and some of the poor, attenuated little Japs, with clumsy clogs on, bear heavy burdens suspended from poles slung across their shoulders. It gives

Hawaii: Waikiki Beach

one the idea of being all very queer and very *mixed* in
its picturesqueness; the presence here and there of an
American store, making it all seem a bit incongruous.
Oh, Civilization! What hast thou not to answer for? I
am afraid that the Hawaiians are taking all too quickly
to the American methods! They seem to be naturally so
sweet-natured, simple, and kindly, that it really seems
a shame to initiate them in our canny ways!

On driving to the Museum we rode through long
stretches of the residential quarter, where each house is
planted in the midst of a wonderful tropical garden.
We passed fields of rice, avenues of royal palms, and
many other kinds of palms, some laden with cocoanuts,
and some with huge bunches of brilliant scarlet and
green berries, two or three feet in circumference, and
long, tassel-like pendants of queer stringy growths, four
or five feet in length, of which some are of a brilliant
orange colour, others bright green. The hedges round
the gardens are of three kinds. Those of hibiscus, those
of dwarf bamboo, and others of a remarkable plant, the
leaf of which is formed like that of the locust tree, only,
instead of being green, it is of a delicate mauve, variegated with white. It is one of the most exquisite and
most curious shrubs I ever saw. Fancy a whole hedge
of mauve and white *foliage* — mark you, not flowers.
Some of the, to us, strange trees we saw were the banyan, the mango, the coffee, the alligator pear, the Pride
of India (which is a large tree as tall as an elm, with
clusters of scarlet blossoms all over it), the monkey-pod
tree, with blossoms very much like the passion flower,
the tamarind, the rubber tree, the guava, the pomela, and
the breadfruit tree. I cannot describe the impression
it made on us to see all these extraordinary trees with
brilliant blossoms, none of which we had ever seen be-

fore. Then there were large numbers of banana trees, laden with fruit, with their huge, feather-shaped leaves, which nearly always present a somewhat ragged appearance, and some very large specimens of the prickly-pear cactus. Most of the common trees, which spring up all around — not in gardens but by the roadsides, have a delicate, feathery little leaf like that variety of acacia called the " sensitive plant." It is named " algeroba." I wish you could have heard our wild cries of delight and wonder as we saw all these new things. It was, " Oh, what is that tree with the yellow trumpet blossoms? " " And that with the bunches of scarlet flowers! " " Oh, look at the kroton bushes! Don't they seem ablaze with colour? " It was scream after scream of excitement from one or other of us most of the time, until we were almost exhausted with our own emotions.

We spent a most thrilling morning in the Museum, where Mr. Brigham acted as guide, philosopher, and friend, showing us wonderful things and explaining their secret history in such a way as to render them of vital interest to us. He and his assistant, Mr. Stokes, an interesting young Australian, were kindness itself. They seemed to feel that they could not do enough for us.

[*Note by* H. M. R. " We were all of us simply delighted and astonished at Brigham's work, for he has been the inspiration and the Director, and to him must be given the highest and almost entire praise. This Museum is a part of a school and college (if you please) for girls and boys, and is a memorial of a Mr. Bishop to his wife, Bernice Panahi Bishop, who was a granddaughter of the royal house of Hawaii. Mr. Bishop is a banker upward of eighty years old, living in San Francisco. Brigham, many years ago — forty and upwards — went to the Islands to study the volcanoes, got tremendously interested in the people, their ways, their arts of weaving, basket making, pottery, traditions, religion, customs, etc. In his wanderings he visited many islands of the group, took voluminous notes, and watched the people at their work of weaving, basket making, etc., they having inherited their knowledge from their ancestry for generations.

" When Brigham came back again, some fifteen years or so ago, he found to his dismay all of these arts in their desuetude — no longer practised, the old people dead, the young people saying it was too much trouble to learn, and was not necessary because of what the *whites* had begun to bring to the Islands in trade. He had been appointed by Mr. Bishop to help arrange the collection that had been made of a few things; soon he got hold of the Government collection, then begged Mr. Bishop for a suitable building, then began to get hold of the oldest natives and tried to reproduce the works their ancestors had done. Finding here and there one survivor, he, from his notes and their help, got hold of everything to illustrate what it was, and ended by taking a *mould* in plaster, *life size,* of the old woman herself, and then had it reproduced and colored, and there one old woman is *in one case* (" case " in a double sense) as large as life and almost breathing in her naturalness, at work on a texture which she is making, and so concentrated that you can almost trace her thoughts.

" He seems to work with the fervor and heat of a steam engine, and with an ingenuity and comprehension that is simply wonderful. As a mere mechanic, draughtsman, architect, cabinet maker, photographer, printer, metal cutter, botanist, weaver, glass stainer, scientist, he would be remarkable; but his lack of means to do all

he wanted, and his determination to have what he
wanted, means or no means, has made him everything
all in one.

" Then to hear him tell of his rows with the trustees;
his row with the Catholic Church, who requested his removal because it was said he had spoken disrespectfully
of Father Damien, whom he knew, I believe, puts you
into fits of laughter, for as he was in his youth, so is he
in sixtieth year — utterly careless what particular corn
he is treading on when he is telling the truth in the most
uncompromising way. I laughed and laughed, for he
and I drove in his wagon, as he told me some of his
experiences.

" The arrangement of the Museum and the opportunities for close observation and study there equal or
surpass anything I have ever seen anywhere, and Mrs.
Hearst was simply delighted with what she saw, and
with Mr. Brigham and his assistant, Mr. Stokes; and,
against her protest, we insisted on putting the dear
Ladye in a wheel chair (she had been working too much
the night before on her mail from Honolulu home), and
taking her around from case to case, letting her walk a
little and ride a good deal, till I said, ' Children, you
must now go to lunch! ' "]

I wish I could give you some idea of the really marvelous colours of the fish that are caught in the waters
of the Hawaiian Islands. In the Museum there is a complete collection of perfect reproductions of them which
is a sight to behold. In colour they are like brilliantly
tinted birds, such as parrots, canaries, etc. only with
scales instead of feathers — bright blue, green, yellow,
purple, pink, silver, and in every conceivable form and
shape — many of them curiously grotesque! It seems to

me that colour — blazing, radiant colour — is the natural key-note of these Islands.

After we had looked and looked till our eyes seemed to have receded to the back of our heads, and Mrs. Hearst was almost ready to faint from exhaustion, we drove back to the town and took lunch at " Young's," a new hotel where everything was modern and immaculate. The dining room was on the roof, commanding a splendid view of mountain and sea. After a delicious luncheon, we returned to the Museum with renewed spirits and vigour to examine the rest of the curiosities. By the way, it was fortunate that we had, in Mr. Brigham, a friend at Court, for it happened that the Museum was closed for repairs, and if he had not been prepared with a special permit from Governor Dole, we could not have gone in at all.

We went afterwards to Mr. Brigham's home to see his fine tropical garden and his aviary of queer birds. He is very proud of his royal palms, which he planted himself when he first came to the Island. He told us that a single leaf of one of these, which fell the other day, measured over 25 feet in length! When he had done the honours of his place, and speeded the parting guests, we found that we had barely time to drive to the ship which was to leave at 5 P.M., and of which we heard the warning as we pelted over the roads. We arrived at the wharf just as the last signal was being blown, and had only time to throw a parting greeting to Mrs. Wheaton, who had driven down to the ship to leave for Mrs. Hearst a farewell offering, which consisted of specimens of all the native fruits in season, collected by her and beautifully arranged in a canoe-shaped thing, about three feet long, constructed out of the thick, smooth, green skin which covers the top of the royal palm. There were the bread fruit, the native pineapple, the pomela, fresh dates, the papaya, which looks something like a melon, and tastes more like a mango, and the guava, which looks like a dumpy little lemon, but is rather soft, and inside is in colour like a miniature watermelon. The flavour is fine. Then there was the fruit of the passion flower, which somewhat resembles a green cocoanut in form. The vine on which it grows is quite different from the passion vine we know; it is larger, stronger, and succulent like that of the melon or cucumber. The blossom is of a rich purple, heavily fringed and very large. The outside of the canoe was decorated with tiny sprays of stephanotes and passion flower, and at the bow and stem there were branches of several varieties of the brilliant kroton and other richly tinted leaves. It was a beautiful thought of Mrs. Wheaton's to leave with us this little tropical note of Hawaii.

There is no denying that it was a disappointment to us all not to be able to drive to the Pali, look into some of the craters, and take in the superb vistas of sea and mountain on the way, though of course it was felt most strongly by Harry and me, as both Mrs. Hearst and Cousin Clara had been over the ground before. I do hope, however, that on our return voyage we shall make up for it. Meanwhile I am thankful for all that we were able to take in between showers. Of course we have seen only one aspect of Honolulu, and that not the best on account of the weather, but I think one could hardly have taken in more in one day. As it is, we were all of us well nigh exhausted and overcome with the intensity of our pleasurable emotions. I carry away with me a lasting impression of rare beauty, fragrance, and brilliant, flaming, radiant colour, and Honolulu will always be associated with necklaces of Frangipani and all sorts

HAWAII: View from Nuuanu Pali (near Honolulu)

of strange blossoms which fill the air with perfume, and the eye with a brightness and splendour quite indescribable. We were all equally enthusiastic, and we agreed that it had been a memorable day. The ship began to roll again as soon as we got outside the harbour, and we are in for a rough night, I trow; but, no matter. We have had at least a glimpse of Honolulu!

October 18th and 19th
DURING the last three days there has been no event of interest. The sea is smoother and the heat greater, — that is all, and we have gone back to our books. This ought to be Sunday but it is actually Monday, which means that in crossing the Meridian — going to the Orient from San Francisco, from October 7th to October 19th — we have lost two hours a day. We crossed the line this morning at eight minutes to nine, and two guns were fired to mark the event. There is to be a tournament this afternoon, and they are planning for a dance on deck tomorrow. It is still very hot.

October 21st
THERE was such a big sea on yesterday and the ship danced about so effectively that all thoughts of other dancing had to be abandoned for the nonce. One does get terribly banged about in this rough weather, but at least it is cooler, which confirms the truth of the proverb, " It's an ill wind," etc.

October 25th
THE night of October 23rd and yesterday were the worst I have ever experienced on any ocean voyage. A gale of wind to cap the climax of a sea which seemed already as heavy as it could be. Every two or three min-

utes we shipped enough water to swamp an ordinary
vessel, and the unfortunate steerage passengers, consisting of nearly four hundred Chinamen and Japanese,
all had to be packed up together and sealed up, as otherwise they would have been washed off! When I think
of their sufferings (for it was very hot and close everywhere) our little discomforts seem as nothing! But today everything is bright and beautiful, and our spirits
have risen accordingly. We shall reach Yokohama some
time tonight, but shall not land till tomorrow, after the
health officers have done with us. There is no wharf
where we can land, so we shall anchor outside, and be
taken off in steam launches.

[*Note by* H. M. R. " I have been thinking a good deal
about the missionaries, as I see them on board, and I
am filled with wonder at the seeming absolute unfitness
of those I see for any possible influence say with the
Chinese. Imagine a delicate man, educated, with an
anemic wife and five small children, and one at the
breast, going out to Christianize anybody. His tenets
are, we will say, Presbyterian. He goes to a Chinaman
and he says, ' You have got to believe so and so.' The
Chinaman says, ' But the father of the Catholic Church
told me that wasn't true.' To which he replies, ' I tell you
what the father says isn't true.' The Chinaman says
' You give me one God; the holy father gives me three
Gods; I have in my religion a thousand gods. What do
you give me that I have not already and more, too? You
and the father don't agree about your Gods, and my
gods we all agree about.'

" Meanwhile the minister goes about the house, as he
goes about the ship, *always* with a baby in his arms.
Another kind on board tends the baby all right, and his

wife looks like a breeding cow. You would not give any of them any child, or one you cared for, to bring up, to educate, to refine. You couldn't do it. You would challenge them on sight. How can you believe that that kind can make an impression on 535,000,000 people? Why should anybody want to Christianize the Chinese, the Japanese, the Siamese? What are they giving to these people better for them than what they have?

" Think of a man who does not know the language of China, the thoughts of a Chinaman, trying to understand what is behind the impenetrable mask of the Chinaman's face! It seems to me a gross absurdity. If they were all educated missionaries of medicine, of healing, of nursing, instead of educated theologians, I could believe in the chance. Then again, the merchants on board say that the Boxer trouble was partly a result of the interference of the priests and preachers who undertook to arbitrate in disputes between natives, and always gave in favor of the native who was called a convert. If I had been a Chinaman I think I should have felt I was doing things pleasant to my gods when I was sweeping such out of the way.

" We have had two or three evenings of talking on board, where missionaries and others have delivered themselves of what they knew of the Chinese or Japanese. As to the Japanese the talk was simply pathetic, so much of it was drivel. The talk on the Chinese was better. One of the missionaries — he of the five children — talked well and understandingly, as far as he went. They all generalize pretty hastily, and I had a talk with him the day after. I asked him how he could tell he got behind those masks? Whether, since he began his remarks by saying they were *liars, liars, liars,* the fair inference might not be they were lying when they said the things to him that they knew he wanted them to say?

" The testimony of Mr. McLeod, a Shanghai merchant who spoke was that his dealings with the Chinese merchants year in and year out, involving millions of taels, showed them to be the most high toned, honest, and trustworthy men that could be found, never breaking their contracts. The Japanese, on the contrary, were absolutely untrustworthy as merchants. It is a curious commentary on this that the Japanese banking houses, native or foreign, have Chinese as managers.

" The purser tells us that the gang of missionaries on this trip are above the average. There are some young girls going out to far-away hospitals of China, as nurses, etc. Of course, I am merely an onlooker, and do not pretend to understand all about it, but I cannot help feeling that with all that there is to be done ' next door ' at home, it is a far-off cry to go to China to find a place to do good. I cannot help thinking constantly of the Vision of Sir Launfal and his quest for the Christ he ultimately found at his own door.

" In trying to account for the broods of children of the missionaries, I am met by the statement that for every child born to the missionary an extra $100. per year is allowed by the Foreign Missions till the child is fourteen years old. I do not know whether this be so or not, and I have not felt justified in asking questions from headquarters. I have to take what is said either by the missionary or the merchant, who do not seem to have anything in common, with a grain of salt.

" A very highly educated and refined lady of Hong Kong, wife of a solicitor there, gives her opinion that the missionaries, on the whole, accomplish some good, and I think I should accept her views. I suppose she has seen more of their school work with children and their hospitals, etc., than some others. What the same expenditure of money and energy might accomplish in Boston or New York or Liverpool or Glasgow or London is an interesting consideration."]

Oriental Hotel, Yokohama, Oct. 26th, 1903
WE STEAMED up to the harbour at 7 A.M. Our ship was surrounded by hundreds of " sampans " — flat bottomed boats, propelled like gondolas. Some of the fishermen had on skirts, capes, and broad, basket-shaped hats, made of thatched straw. You never saw such queer-looking things! They looked like the wildest sort of savages. A Mr. Brockhurst, to whom a friend in San Francisco had written on our behalf, came on board to meet us, bringing with him a guide he had engaged for us, who is supposed to speak English, a dapper little man who bows and smiles obsequiously. His name is Fujii — easy to remember! Mr. Brockhurst had also engaged some beautiful rooms for us at this hotel overlooking the harbour, and had in fact done everything that a good friend could do.

Arrived at the landing stage in the little steam launch sent out by the hotel, we all got into separate jinrikishas. If only some of our Boston friends could have seen our imposing procession! We mounted and leaned back with an aplomb which would have done credit to dyed-in-the-wool Japanese folk. Women look really quite distinguished and quaintly dignified in them, but men look clumsy and terribly out of place. It really seems awfully queer and uncanny being carried about by these funny little men, who get outside the shafts, taking one in each hand and trot as fast as ponies. I cannot quite reconcile myself to the ignominy of it! It is unpleasant to contemplate these human horses, although in truth they hardly seem like real men, but rather like some strange little nondescript beasties! Still it does cross one's mind now and then that they are really human beings!

After settling ourselves in our delightful rooms in this clean, fresh, and new hotel, we went at once to a famous tailoring establishment, named Tom's, to select and order some very necessary garments which, we were told, we would better provide ourselves with at Yoko-hama to suit the different climates to which we shall be exposed, and we were greatly impressed by the exquisite Chinese and Japanese silks, magnificently embroidered to order, which we could get for very little money. If we did not begrudge the time from sight-seeing, we all of us concluded that we should like to order an entire trous-seau!

We then took to our jinrikishas again, and poked around the queer, narrow side streets, where we saw all sorts of interesting and utterly novel sights, which would take hours to describe. Then we returned to the hotel for tiffin. In the afternoon we started forth again and wound up at a famous curio shop, kept by Yozo Nomura, to whom Harry happened to have an introduction from Joe Millet, who said that we ought not to miss seeing his rare things. He was so nice to us, presenting each of us ladies with a silver hat-pin with a Buddha on top, and before leaving he asked us to honour him at his house for tea, which we gladly did, for it was a speedier oppor-tunity than we had expected to see a real Japanese interior.

It was a little gem of a house, situated in such a charming little garden, trees and everything being in miniature. The whole front of the house was open, and cushions were placed for us on the outer rim, so that our

TOKYO: The Flower Festival

feet hung over into the garden, and we did not have to remove our shoes. Had we entered the room we should of course have felt obliged to do so, for one would no more think of walking over those exquisite polished floors and delicate mats than one would of treading on brocaded sofas and chairs with one's walking shoes. Everything was dainty and in exquisite taste, a thoroughly characteristic Jap house, more like an overgrown jewel box than a dwelling house. We were served with tea in true Japanese style by a reduced specimen of womankind who went through all the forms of true Japanese politeness. In addition to the tiny cups of choice green tea, of which there was not more than a spoonful served to each person, there was a plate of some inviting looking stuff which looked like blocks of jade, but which turned out to be a pastel made of bean meal, sweet and sticky, but nice.

It was rather late when we returned to the hotel, and we only just had time to get dressed for dinner. I have always heard that there was nothing of particular interest to be seen at Yokohama, but I cannot understand how any one with eyes to see could say such a thing. As soon as one gets off the " Bund," and turns into some of the side and back streets, one is in veritable Japan, without any European alloy. The streets are narrow, and some of them have avenues of curious little scrub pines on either side in front of the little, low-roofed shops, no two of which are alike in structure, colour, or material. The eye is attracted at every turn by something quaint, picturesque, and novel. But dominating all one's sensations is a sense of queerness and topsy-turvy-ness. You see hundreds of jinrikisha men running like mad in all directions, shouting to people to get out of the way, and hundreds of coolies in butcher-blue linen blouses, with the name and monogram of their employer marked over the back in large Chinese characters. They all cry out and jabber and quarrel among themselves. Everything here is different from anywhere else. The little tip carts, the funny, primitive, little watering carts — all covered with Chinese characters; the women shuffling about in their clogs with the inevitable baby tucked in the back of their kimonos.

While we were in Nomura's store, our five jinrikisha men got into a regular fight with a coolie. They clung to each other and fought fiercely like bull dogs; it was equally difficult to separate them. Meanwhile they kept up a jabbering that would have out-monkeyed a monkey-pen at the Zoo. Our courier-guide, Fujii, is a kindly little man and very obsequious, but I don't know which is hardest to understand, his Japanese or his English! I really think we shall have to hire some one else to interpret him!

October 27th

A REGULAR hopeless rainy day! And a rainy day in Japan is worse than anywhere else. Sidewalks are infrequent, and if you want to walk at all you must do it in the road, which is well coated with rich, black mud. We had planned for today a beautiful excursion to Kamakura and the Daibutsu, — the colossal bronze Buddha, — the temple of Hachiman, and the great image of the Goddess Kwaunon, but of course it is out of the question to go in this downpour. Oh, for the skies of California! So we are to leave here today at three for Tokyo. We should stay on here a day or two longer, as we like it so much and are so comfortable at this hotel, but unfortunately we have accepted an invitation to dine at the American Legation tonight in Tokyo. We had, or rather

Mrs. Hearst had, a letter to the American Ambassador, Mr. Griscom, and his wife, and so we are to be dined and wined, and must put on our best bibs and tuckers as soon as we reach Tokyo. We hope to obtain through Mr. Griscom an invitation from the Emperor to his garden party, which takes place at the precise moment when the Imperial chrysanthemums are in their glory, the date being set, not by the Emperor but by his gardener.

Imperial Hotel, Tokyo, Oct. 28th, 1903

AT THE Ambassador's dinner last night there were some distinguished people such as Baron Rosen, the Russian Ambassador, and his wife, General Winslow, and others. The house was beautiful, but European in style; the dinner was good and served by Japanese butlers in their long robes, with the Embassy monogram embroidered on the back, which gave them the dignified bearing of priests. The conversation was not brilliant, however, and I like our own dinner parties in Boston better! We learned that the garden party was to be postponed till the 15th of November on account of the lateness of the chrysanthemums blossoming, and as we must either sail for China and India on the " Hamburg," which leaves Kobe on the 15th, or upset our whole itinerary, besides losing our one chance of getting good accommodations on a fine boat, I am afraid we must give up all idea of the garden party! It is a pity to miss the sight, but I do not see how we can help it. We are to be invited to the Emperor's ball on the 3rd, but I want to see the chrysanthemums more than I do the royal family!

Today it is bright and beautiful, and we are crying " Heaven be praised " ! We will hie us to Shiba Park and visit the Temples and tombs of the Shoguns. Mrs.

Hearst is not feeling well today — too much Embassy last night, I fear, so Harry and Cousin Clara and I are to start off without her, and see the sights.

[*Note by* H. M. R. " When you see the jinrikisha men running around, through the mud, with only a light sandal sole on the bottom of their feet, and this tied on only by a wisp of grass cord between the great toe and ' the next gentleman,' with legs bare half way above the knee to the thigh, and only light drawers and a shirt, often open and showing their dark skins underneath, and the whole crowned with an inverted washbowl bamboo hat, with the name of the hotel, or the number of the ' jin ' man himself upon it, and when the rain is beating down and you are behind this human being, enveloped in a rug and with a boot drawn up so you look through the opening between the end of it and the top of the ' jin,' as you would ride in a buggy with the boot drawn way up, you can get an idea of the way my thoughts get ' a-going,' and how my sympathies get enlisted; and yet, I understand they are wasted, to all intents and purposes, for the ' jin ' man is a favored being, having a regular trade, with cash paid him for his work, and much, much more of it than the ordinary run of coolies. Therefore, I ride behind them as often as I can, despite all previously ventilated views upon the subject.

" *All* women in Japan carry babies on their backs — all females, I may say, without much regard to age or size, either of themselves or babies, for it seems to be indigenous to the female of Japan. The children are carried in what would seem to be a shawl, and with straps going over the carrier's shoulders. The baby is near the carrier or far off, according to circumstances, close to the back, or lolling helplessly around farther off. As the women are all short and all bend forward and have to

Tokyo: The Jinrickisha Procession

shuffle along in their wooden clogs, ' clampity —
clamp,' you will at once perceive there can be neither
grace of form nor of carriage in them. Poor things! I
suppose it is not ' style,' unless it be the Irishman's
' round shouldered with style,' they are after. Now
the women do not *prefer* to carry their babies probably,
and this is shown (not to generalize too hastily) by the
occasional baby wagon. I learn on inquiry that the aim
of women is to get a baby carriage — apparently there is
no doubt on the subject of getting babies enough to fill
it, *but* here is the rub! A baby carriage costs say 5 yen
($2.50), and no ordinary woman can save five yen dur-
ing the infancy of the present child, and the next comes
before she gets her mind made up about a carriage.

" Everything seems so upside down — wrong side up
— that you get into a ' bewilderness ' notwithstanding
you are made familiar by books, pictures, descriptions
of all you see. One look at the teeming, small, dwarf-
like people, their tiny bits of shops, houses, gardens,
their lack of so many things that seem to us necessaries,
and you feel it is all new — a revelation.

" Did you ever eat canned butter, for example? They
do not make butter that is good for anything in Japan —
absence of cows, knowledge of agriculture in its best
forms and dairy conveniences, etc. So the butter comes
in *tins* from the United States, France, Germany, Aus-
tralia, and it only varies in *badness,* so far as our experience goes. We have given up milk and butter! The eggs
are good, the fish delicious — the best thing for breakfast is a small sole — English sole at that — it is bully.
I have just had one. The fruit is not good; apples, pears
and grapes very so-so. The persimmons are said to be
fair — I have not tried them yet; they have not seemed
to me ripe."]

October 29th

WE SPENT the morning in Shiba Park, visiting the temples and tombs of the Shoguns, and it has been indeed a day of wonders! The park itself and everything about it is intensely Japanese — the trees, cedars, pines, etc., bending over and crawling on their bellies in most grotesque forms, greatly in contrast with the large, erect cryptomerias, which look like the California sequoias and which seem strangely out of proportion to their stunted surroundings. Arrived at the entrance of the first temple, that of Zo jo ju, some attendants drew over our shoes something that looked like bed socks made of canvas, which was better than having to remove our shoes and walk around in our stocking feet. The presiding genius of the temple was the Goddess Amida, a fat lady in gilt, enshrined in gorgeousness untold. There were three priests offering prayers outside the shrine, one at each side and one in front, their positions describing a triangle. Each one had beside him a low, lacquered table, on which were prayer boxes, containing the scrolls on which the different prayers to be offered are written. The priest on the left of the shrine had a metal plate beside him, on which he kept incessantly hammering to attract and hold the attention of the gilded lady in the shrine (perhaps he was afraid we might distract her!). When a prayer was finished he struck a gong. One of the people came in and knelt while he muttered a prayer, presumably for some dying or dead relation or friend. He remained in that position a long time, mumbling mechanically, with an utterly expressionless and vacant face. I would have given a great deal to know what was passing in his mind — if anything!

I will not attempt to describe the marvelous metal

work, wood carvings, gold-lacquer vases, and pillars. It would take days. We saw a number of temples today, and many different shrines, but lawks!, one would have to visit them again and again to take in even half the significance of all the symbolic carvings which fill the eye at every turn. I only got a general idea of splendour —barbaric in its conception, superb and artistic in its execution, a veritable orgy of beauty and barbarism.

But I shall never forget a small, bronze Buddha in a secluded corner of the temple — in a standing position. The dignity and the mystery of it were indescribable. The large, squatting Buddha near by looked positively vulgar beside it. In one of the temples there was a yellow-robed priest who spoke a little English, and who kindly took us in tow and told us many things we wanted to know. He also struck the famous war-drum for us, which I think was stretching a point, as it is only sounded in time of war. It is made of tiger skin, and it certainly does give forth a very threatening and savage boom! While he was conducting us about in the Mortuary Temple two or three Japs came in to offer prayers, whereupon our yellow priest, without any preliminary, suddenly squatted down with them and muttered three or four prayers in the most unconcerned and perfunctory way; then, without any change of expression, got up and continued escorting us over the temple. There seems to me to be nothing really devotional in their praying except the mere attitude itself. Their faces are perfectly impassive, and they even stare vacantly about while they mumble their prayers. We bought some of their little pictures and prayers done up in envelopes with incense enclosed as we left the temple.

All that we saw today was thoroughly Japanese in spirit, and the tiny chrysanthemums (the blossoms being

smaller than the smallest of wild asters) outside the
temples, the pink Japonica petals with which the steps
were bestrewed, and here and there a huge crow which
balanced itself on the edge of the overhanging roof, jeer-
ing at us with a sardonic " Cawk, Cawhi! ", completed
the bizarre effect.

After dinner Fujii came to tell us that there was to be
a flower market tonight in the " Ginga," which is the
Broadway of Tokyo. Of course we wanted to see it, but
as Mrs. H. and Clara did not feel equal to going, — for
it could only be seen on foot, — Harry and I, accompanied by Fujii, sallied forth without them. It was really
a startling sight to see whole streets banked up with
chrysanthemums of every colour, about six feet deep and
illuminated by torches. In the size of the blossoms we
can certainly beat them in America, but here were numberless curious, de-natured plants which one never could
expect to see elsewhere. For instance, those reduced to
a size even smaller than our pansy blossoms. These
minute specimens are much more highly prized in Japan
than the most magnificent of the mammoth blossoms
which in America it is our pride to cultivate. The Japanese seem to take particular delight in reversing the
natural order of things — in twisting into a crooked
shape trees which tend to grow up straight, and many
other forms of distortion too numerous for the casual
observer to note.

I wish you could see the two dear little dishes of miniature chrysanthemums which we bought to take home to
Mrs. Hearst and Clara. The china dishes were no larger
than the usual canary-bird bath, yet each dish contained
five matured plants of different colours in full bloom!
The price was 25 sen (twelve and a half cents) and,
would you believe it, that wretch, Fujii, beat it down

to 15 sen! There were other wares besides flowers and fruit for sale, such as the poorer classes buy — spread out on mats, laid on the ground in side streets, the owners sitting on their heels beside them.

We were greatly annoyed at the people crowding around us and staring right into our faces as if we were some new and curious sort of animals in a show! They came so near that their faces actually rubbed up against our shoulders; not by any means a pleasant proceeding where so many of them are afflicted with unsightly skin diseases, suggestive of a general unwholesomeness. But, I suppose, if the truth were known, we should find that we are far stranger animals to them than they are to us, and that is saying a good deal!

[*Note by* H. M. R. " I wonder if I can describe our visit to a great emporium. We drove to the shop, into which we looked from the sidewalk. First we met some half dozen coolies — servants — squatted around an open brazier warming their bare legs and hands. This space where they were was covered with a wooden awning, and the space itself was level with the sidewalk. Here ' the people ' take off their shoes, their clogs, and outer coverings, and leave their umbrellas, which the coolies fasten and mark with a wooden tag, and give duplicate to the owner. ' We uns ' had shoes of felt put over our shoes. We then stepped up one step into the store proper, covered everywhere with straw matting, and began our ' walk around.'

" The attendants are both women and men; some speak English. They all bow, with hands hanging down or else resting on the front of their legs, and bend their hips. The women are, *so far as my observation goes thus far,* knock kneed and pigeon toed. They were all small bits of things; they all stoop forward, or do not bend backward. The men are small, too, with only rare exceptions. Here and there you see a fine face and good figure. The manners of all are most gracious and pleasing, sympathetic and not aggressive. They never urge you to purchase, and do not show their best goods first. They ' size you up ' to get an idea of the quality and price of things you are after.

"There are three stories to the store, I believe, and they only took us over two. The third, where the richest and rarest things are, as we understand, they did not offer to show us. Mrs. Hearst bought some rather fine silks (I believe), but there was nothing so rare there in sight as to make it worth while to ' blow it in.' She is so gentle and simple in her manners, and so wise; she sees a good thing instantly, and knows it, and you cannot fool her one bit as to quality. At the Museum the other day she saw some wonderful things and was all of a glow. She had the equal of some, but others she had not; but she knew the rare and wonderful at sight.

"We came out of this store and went to another, where they sell silks and velvets, and things of that kind, in the piece. Here it was different. We went into an open showroom, exposed to the street. The floor of large blocks of stone, and everywhere the boys had hand braziers to keep their fingers warm. We got to the edge of a platform, and there were placed stools. We did not go up on the platform, but some dozen of shopmen, apprentices, and cash boys were there. We saw no goods displayed there, though there were goods in cases, samples, in the great open space. We asked through Fujii to bring on their show, and from the main warehouse (the ' Go Down ' as it is called) roll after roll, and roll after roll of silks and stuffs were brought out and shown. If bought, they were put aside; if not, they were rolled up and put in the great boxes from which these many rolls were taken. There are always crowds of apprentices learning the business and boys around, and our experience is that there is none of that fine touch that some of our salesmen have in displaying goods. There is not, either, praise the Lord, any urging to buy anything. You take it or leave it."]

October 30th

A RAINY day, so we elected to spend the morning in a Daimio Museum (not to be confused with a Dime Museum!). We accordingly hired a closed carriage and drove out to Uyeno Park where there are several Government museums, containing beautiful and rare objects of all kinds. We spent a delightful morning there, and felt satisfied that it was the best way to spend a rainy day.

When one hires a closed carriage here it includes an outrunner — that is, a man who runs behind the conveyance, and every now and then to the front of it, uttering unearthly cries — a sort of scooping " hee-oup " sound — to warn everyone in the street to make way. This proceeding took us so much by surprise, and we got into such a gale of laughter as to become almost hysterical. When one drives in a carriage here, one seems to have the air of royalty — " Out of the way, their Majesties are coming! " — that is what the air and the cry of the outrunner suggest! Our runner had to me a very familiar face; I am sure I have met with him before on a kakemono!

We saw on our way the large Lotus pond which surrounds the little island temple of Beuten, but alas! the large lotus leaves were all hanging their heads and turning brown. On our return we left cards on Baron Kamura, the Minister of Foreign Affairs, who has procured us invitations for the Emperor's ball, — in celebration of his birthday — to take place November 3rd. We had a letter to Kamura. We also paid our party call on the American Ambassador and his lady. Later in the afternoon we received a visit from Baron Kaneko of the House of Peers. He was educated in America, at Harvard College, but in spite of it he speaks English with difficulty. In appearance one would hardly describe him as " every inch a King! " For, where nature has refused to cooperate, it is hard to be properly impressed even by dignity of bearing and extreme courtesy. He proved to be, however, a charming gentleman and extremely obliging. His wife is in bad health, and they are leaving tomorrow for the seashore, at Kamakura, so we must wait till our return here in the spring to improve our acquaintance.

October 31st

TODAY it is again raining hard. It is truly disappointing to see Tokyo at such a disadvantage! We have no idea what the surrounding scenery is like, and as for Fujiyama, the only glimpse we have had of it so far was on our arrival at Yokohama, — half veiled in mist at that!

We indulged in a closed carriage again this morning instead of taking jinrikishas, and we contented ourselves with spending an hour or so in an emporium of wonderful brocades, which we were told we must on no account miss seeing. It was certainly worth the trouble, there were so many startlingly beautiful things. We made some purchases, of course, and on leaving there was handed to each of us a present, exquisitely done up. It was only a square of some pretty Japanese material, but very attractive. The pretty little Japanese woman, who made the presentation with perfectly fascinating manners, sank down on her heels and implored me to take her with us to America in our service!

Over fifty people collected outside the shop and stayed around just to see us get in and out, although they had to stand in the pouring rain to do it. But their large, oiled-paper umbrellas overhead, and clogs underfoot, rendered them apparently indifferent to the elements. It is astounding that at Tokyo, the Eastern Capital, where so many foreigners are constantly coming and going, such curiosity still prevails. I had no idea that the Japanese were so childish!

This afternoon we received a visit from the Marchioness Oyama, to whom we had brought a letter of introduction — a charming woman! She was educated in America, at Vassar College and speaks English perfectly, though she is thoroughly Japanese in all other essentials. She wore her native costume consisting of three or four kimonos, one over the other, showing the borders of each one in front. The outer one, with the family crest embroidered on it in medallions, was of a dark-grey cloth, the inner ones of a somewhat lighter shade. A fine brocaded obi and *straw sandals* completed the costume. We were delighted with her manners and conversation, so full of intelligent comprehension — in fact we found her fascinating. She invited us to an entertainment at a Japanese ladies' school this evening, and we mean to go, because it is precisely one of the things which will give us an opportunity to see a phase of Japanese civilization which we could not get on the beaten track.

November 1st
THE SCHOOL entertainment last night proved to be most interesting, and I am glad we made the effort to go,

though it involved missing our dinner. We had a fine
chance to see a bevy of Japanese school girls in all their
war paint. There were some beautiful tableaux, two
duets on kotos, two vocal recitations accompanied on
the biwa, and some remarkable exhibitions of fencing
between individual girls and their teacher, — an old
woman named Komatsuzaki, — who is one of the few
remaining experts in this ancient accomplishment, for
it was not the fencing as we know it, but something quite
different and with strange weapons. There was also a
sword dance, the music to which was a song of warfare
sung by a man behind the scenes. The old fencing teacher
was as agile as a cat and quite remarkable in skill. I
asked one of the school teachers about her, and learned
that she was extremely poor, and that all she gets for her
lessons in fencing is 50 sen (25 cents) a month for a
lesson every day! That is at the rate of less than a penny
an hour. When Mrs. Hearst learned this, her big heart
was touched, and she asked to be allowed to present the
little old lady with 50 jen ($25.00). You can imagine
what this meant to the poor old lady who had never seen
so much money in her life! It was all very sweet and
touching, and Mrs. Hearst is the dearest woman in the
world.

Another day of pouring rain! I blush for the climate
of Japan! We stayed at home this morning to do up our
correspondence, and in the afternoon we rode out to pay
a call on the Emersons. Mr. Emerson is an archeologist
who has done some work for Mrs. H. in the past. His
sister has been very nice to us since we have been here.
We have received various invitations to dinner, but have
declined them, as we do not want to be entertained by
Americans. Our Japanese friends are afraid to invite us
to their houses because they cannot offer us hospitality

after the European style. They don't seem to be able to imagine that the very thing above all others we should like would be to sit on our heels and use chop-sticks! And just think of it, they kept saying apologetically at the school last night that they were so sorry not to have some European music on the programme on our account!

There is a little rift in the clouds this evening, and I really do think it will be fine to-morrow. Oh joy! We are invited by the Marchioness Oyama to tea in a wonderful old Daimio garden tomorrow afternoon. General and Mrs. Winslow and two or three others are to be of the party, I believe. In the evening we have planned to dine at the Maple Club and see some geisha dancing.

November 2d

I NEVER enjoyed anything more than our visit to the old Daimio's garden this afternoon. It is a dream of a garden of ancient times — on a grand scale, with nothing of the more modern-artificial style of landscape gardening, but rather that of the old days, when the Japanese nobles wielded swords, twice the size of a Japanese warrior of today. The fine old trees were magnificent! We were led down over old stone bridges and by little temples, exquisite in form and decoration. There was a large pond into which a waterfall emptied itself, and in it, swaying to and fro, were some magnificent lotus leaves still untouched by the frost.

We were charmingly entertained by the Marchioness and her pretty daughter, in a lovely garden house, though, alas! *not* in Japanese style. The tea we drank however, was both gathered and cured on the estate of the Marquis Oyama, and was delicious. We like the Oyamas so much, they are so cordial, genial, and simple. When I happened to see the bare legs of the Marchioness, as she slightly raised her kimono in a damp spot in the garden — legs which were brown and rough like a peasant's, it needed a stretch of imagination to place her where she really belongs, among the *crème de la crème* of the Japanese nobility. We bade them farewell with real regret, and we shall long remember our afternoon in that ancient garden, and see in our mind's eye the grand old trees and swaying bamboos!

We have abandoned the plan of dining at the Maple Club and seeing geisha dancing, it would really be too much with what we have on hand for tomorrow. We begin with the grand review, in celebration of the Emperor's 52nd birthday, where we are invited to the grandstand of the Legation by Mr. Griscom, the American Ambassador, and we finish up with the Emperor's ball in the evening, after which we must pack and make ready for an early start for Nikko in the morning of Wednesday.

November 3rd
WE ARE making history so fast that I can with difficulty find the time to chronicle the events as they happen. The review was splendid this morning, and it was really most entertaining to watch the Japanese troops, who looked like the little tin soldiers in a toy box — I might call them military microbes! But they seemed very sturdy and warlike in their own Japanese way. There was an enormous crowd, yet not a sound was heard except the neighing of the cavalry horses. The Japanese evidently express their enthusiasm by dead silence. They did not cheer their Emperor when he arrived on the field, nor afterwards, they merely stood up and raised their hats. His Majesty is certainly not pretty to look at. He is distinctly inelegant and lumpy. This may be partly due, however, to the fact that he is never measured for his

clothes or uniform, as it would be a sacrilege for his august body to be touched by a tailor. So his garments have always to be too large, and a misfit generally. You can conceive of nothing more awkward than his appearance on horseback as he stooped over and held on to the saddle. The horse was led by a groom, and another stood at the tail, so it gave one the impression that the Emperor had never been on a horse before, and did not know how to ride. When I made some such comment to Mr. Emerson, he said that His Majesty had probably been celebrating his birthday early in the morning! We saw him receive the diplomats and ambassadors in his open tent, and after that he was served with tea before mounting.

The tremendous concourse of officers and dignitaries of every nationality made the occasion doubly interesting and gay. There were Russians, Prussians, Belgians, Frenchmen, English, etc., all in full uniform with all their decorations. Some of the Chinese dignitaries were simply splendid and gorgeous. As I looked first at the brilliant array of European officers who were onlookers, and then at the Japanese nobles and officers, I could understand for the first time why they are trying so hard to be European in their way of living, for the Europeans looked verily like a race of kings among them. It will take a long time, thank heaven! but I fear the Europeanization of Japan is inevitable. The race, in its present condition, seems to be somewhat degenerate — at least to casual observers like ourselves, and perhaps a new current of life has become a necessity for its further development. Who knows?

[*Note by* H. M. R. " It is astonishing how few people of distinction one sees, and among the Japs I have not seen a single one, man or woman. They are not a virile looking race, in the higher classes, certainly. Here and there you see fine looking men in the streets, coolies or others.

" The insufficient food or the quality of it through centuries, the curiously primitive ways, the slowness of apprehension as compared with people who do not understand you or your language better than the Japs, all make them seem to me unreal, diminutive, half baked — just awakening, perhaps. The Marchioness Oyama told us that the young and coming generation would probably be better physically, for where the nobles sent their children to England, for example, the good food, the out-of-door life and the English living developed them immensely, and made them, though of diminutive fathers and mothers, tall and strong men and women when they returned."]

The band played only European music, much to my disgust, the Japanese National Hymn being the only native selection, and that even was harmonized in such a way as to make it sound like a Cossack dirge. After the Review we drove out to Shiba Park, to see the chrysanthemum show, where there were curious tableaux of revolving figures, representing episodes of warfare and of the lives of the Samurai. The garments of these life-size figures were all composed of small chrysanthemums woven together to look like tapestries and brocades, and the flowers were *growing*, mind you! They are carefully uprooted and wrapped in moss, the roots being stuck out of sight in the shoes, or some other part of the dress. It was indeed a very wondrous and curious sight. In the afternoon we drove to Uyeno Park to see some collections of modern Japanese paintings, which we found to be extremely poor, and afterwards we visited a fine temple. Rather a full day, considering we are to top off with

the Emperor's ball. We have been duly called on by
" Le Baron et la Baronne Y. Sannomiya — *Grand
Maître des cérémonies de sa Majesté l'Empereur*, but
we were out and only have their cards.

Kanaya Hotel, Nikko, Japan, Nov. 4th, 1903
As we are in Nikko the beautiful, up among these mountain peaks, and far from the madding crowd, it goes
against the grain to descend to anything so material as
the Emperor's ball last night, so I must make short work
of it! Of course it was a " crush," also a fine sight, and
quite interesting on account of the enormous number
of different nationalities represented, which furnished
us with an opportunity to compare the different types.
The nobility of all nations were rampant, and all of the
Chinese grandees whom we saw at the review in the
morning were at the ball. We never say now that anything is strange or anomalous, we simply say it is Japanese! The Emperor never attends his ball, although it is
given in his honour — to celebrate his birthday; he
never appears nor does the Empress nor the Crown
Prince. All the rest of the royal household, however,
were present in full force, and they all danced like mad.
I am compelled, much against my will, to admit that
these, one and all, looked strikingly insignificant in their
European dresses, and the more bejewelled they were,
the more gorgeous the brocades and laces they wore, the
more they looked like penny dolls. Why, oh why will
they do it? There were also numbers of Japanese ladies
in their native costume, and how much better they
looked — how much more in keeping with their type,
although I confess that the quiet colours of their kimonos — the correct fashion at present — seemed
hardly decorative enough for an Emperor's ball.

The supper was very bad, the service quite inadequate; but champagne flowed like water, and the Japanese contingent soon showed the effects thereof. They were very funny in their cups! They lost all restraint, and quite forgot their good manners — tearing away the floral decorations from the walls and arches, and distributing them among their friends. We were greatly shocked at the proceeding. Nevertheless, it was very interesting to us to see the Japanese gentry *au naturel* — stripped of all their conventional ways and artificialities, and so completely under the law of " In Vino Veritas." Mrs. Hearst and Clara retired early in the evening, rather exhausted after the long and busy day, but Harry thought we might as well make a night of it and see the thing through, so we did.

The journey from Tokyo to Nikko was quite pleasant and full of novelty — past rice fields and groups of peasants weirdly attired, persimmon orchards, etc. In Europe or America, however, we should have made the same distance in less than half the time. We left Tokyo at 9 A.M., arriving here at 2 P.M. We were very comfortable, however, as we had a double, first-class compartment nearly to ourselves, and were served frequently with tea on the way. There were only two Frenchmen in the car besides our party, and Harry, of course, became intimate with them — in French, for they spoke no English. They proved very interesting travelers.

Our guide had written to the Kanaya Hotel at Nikko to send some one to meet us at the " tmaichi " station, in order that we might take the famous four-mile ride through the avenue of gigantic cryptomerias, planted three hundred years ago. Sure enough, there was the hotel porter but no jinrikishas! We had left the train, taking it for granted that he had provided the necessary conveyances, but no; he had, with native literalness, come in response to the order, without ever asking why, and we came, in consequence, within an ace of losing our train. We had to hustle, I can tell you, to get back into our compartment before the train moved off. Had we been left behind there would have been no alternative but to walk all the way to Nikko — which for Clara and Mrs. Hearst would have been an impossibility, — or else wait at the station for the evening train.

The stupidity and dulness of apprehension of the average Japanese that one comes into contact with on a day's journey are beyond words! They never seem to reason or draw inferences, no matter how obvious. Their minds seem only to work literally. They observe, remember, and repeat whatever one may have shown them or told them to do once, but they do it blindly and without reflecting that different conditions demand different action. This makes it very trying at times. However, once arrived at Nikko, the surpassing beauty of it all made us forget everything else.

As soon as we had settled ourselves in our spacious rooms, Harry and I sallied forth together — the others preferring a nap. We walked along the winding river-side for a few miles, having crossed a bridge about a hundred feet from the remains of the sacred, red-lacquer bridge which was, alas! swept away by the great flood in 1902. The road, or rather path, was shockingly bad and difficult to walk on without tumbling into the river, but the scenery made up for it. To the left of us, a range of beauteous mountains, covered with the wonderful Japanese maple in its flaming autumn dress, and beyond, higher mountains, striped with snow. In the boisterous river huge boulders of volcanic rock of many shades angered the waters to a fury. We came upon a curious old temple in a garden which must have been beautiful once, but which had been swept by the flood. There were many stone images of Buddha in different incarnations, but many of them wore their heads on the ground either beside or behind them. We raised and reinstated some of them, but I fear they will shed them again all too soon!

We found a lovely road through the mountain woodlands back of the river, and went back that way for a change. I gathered some blue gentian and fine branches of crimson maple, and we felt as much at home on that ramble as though we belonged in Japan. There is nothing like going about on your two feet! It is difficult for us to find opportunities for this, as Mrs. Hearst and Clara are not walkers, and feel that they must ride everywhere. So we have been rushed through the streets, either in jinrikishas or carriages, since we have been in Japan. Of course one saves time that way, but one also misses many interesting details of Japanese life. Harry and I love to prowl about at leisure and take it all in — stopping before the funny little shops and stalls to see the queer things they sell to eat, and the queer unwholesome people who buy them.

The view from our hotel windows is enchanting. Snow peaks with foot-hills bedecked with tinted maples, and the curving, rushing river at our feet, for we are on a high hill, and Nikko itself is over two thousand feet above sea level. We shall sleep without rocking tonight!

November 5th
THE SAYING goes, " He who has not seen Nikko, has no right to use the word " Kekko " (magnificent and beauteous in one). I am glad we have a right to say " Kekko "!

I have read many descriptions of Nikko and its mar-

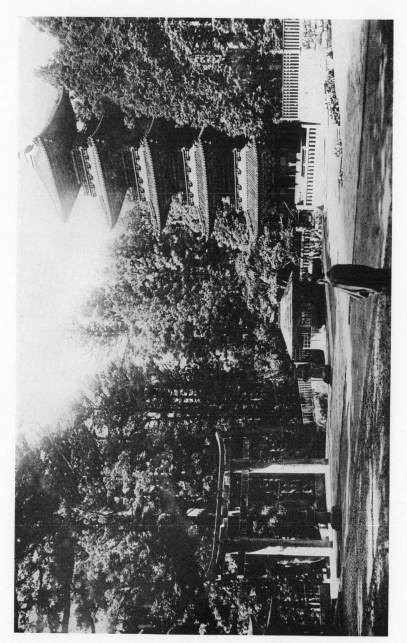

JAPAN: The Pagoda of Nikko

velous avenues of cryptomerias, its mountains and its temples of splendour untold, perched on high ridges. These have been compared to Oriental princesses, and every rich, graceful, gorgeous thing under the sun; but such descriptions mean literally nothing till you see it all for yourself! I never really understood before what it was for Nature and Art to combine and co-operate so wondrously — so intelligently, so harmoniously. It is more than poetic and splendid. It is a dream of heaven! I would not presume to give a description of the temples themselves or their surroundings. There are no words which correspond to certain emotions.

We started off after breakfast up the grand avenue to the sacred enclosure of the great Shinto Temple — all in red lacquer, with its numerous adjoining shrines. The Temple is dedicated to the great Shogun Jeyasu, and on mounting two hundred and fifty steps a little way beyond, you come to his beautiful mausoleum. In the Temple we induced the priests to perform the Shinto service for us — on payment of a moderate sum, — so they got into their gorgeous robes — there were five of them — and went through the whole ceremony of opening the sacred shrine, — the Holy of Holies, — meanwhile reciting the Shinto prayers and invocations in a sort of low chant. It was extremely impressive! Before the ceremony three priests, robed in wonderful, peacock, changeable silk, entered and sat on their heels near us, outside the shrine, and played on weird wood wind-instruments. The first produced discordant sounds exactly like a creaking door-hinge, the second I cannot recall, the third was like a primitive sort of flute, the scale of which seemed to be in quarter tones. To our ears the effect was most untuneful. But the queerness of it redeemed it and made us take it all in with vivid interest.

We were served with holy sake and sacred rice cakes, pink and white, and deadly looking. If you only could have seen us assisting at this shrine!

We comported ourselves with becoming respect and reverence of course, having removed our shoes before entering the Temple. But before the ceremony of opening the Sacred Shrine, we were told that we must remove our coats also! The four of us squatted on our heels (which, let me tell you, is much easier to do in one's stocking feet than with shoes on). Harry, who had drawn his green sweater over his vest, looked funnier than anything I have ever beheld. He seemed two yards long from his head to his knees — all in one straight line, " incongruous " faintly expresses it. I nearly rolled over my heels backward with laughter as I contemplated his long, straight, green body and earnest face, and when Clara, on rising painfully from her unwonted position, facetiously trod on the upturned soles of his feet, that finished me! After this we moved away and took to our shoes again on the outside. We visited many smaller temples in the same enclosure, and in one we saw a Shinto dance, performed by a Shinto priestess, which was very weird and mysterious.

We returned to the hotel to lunch in the afternoon, rather tired, particularly of taking our shoes off and putting them on again, although our kurumayos (carrier men) did it for us. We could not make use of jinrikishas for this visit to the temples on account of some of the avenues being broken up by steps, which do not agree with wheels, but Mrs. Hearst and Clara were carried by four men each in a bamboo chair fastened on strong bamboo poles, and lifted up on their shoulders. They looked very exalted and proud. Our guide had engaged four men and a chair for me also, but I scorned the con-

veyance and preferred to walk. We had in all sixteen
bearers in our train! In the afternoon we were enterprising enough to start off again to see more temples, but
it came on to rain lustily — real mountain rain, which
means business, so we had to give it up.

November 6th

This morning we started forth again, the weather being
clear and cold, to visit some Buddhist temples, and it
was most interesting to compare them with the Shinto
temples of yesterday. One of the most interesting things
we saw was a group of rude stone images in a hollow
formed by an overhanging rock. It was one of the primitive places of worship, in use long before there were any
temples. We had a most fatiguing morning, as we had to
go up a mountain to the Takino-o Temple, and Harry
and I had to do this and mount over a thousand rough
stone steps in all on our two feet, because, in view of
the fact that we made no use of the chair's bearers yesterday, we dispensed with them today, which our feet
sorely regretted afterwards! Our guide, old, stupid that
he is, when we ask him what particular temple this or
that is, never knows whether it is dedicated to Jemitsu,
Sannomiye, Ieyasu, or who, always answers " Red-
racquer Temper " the pronunciation of the letter *l* being impossible to the Japanese tongue, and that being
the nearest he can get to " Red Lacquer Temple." We
find it such a picturesque expression for the angry emotions, that if Mrs. Hearst ever gets impatient with the
colossal stupidity of Fujii and others, we cry out, " She
is in a red-racquer temper! " We have quite adopted the
saying!

Every night, after dinner, all sorts of curio dealers
waylay us at the hotel. They bring with them bales of

goods, which they insist on spreading out either in the hotel office or parlour, and very interesting things they bring too. We have bought quite a number of Netzkis and Ogimes, and some quite interesting old pieces of ivory, lacquer, etc. The dealers bother us to death, however, and invade us in our rooms even before breakfast, so bent are they on making a trade. But they are the personification of patience and courtesy, for if, after they have taken a half an hour to show their wares, which they have perhaps brought from a distant " Go down " (warehouse), or lugged up a hill, you do not choose to purchase anything, they show no disappointment whatever, but, placing a hand on each knee, they bow down to the ground and draw in their breath respectfully, seeming just as pleased as though you had bought hundreds of yens' worth of goods. I am sorry to say, however, that they are intensely unreliable. Woe to him who buys without having any idea of the real value of their articles — he will surely get cheated up to the hilt!

November 7th

TODAY we made an excursion to the beautiful mountain lake Chuzenji, 4375 feet above sea level, in jinrikishas, with two extra men each to push them up hill and pull back with a rope on coming down. I must give up in despair! There are no words to describe the loveliness and individuality of the scenes we passed through — the extraordinary autumn colours of the maples, beeches, wild cherry, etc. We have really nothing so resplendent in the way of autumn tints in America! Then the forms of the trees are so different from anywhere else. They lean over at such queer angles, and form such weird pictures. These, the noble cryptomerias, the bamboo groves, and the tall, variegated bamboo grass that covers the mountain sides, the strange shrubs bearing beautiful berries, the grand waterfalls, the stony and boulder-laden river bed, thousands of feet below, and the raucous cry of monkeys hidden away in the forest, all combined to create in us sensations hitherto unknown.

We stopped several times on our way up the mountain at country yadoyas (inns or resting places) for our bearers to refresh themselves with a bowl of rice, and for the purchase of some straw sandals (price two cents), a process which had to be repeated several times during our progress up the mountain. On the last stretch before reaching the summit, Harry, in a sudden fit of exhilaration, burst into song, accompanying the monotonous tread of our bearers by vigorously intoning the classic lines:

> " *The hens and chickens went to roost,*
> *A hawk flew down an' bit de goose."*

But when he reached the refrain:

> " *Get out of de way, Daniel Tucker.*
> *You'm too late to come to supper* "

he improvised a prolonged

> " *Tewit-tewoooo* "

the coolies had to set down their burdens and hold their sides for laughing. The fascination that the tune had for them knew no bounds. They simply yelled with delight, and had a try at every sort of sound their throats could produce till they succeeded in imitating the " tewit-tewoooo." That scooping sound, which lost nothing in Harry's rendering of it, apparently awakened in these queer little men every dormant sense of humour and wild spirits. They kept urging Harry to repeat it again and again — at every mountain inn, calling together the inmates to hear it and their own version of it. Till we left Nikko, and even at the station, Harry was saluted at every turn by a " tewit-tewoooo " from some coolie who had been initiated into the art by our bearers.

As soon as we reached each mountain inn, dainty little trays with a tiny teapot and saki cups were brought out to us, together with some fat peppermint jumbles, while cushions were placed for us to sit on the edge of the veranda. We reached our destination, Lake Chuzenji, at a little before two, and had a very fair luncheon at the Lake Side Hotel, which is fascinating, and thoroughly Japanese, though it tries to be European.

After lunch we played with a pretty little native monkey in the office, and then took to our jinrikishas again, to be rushed down hill at full gallop. On our way we met several people coming up the hill in a different kind of conveyance, a sort of hanging, reclining chair, in which the occupant is covered up to the chin with rugs, suggesting an improvised hospital ambulance. It is so short that they have to double themselves up in it. They are carried by two men. These conveyances are called " kagos." I shouldn't like to get into one unless I owned the fittings, for so many people in these parts have horrible skin diseases, and the Japanese are so unsanitary in certain of their ways.

It began to rain as we neared the hotel, and it looks as if we were in for a rainy day tomorrow, when we are to leave at 7 A.M. for Myanoshita, a lovely mountain region, where there are all sorts of hot springs, and where people with skin diseases and rheumatism flock for the baths. We are only going to stay there over night.

November 8th

IT WAS a rainy day and no mistake! Our journey was rendered interesting, however, by our having for travel-

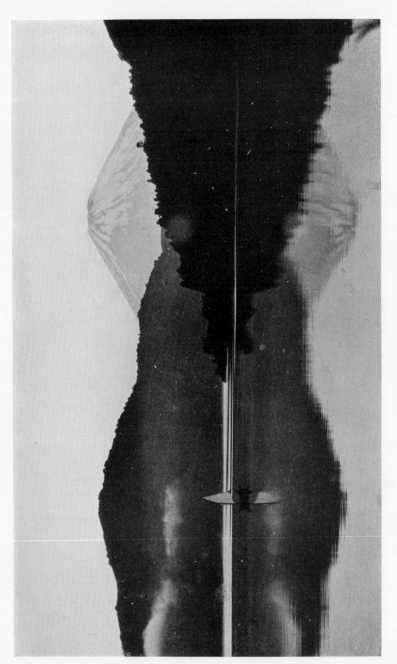

JAPAN: Mount Fujiyama

ling companions some high caste Chinese who had been entertained at Tokyo during the Emperor's birthday festivals. One of them was the Governor of Tientsin. We conversed by medium of their interpreter — a really intelligent Japanese. The Governor was evidently one of the reform party, and was quite affable for a Chinese. We were informed by the Japanese interpreter, who apparently took a fancy to Harry, that Governor See would put the town at our disposal if we would go to Tientsin! It was pitch dark when we finally reached Hakone.

After an hour's ride in an electric car, we took jinrikishas to go up the mountain to the Fujiya Hotel, each with two pushers besides the man-horse. All the jinrikisha men were dressed in white, from their broad, mushroom hats down to their feet, that they might be visible in the darkness. Every jinrikisha was furnished with a coloured paper lantern, and I never saw any prettier, or more picturesque procession than ours as it wended its way up the steep, winding mountain paths, casting the lantern light into the black darkness of the night. The hotel is charming, and the situation, right among the mountain hearts, is — well, I won't attempt to say what! The rain is ceasing, the moon is trying to come out, it will be fine tomorrow, hurrah!

November 9th
IT WAS fine this morning, gloriously clear and bright, and the run down the mountain in jinrikishas was most exhilarating. On my way I observed several varieties of hydrangias growing wild on the mountain slopes. At Hakone we took to the train, and a little beyond we got our first really perfect view of Mount Fujiyama — the

presiding genius of Japan. It was wonderful, dressed in its deep snow cape! On our way to Nangoya we passed acres and acres of rice fields where they were harvesting — an interesting sight. Also numberless tea plantations, many of them in terraces up the hill slopes, like the vineyards in Switzerland and on the Rhine. The tea trees look something like close-cut box bushes — about three to four feet high, only the leaf is larger. The blossom is something like a small wild rose, white, with a yellow centre, only thicker and more substantial. We passed whole groves of trees laden with the golden persimmon, which grows here as large as the apple. It is the fruit of the country apparently. They are beautiful to look at as a note of gold in the landscape.

We were very uncomfortable in the train, which was crowded, and I never in my life was in a country where in a first-class carriage one met people with such brutally bad manners. There were a number of Japanese army officers, who were rough and uncouth in the extreme, and, moreover, they made us nearly sick with their nasty ways! One little man, who sat next to Clara and entered into a pidgin English conversation with her, being superior to the rest in education and dressed in European clothes, did nothing worse than take his boots off and travel in his stocking feet, which he made conspicuous by crossing his legs and sometimes drawing them up onto the seat! How glad we were that we had determined to break our journey to Kyoto, by stopping over a night at Nangoya! We have ordered Fujii to engage a private compartment for our party between here and Kyoto, tomorrow, seeing that in first class carriages one cannot have immunity from the genus *Hogg* who elsewhere would belong in the third class!

Kyoto, Nov. 10*th,* 1903

As WE did not leave Nangoya till noon, we had time to drive up to the castle, which is very fine, with its splendid moat and massive walls. We also visited a Buddhist temple, famous for its wood carvings (the Higashi Hongwongi). There happened to be a service in progress, for which we were glad. It really is very much like that of the Roman Catholic Church — to the naked eye, at least. We induced a young priest in one of the corridors to sell us his prayer beads by giving him a small advance on what he said he paid for them.

Lastly we went to see a chrysanthemum show, which was quite wonderful. Mrs. Hearst herself, who has such a grand collection of them at her Hacienda, owned that she had never seen nor conceived anything like these. They were vastly superior to those we saw at Tokyo. They are not so beautiful as they are weird and curious. The Japanese seem to delight in making everything look like something else, not itself. To make art as separate from and unlike Nature as possible. This seems really to be their principal aim, especially in their cultivation of trees and flowers. The result is always interesting though not necessarily beautiful, but the effect is certainly picturesque and artistic. I verily believe they have a secret way of hypnotizing their plants and forcing them to grow the way they want them to.

We arrived here at five. The hotel is beautiful, but the view also of the city and surrounding mountains is magnificent! We have a fine drawing room and five large bedrooms *en suite* for our party, and are very comfortable. I wish we had time to settle down here for a couple of weeks, there is so much to see and do, and Kyoto is such a representative Japanese city. But alas, our ship

for China and India sails from Kobe relentlessly on the
15th. However, in April, on our return we shall try to
make up for it.

November 11th

THIS is the day of days to see Kyoto — clear, bright,
and beautiful! I think the weather is going to be kind
to us at last!

Harry scraped acquaintance with some American
ladies in the hotel last night, and was introduced by
them to another compatriot, who is at the head of a large
girls' school in Japan — a Miss Denton, who happened
to know all about Mrs. Hearst and her good works, so
she begged to have the privilege of showing us around
Kyoto, and of bringing with her one of her Japanese
professors to explain things to us. So we four, accompanied by Miss Denton and the Professor, started forth
after breakfast in two carriages for the castle and the
Emperor's palace, for which the American Ambassador
at Tokyo had given us a special permit.

The Professor and our guide Fujii were instinctively
antagonistic, therefore his presence, on the whole, did
not add to the gaiety of nations! He pointed out to us,
however, a number of the fine old paintings of Kanna,
which our stupid Fujii knew nothing about. On contemplating them one could but feel that the modern Japanese painters cannot touch the fringes of the old art! We
had an interesting and memorable morning, slightly
marred by the discomfort of cold feet from walking
about so much without our shoes. If I were to stay long
in Japan, I certainly should adopt the native custom of
wearing thick socks with a separate compartment for the
big toe, and sandals, as one expends too much time and
energy in taking off and putting on one's shoes. One has

to do it even in many of the stores, and always in private houses.

In the afternoon Harry and I strolled about the quaint and picturesque streets, which all look alike for miles and miles, but which smell variously! Mrs. Hearst, meanwhile, spent the time in some curio shops with Miss Denton. A very nice young man who is studying Japanese art here, and who lives in a Japanese house in Japanese style, has invited us to see the " tea ceremony " tomorrow afternoon. He is a collector of precious Japanese and Chinese curios. Mrs. Hearst has had dealings with him in San Francisco, and has great confidence in him — so much so that she has given him commissions to collect certain objects for her Museum.

November 12th

THIS has been a full day! In the morning there were several Buddhist temples to be visited, and fine ones they were! Miss Denton went with us and added much to our enjoyment. She is a most intelligent woman and speaks Japanese well. In the afternoon we went to the tea ceremony at Mr. Jaehna's house, which we were all much interested in seeing. It is the most formal, cut and dried, deliberate, and — I may add — tiresome performance imaginable. It is hard to guess how such a ceremony ever came to be! The Japanese seem to take it all very seriously, however. You have to hold your cup in a particular manner, and, after turning it around just so many times, you raise it to your lips, and you must drink the whole of it in just three swallows and a half. If you leave a drop, it is regarded as an offense to the tea brewer, who has also gone through the ceremony of washing the utensils, preparatory to making the tea. The silk cloth with which they are wiped must be folded in a certain way, and differently for each one. Every gesture and action appears to be strictly rhythmic, as in a Wagner opera. No wonder the Japanese girls study the ceremony under teachers for three years! It is part of their education — every properly equipped person must know how. The pretty daughter of the Marchioness Oyama told us that she was only a beginner, having studied it only one year.

I am more and more impressed with the fact that time is of no importance to the Japanese. We have not dared to go to the theatre yet because it takes over six hours to see a performance — in the right way, and it is as much as one's life is worth to cope with Japanese etiquette. Amongst other things I have seen here, is, that if you make a little present to a Japanese, you are immediately asked how much you paid for it, in order that the recipient may get something for you of precisely the same value. We, in the West, often do the same in spirit, though not in quite such a barefaced way! Tonight, after dinner, we are to go to a Geisha performance. We told Fujii to announce our coming at one of the principal tea houses, and to tell them to have the best Geishas in Kyoto engaged for us.

Well! Now we know what a geisha girl is! We have seen them do all their different dances, we have heard them sing(?), play on the samosen, the koto, and on a queer little sort of drum, the name of which I forget. It was a long entertainment — far too long — beginning with the tea ceremony, which we begged them to curtail as we had seen it once already. We sat on the floor — on our heels, as long as we could bear it, and then we ignobly settled on the base of our spines and stuck our feet out.

There were about ten Geishas in all to entertain us,

JAPAN: Geisha Girls

and they danced, one at a time, while three played and sang the music. The ones whose turn it was not to dance, came and squatted down beside us — one between each pair of us, and proceeded to " entertain " us. This they did principally by fingering our clothes and asking questions about everything we had on. My green necklace and Mrs. Hearst's amethyst hatpin seemed particularly to take their fancy, and one of the Geishas drew the pin out of Mrs. Hearst's head and scratched her own head with it! We could not understand them nor they us, but Mr. Jaehna, who went with us, was able to talk a little and interpret. They were very merry and laughed in a high, rippling cadence. They seemed a good sort in many ways, and did not impress us at all as being otherwise than modest, but simply silly and childish. Their merriment, however, while of course it was, in a way, artificial, did not appear forced, which was the saving clause. I am glad to have seen them in all their war paint, and to have seen so many different types, but I confess I do not hanker after any more geisha entertainments for the present!

November 13th
THIS morning we drove to the Emperor's garden — four miles out, having first obtained a special permit from the American Ambassador at Tokyo. It is a paradise of a place, and a triumph of landscape gardening — all the more so that you get the impression that Nature has done it all. I never saw such tinted maples in my life, and they did not appear indiscriminately, but always in the right places. The garden is partly constructed on a hillside — in terraces. There is a beautiful little lake of liquid jade, and here and there a flaming maple has been made to hang over it at just the right angle to cast its

reflection in the water. There is a long avenue of very old pine trees leading up to the terrace garden, but none of these has been permitted to grow more than three or four feet high, as otherwise they would obstruct the view of the grand mountains — the frame in which beautiful Kyoto is set. It made me sad to think that such a wonderful garden should only be enjoyed now and then by a few individuals armed with permits — never by the people, and very seldom even by the Emperor himself. The spirit of altruism has, I fear, not yet sprouted in Japan!

This afternoon we were invited to Miss Denton's school house to see what good work she is doing with her little army of Japanese girls — mostly merchants' daughters, of Kyoto. Although they are all taught English, their education is thoroughly Japanese — their rooms being without furniture, the same as in their own homes, and their lives lived on the floor. The only innovation I could find was a sort of military drill for the development of muscle. Their bath tubs, which are very little larger than our own, are occupied by three or four girls at a time, and the same water is used by the next bevy and yet the next, until it is too dirty even for their taste! Miss D. assured us that they prefer it so, as that is what they are accustomed to.

We saw a class of girls taking a lesson from a learned professor in arranging flowers, a process which was truly interesting. I should have liked to join the class myself so artistic were the results. Every branch was compelled to bend over the way the professor said it should go, and when a twig was restive it was soaked in hot water till it became pliable. Only three or four flowers were allowed in each vase, and I must say that, as I surveyed these vases, it made our crowding of flowers together in masses seem very vulgar. We have much to learn from these artistic little people!

We were all invited out to dinner at the house of a Mr. Phelps, an American, settled in Kyoto, who had known Mrs. Hearst elsewhere; but Clara and I, who wanted to do some writing and packing, declined the invitation, and let Mrs. Hearst and Harry do duty for us all. We leave for Kobe tomorrow morning. It is only two hours distant from Kyoto, and there we are to board our good ship " Hamburg " *en route* for China tomorrow.

We have seen far too little of Kyoto, which is really the finest and most representative city of Japan, besides being full of interest and extraordinary beauty. Its position in the landscape is unequalled, surrounded as it is on all sides by magnificent mountains, which are agreeably accessible. Add to that miles and miles of most picturesque and purely Japanese streets and numerous gorgeous temples, gardens, etc., and you have something unique. Europeanism has not touched Kyoto so far, and, now that I have sampled it, I am not surprised at people who enter Japan from this end, saying that Yokohama and Tokyo are not particularly interesting. By comparison with Kyoto, they certainly are not.

Kobe, Nov. 14th, 1903

Kobe is a quasi-European city, something after the style of Yokohama; a very large portion of it is purely Japanese. I strolled out this afternoon with Marie, the maid, to make some necessary purchases, and, to my delight, there passed a characteristic bridal procession, the bride's trousseau and belongings being carried to

the house of the bridegroom in chests suspended from
bamboo poles, and hoisted on the shoulders of two men.
I had read descriptions of such processions, and I thought
it was quite a piece of good luck to run into one. I think
I should like to spend a few days in Kobe on our return.
It is charmingly situated, in a frame work of fine mountains, and there must be some lovely walks and drives in
its neighbourhood.

November 16*th*

WE WENT on board the " Hamburg " soon after four,
yesterday afternoon, in the hotel tug, and passed the
American warship, " Kentucky," in the harbour. There
was a great waving of our flag and hearty cheering. The
" Hamburg " is a magnificent ship, a perfect monster.
I should think that wave and wind would make but little
impression on her. We had to mount a three-story stair-
way to get to the first deck! I never saw anything like
the height of it. Our stateroom is large and commodious,
and I think we shall be very comfortable on our long
voyage. Mrs. Hearst has a beautiful suite of sitting-
room, bedroom, and bath, on the promenade deck.

We are now in the Inland Sea, *en route* for Nagasaki,
and oh, what scenery! Tier upon tier of mountains, and
such beautiful islands springing up out of the water. It
would be worth any one's while to go to Japan just for
the Inland Sea. The channel is very narrow in parts, and
the ship seems to go close up to the mountain bases.
The weather is still fine. At four o'clock we went
through the " narrows " — very dangerous on account
of close quarters with the coast. There were hundreds
of Japanese junks apparently filling up the narrow passage, and it seemed a problem how our great steamer
could get in between them. They say that the junks

often get in the way of the " liners " on purpose to get
run down and recover damages. We passed two leper
islands — sad to think about, beautiful to look at. One
could almost feel our ship heave a sigh of relief when
she got outside the narrows into the open again. We are
to reach Nagasaki tonight some time.

Anchored at Nagasaki, Nov. 17th, 1903

A RAINY day, as I predicted! The shores of Nagasaki
are very attractive, but alas! it is no place for us women
in such a pouring rain. We should be soaked to the waist
in dragging our skirts over the three flights of perpendicular steps to get to a sampan or a tug to take us
ashore. So we can only look and long. From here, Nagasaki looks all mountains, which sprout from the water's
edge, with rows of pretty, low-roofed houses, in terraces
on their slopes.

This is our chief coaling station, and there are over
fifty coal barges surrounding our ship. In these are
stationed hundreds of little Japs, men and women,
shovelling the coal into small baskets and putting the
contents into a hoist. I should think it would take a
week to put the two thousand tons in. However, they
say we are to leave for Shanghai at eight this evening.

November 18th

THE COAL was not all put in till nearly noon today, and
no wonder, when we consider the primitively laborious
way in which the work was done. We are now looking
our last at the beautiful shores of Japan, which I leave
with keen regret. We had only two earthquakes during
our stay there, and neither shock was violent. Our exit
from the bay was a repetition of the beauty of the Inland Sea of yesterday. And now we are out in the open

again, the ocean is beginning to kick up, and the ship to pitch.

November 19*th*

WE ARE in the Yellow Sea today. The weather fair but cloudy and quite cold. At six we sighted the shores of outlying islands of Shanghai. We shall anchor outside the bar some time tonight. The ship does not cross the bar at all, so we shall have to cross in a tug.

[*Note by* H. M. R. " The ' Hamburg ' came to anchor off Wusung last night at about eleven o'clock, and began to take cargo on board immediately, I judge, by the sounds of the night. At 8.30 we took the tender tug and came to Shanghai, a trip of about two hours and such river scenes as are impressed for all time on my mind and memory! Great junks, with elaborate ornamentation and each with two eyes in the bows, one 'on each side, for ' no eyes, no see; no see, no walkee; no walkee, no get along '; hence the eyes; pointed sampans (meaning literally three boards) with the high sculling oar, and differing essentially from the Japanese we left a couple of days ago; Chinese men of war, both junks and modern iron vessels like the American, English, German and French and flying the flag of the five-footed dragon."]

Shanghai, China, Nov. 20*th*, 1903

OUR SHIP having anchored outside the bar, an hour and a half distant from Shanghai, we took the tug this morning at 8.30, to go up to the city. The weather was fair, I am happy to say, as otherwise it would not have been a pleasant excursion.

The Yellow Sea grows more and more yellow as one approaches the shores of Shanghai. This is because of the river Yangtze Kiang, which flows into it from its distant mountain bed, where it becomes charged with yellow mud. These shores present a powerful contrast to those of beautiful, undulating, and mountainous Japan. They are perfectly flat, and you could easily imagine yourself in Holland but for the plantations of sugar cane, the blue-gowned natives, and the absence of windmills. The harbour presented a lively and quaintly picturesque sight with its hundreds of brown-sailed junks, its gaily painted gunboats and sampans, interspersed with warships of many different national-ities. There was something unusual and interesting to arrest the eye every moment, so that we almost grew weary of looking. One thing I noticed was that there was not a single boat of any kind with a *white* sail. They were all tinted a rich sepia or a golden brown.

Arrived at the Bund, our bags were taken charge of by the Chinese porter of the *not* Chinese " Astor House," and we followed in rikshas. The Bund, along which we were trundled, is a very fine road, facing the harbour, with large, semi-European buildings, mostly public, on the side opposite the embankment. It was thronged with carriages containing European residents and high class Chinese in gorgeous robes; the Chinese drivers in their blue gowns, with a touch of red on their waistbands and caps, and the footmen similarly equipped, looking very grand and decorative. At nearly every street corner there stood a tawny, turbaned Sikh, with black mustache and short beard, looking very dig-nified and a little fierce. I suppose the Chinese use these Indians for policemen because they think they are more awe-inspiring to the quarrelsome coolies than their fellow-Chinamen.

There were hundreds of rickshas in swarms, and a

great many wheelbarrows — a sort of wooden platform on a wheel, with a division in the centre, on which the natives ride on either side, sometimes six or seven at a time, wheeled by one man. This is the cheapest mode of conveyance for the poor people. We passed several men with round, flat baskets full of live muscovy ducks huddled together, their long yellow beaks sticking out and hanging over in all directions. Each man carried two baskets suspended from a bamboo pole slung across his shoulders. It was impossible to take note of all the strange things that were going on in this novel and animated scene. I wished for eyes behind as well as before, and at the sides as well.

Arrived at our hotel, we settled ourselves in a suite of five very large rooms, each with bathroom and toilet attached, the bath being a huge, earthenware pot, framed in wood, in which you can only squat. After a very good lunch we started off in rickshas to see a sight that the European residents of Shanghai know nothing about, we are told, *viz.* a walled Chinese city within Shanghai but entirely apart from the European concession. It is a city with its own laws and rulings, its own temples, Government House, prisons, un-sanitary habits, water supply, amusements, and commerce. There are over four hundred thousand inhabitants crowded together therein. We should not have dared to penetrate into this quarter had we not been under the guidance and protection of an American missionary who, with his wife, has lived in China for over twenty years, who speaks Chinese and knows the people thoroughly. His name is Upcraft, and, out of all the missionaries who have crossed with us this trip, he is the only one who has seemed enlightened enough and broad enough for his work. He is a man of rare courage, endurance, and humanity. We made

SHANGHAI: A Funeral Cortège

friends with him and his wife on the ship, and he volunteered to show us the *heart and soul* of Shanghai. Just before we reached the bridge across which lay the hidden city, we had to dismount from our rickshas and take to little sedan chairs, carried on the shoulders of two men — rickshas being forbidden within the walls of the crowded city and in the narrow streets.

" Oh, for the eyes of Argus! " That was our cry as we were borne through the narrow passage ways, they can hardly be called streets, where, with outstretched arms one can touch the counters of the shops on either side of the way. Shops replete with costly jade ornaments, ivory carvings, silks and embroideries, all huddled up alongside unsavoury little shops where they cook and sell loathly things to eat — nameless fried and boiled fish, cakes, poultry, and pork — alla Chinoise! Ye Gods!

And when you consider that the cooking is done with the dirty water of the little narrow ditches, which run through many of the streets, ditches into which all refuse is dumped, you wonder that typhoid fever and cholera are not raging *always* instead of *sometimes!* The curious part of it is that they say that cholera is always worse in European Shanghai, where everything is supposed to be sanitary and the water supply pure. That seems to put a premium on filth, doesn't it? One saving grace in the Chinese city, however, is that the ditch water is tidal, so that the Whang Poo river periodically claims the sewage. But when the tide is low and the water in the ditches ditto, for the first time in your life you know the full force of the word *stench!*

If the Chinese people were really as wicked as report says, our party never would have got out alive! We were surrounded by swarms of natives at all times, and they could easily have murdered us just for the value of our clothes and cash, had they wanted to, or maltreated us as *foreign devils;* but I must own, to their credit, that not a discourteous look or gesture once escaped them. We had only to cope with their invincible curiosity which led them to come up close, finger our clothes, and stare us out of countenance. How far our immunity from insult or disaster may have been due to the protection of Mr. Upcraft, of course I cannot say. He certainly seemed to have great influence over them, and many natives recognized him as an old friend of former days up in the Western County of China.

He took us into a queer and dirty little temple, right in the heart of the city, named " Tsen Huang Miao," which means " Temple of the Chinese City Ruler." It is always open, and the people flock in there at all hours of the day, and, prostrating themselves before the altar, confide their secrets to the god, beseeching his aid and counsel in their business affairs. They coax and plead, and sometimes they threaten! The altar is bedizened with tawdry offerings, tinsel scarves and every sort of trash, and every one who makes a prayer burns a string of paper money, made of tinfoil and white paper in little cup shapes. This money is supposed to become of value in the spirit world after it is burnt, and strings of it are for sale inside the temple, out in the court, and in many shops in the city. The temple is disgustingly dirty and out of repair, noisy and un-sacred in its atmosphere. People crowd into its narrow space as much to chatter and be amused with what is going on as to worship. I saw one woman prostrate herself twenty-one times before the rude, painted image of a canonized mandarin, after which she got up smiling and went out. There was a choir of *noise-icians,* squawking, banging, and rasping on Chinese fiddles. I could not see them at first, and

I thought it was a cat fight, but it turned out to be only the choir!

After this we went to the " Official House," where justice (!) is administered every day from a platform in an inner court in the open air. Justice often takes the form of tortures of various descriptions. As it is illegal to condemn to death until the culprit has confessed his crime, they torture him till he is only too glad to say anything that will put an end to it. The official residence, the courts, and the prisons were all dilapidated and dirty, and even the wooden cages in which they hang the condemned looked out of repair.

We next betook ourselves to a tea house, or pavilion, situated in the midst of a slimy, green pond, and reached by a series of zigzag bridges. We mounted a quasi per-pendicular flight of stairs — worn, dirty, and dangerous, to the upper tearoom looking out on the green pond, and beyond to a little open space where some fakirs were dancing and doing juggling tricks for the crowd. We were served with Chinese tea, peanuts, and pumpkin seeds, and we bought strange, nameless things which looked like candied crab apples on sticks. Near the middle of the room a Chinese barber was plying his trade, and a small baby was having its head shaved. The little thing bore it heroically, only blinking, never whining. Afterwards a fat Chinaman took the baby's place in the barber's chair.

It was curious to note the beauty of the woodwork and ornate windows of the pavilion, now absolutely uncared for and allowed to fall into decay, although it is in constant use and drives a thrifty trade. What can be the cause of such carelessness and indifference? Opium, I wonder? When we quitted the Chinese City, and found ourselves on the other side of the bridge in the French settlement, where we took to our rickshas again, it was as though we had just left behind us a fantastic dream-world, with just a touch of nightmare in it!

We then hied us to a livery stable in European Shanghai and secured three victorias, as two nice American girls, fellow-passengers — Miss Booth and Miss Leighton — had requested us to let them join our party, and we took a drive, the length of the principality, past the " bubbling well," the Country Club, and all the fine residences of the European inhabitants. The contrast with what we had seen in the morning was powerful, our interest in it feeble, and we were glad when Mr. Upcraft proposed that we should return to the hotel and rest for an hour before dinner.

At about nine, after dinner, Mr. U. started forth with us again in rickshas to show us something of nocturnal Chinese life. He knew that we were none of us squeamish, and that we all wanted to gain as intimate a knowledge as possible of the countries we are travelling in; so he did not hesitate to conduct us into places where respectable tourists as a rule would never think of going. The Foochow Road, which is the principal scene of operations of the Chinese *demimonde* and naughty places and people generally, has nothing to do with the Chinese city we visited in the morning, but is a part of Shanghai proper, or rather improper, I should say. It is a fairly wide and handsome street — for China, with attractive Chinese shops and gaudily decorated teahouses on either side, brilliantly illuminated with Chinese lanterns.

Everything teemed with life and activity. In the teahouses fiddles were scraping and women were squawking, drums beating, Chinese robes and vests were being sold at auction in the open shops, thronged with bidders.

Chinese women in rich brocaded trousers, and men in handsome gowns were running to and fro, jabbering together, and coolies were shouting at the top of their voices to make way for the sedan chairs. We were on foot, as rickshas are not allowed at night in the crowded streets of Shanghai Vanity Fair, and of course we could see more of what was going on than in any other way.

A scene more wildly gay and animated cannot well be imagined. A number of private sedan chairs, with rich fittings of blue, scarlet, green, and yellow brocades, rushed past us, and from each of these a painted lady dismounted at one of the teahouses or opium dens. Our attention was attracted to a number of well dressed Chinamen bearing young girls on their shoulders. These girls were gorgeously dressed in rich satins and brocades, with jewels in their hair and their faces painted. Some of them looked like mere children, not over twelve years of age, and we thought at first that they were being carried on the shoulders of a goodnatured relative, in order that they might the better see the fun, but we learned, to our horror, that these young girls were literally being exhibited on the street, and were for sale to the highest bidder! This sight struck horror and pity into my very soul! For the faces of these girls were not bold nor bad, but innocent and pathetically childlike and helpless.

Perhaps this is, in essence, no worse than what actually takes place in similar quarters of Paris and London, but the bare-faced, shameless way of such things here stands for the fact that the whole thing is regarded as perfectly natural and therefore not worth hiding or veiling in any way. That's the dreadful side of it! The girls on the shoulders of the men are mostly novices, many of whom had not yet found a market, while the

painted ladies in the sedan chairs were the first class
courtezans and recognized beauties of the town. We
actually went up, in the tracks of one of these abandoned
creatures, to the upper story, which was a crowded teahouse, ordered tea, and sat there to watch the gruesome
proceedings.

Mr. Upcraft took us, one at a time, to look into an
opium den adjoining, where we saw quite young, fine
looking men lying in the little bunks, giving themselves
up to the effects of the drug. There were girls replenish-
ing the opium pipes, and also some lookers on — no-
tably some Koreans with their queer tall hats, who
seemed to be interested in watching the effects of the
opium on others.

The table we occupied in the teahouse was in a win-
dow-recess apart from the seething mass of Chinese
humanity. These were lolling in their chairs and smoking their pipes. Their faces, which looked as though they
had been roughly moulded in putty, remained absolutely impassive and expressionless. We thought, very
naturally, that we might be regarded by them as intruders, or, at least, as objects of curiosity. But no, not at
all! They were, to all appearances, not even aware of
our presence. If their eyes happened to be turned in our
direction they seemed to be looking *through* us into
the space beyond, as though we did not exist. It is difficult to conceive such total unawareness of the intrusive
presence of eight strangers! At short intervals, a white
robed attendant came around with a large bowl of
steaming hot water. With this he saturated a cloth and
clapped it on the head of the first Chinaman in the row,
and, after leaving it there for about half a minute, he
withdrew it and repeated the performance all along the
line.

After we had seen enough of this to give us bad dreams, we left the wicked teahouse, walked to the side street where our rickshas awaited us, and went home and to our beds with a lurid picture of Chinese life and im-morals, and with sore hearts for the piteous " Welt Schmerzen," which alas! is everywhere! I could not help thinking, as I recalled the picture of that dear, re-fined, dainty little Mrs. Hearst, dignified, wholesome-minded Clara Anthony, the two ultra respectable American women, Miss Booth and Miss Leighton, and last, not least, Mrs. Upcraft, a Baptist missionary's wife, sitting there in that hell, surrounded by Chinese *roués* and wantons, what can we not be induced to do in foreign lands that no power on earth could tempt us to do at home!

S. S. Hamburg, Nov. 21st, 1903

WE RETURNED to our ship this morning at eleven in the tug which left Shanghai at nine. Our stay was all too short, we expected to have two days there, but we were delayed at Nagasaki, and time had to be made up. We are now under way for Hong Kong, where, I fear, we shall only have one day to reconnoitre. We are rushing through China now, in order to make the journey to Colombo on this comfortable boat, but on our return from India we shall make up for it. The weather is grey and cold, but fair. We were indeed fortunate to have good weather in Shanghai, where it always rains, they say, for we were able to see as much in one day as most people manage to do in a week.

November 23rd

WE HAVE not lost sight of the shore for the last two days since leaving Shanghai, but the flatness has given

way to undulations and attractive islands, which I cannot find on the map, with names attached. This morning
we were surrounded by a fishing fleet, hundreds and
hundreds of boats, and in the near distance was Foo
Chow, the shores of which look very attractive, with fine
headlands and broad expanses of sandy beach. We shall
reach Hong Kong tomorrow morning.

[*Note by* H. M. R. " The Japanese do not take hold of
me as do the Chinese, the Cingalese, or the northern
Indians. They are not a handsome race, but the very
reverse, and I find it difficult to take them at the esti-
mate that they take of themselves. I grant all that may
be said of the wonderful strides they have made in
the adoption of certain things belonging to other peoples whose civilizations are as different from theirs as
are their looks, manners, customs, traditions, habits of
thought, points of view.

" When an attempt is made by a people to manufac-
ture itself and not to evolve itself, I think they run
against the everlasting foundations: that, for example,
peoples are never manufactured, they are evolved or
do evolve. Now, these adaptions of other peoples —
clothes, material things, I mean — cannot change the
great mass of the people in their manners, methods, customs, traditions, or their moral bent or cast, excepting,
if at all, after centuries. A Japanese in English clothes
is a Japanese. He looks it; he is it. And when, after being
elsewhere than in Japan for his education and training,
he comes home again, he will have to sit on the floor,
on his heels, with the rest of the family, whatever else
he may sit upon when among Europeans, and you will
not get out of him for many a century yet to come that
woman is, of course, subordinate to the man or husband;

and she, on her part, will stand pigeon-toed before him in womanly recognition of his superiority.

" I regard them myself, and I have the concurrence of an intelligent Japanese to back my opinion, that they are flighty, superficial, ready-witted, rather untrustworthy as merchants as compared with the Chinese, and, at present, I think, suffering from ' big head,' because of what they did with China; and I believe if England does not interfere, and Japan does get into a fight with Russia, she will get licked! The people are amiable, and have many very interesting qualities, and of course we would like to see more of them. But depend upon it, the religion of the people, the customs of the people, the traditions of the people, the points of view of the people, are not going to be changed in any limited time, any more than the language, by a few people being educated in Germany, England, and America."]

Hong Kong, Nov. 24th, 1903

I SHALL never forget Hong Kong harbour as it appeared in all its exquisite beauty this morning soon after daybreak, when I first looked out of my stateroom window. The atmosphere was clearer and more beautiful than it has been at any time during our travels, and the majestic mountains, which almost surround the harbour, loomed up grandly — their alternately sharp and rounded peaks glistening in the morning sun.

The harbour was alive with junks, sampans, gunboats, steamers, launches, and tugs of all kinds and sizes. Everything here looks entirely different from the harbour at Shanghai. Besides the contrast between flatness and gorgeous mountain scenery, the boats are differently rigged, their sails being differently shaped and coloured. Here they are shaped something like a

Japanese persimmon and a dull yellow in colour, and occasionally one sees some white sails, which one never does at Shanghai.

On the mountain slopes, plateaux, and even on the very peaks themselves, are erected fine residences, many of them of an imposing character. At first I thought these must be summer hotels, hospitals, or government buildings of some kind, but I learned that they were the private houses and bungalows of Hong Kong residents who are absolutely unable to bear the heat and humidity of the city during the hot season, and who have to fly for their lives up to the heights. They say that if you leave any object over night that is not either enclosed in tin or oil-paper, next morning there will be an inch of mildew on it! It is difficult to realize this on such a balmy day of Italian sunshine. But we are told that days like this are quite exceptional at Hong Kong — that the mountains, the beauteous islands, and peninsulas are seldom to be seen because of the persistent and all-pervading fog. What a pity that there should be such a blot on such a heavenly spot! I had been thinking that it would be a joy to come here and live, and was almost envying the English officers and government officials and their families whose lot is cast in Victoria City. But it seems there are two sides to this as to everything else.

Our ship anchored at Kowloon on the main coast last night, and this morning at nine we took the ferry over to Victoria City to spend the day. First we went to the bank to get our letters and draw some money, and we were kept waiting there for over an hour while the business was transacted at a snail's pace, which gets on the nerves of a good American. It was interesting, however, to see the Chinese officials passing to and fro in their handsome robes, with their fans stuck in the neck-rim thereof. Their carriage is so dignified, so majestic, and their expression, for the most part, so serene that it is a pleasure to look at them, especially after coming from Japan where dignity of carriage is certainly not a distinguishing feature. There were also many fine looking Indians and Parsees with their strange and striking head-gear, going in and out of the bank, and this, united to the fact that we all of us found letters from our respective homes, made our long delay quite bearable. It will take me some time to get used to the idea of news being so behindhand.

Harry went to look up an old classmate of his, Mr. Jeffries, whose office was in an adjoining building, and, after poking about with Mrs. Hearst and Clara among the curio shops and picture-card vendors under the porticoes of the principal street, I joined him in Jeff's office. Jeff looked like an old, old man, with his long, white beard, and skin tightly drawn over his face. While in reality he is younger than Harry, he looked twenty years older. So much for a trying climate and a ruined digestion! He was too lame and also too busy to take us in tow himself, but he told us where to find a Chinese guide, and advised us to take the perpendicular electric railway — as I think it should be called — up to the top of Mount Kellet, and lunch at the Peak Hotel. This we did and were repaid by a magnificent outlook on the harbour and surrounding mountains.

After lunch we took the comfortable local conveyances — chairs on bamboo poles, carried on the shoulders of two men, and were trotted around the mountain and shown the private residences of the city people. Besides the houses, every window of which has a *loggia* outside (the distinguishing feature of all the European houses in China), there was perpetual inter-

est in the flora, which, even at this advanced season,
was most varied and unusual. Every turn of the mountain road, disclosed some fern, shrub, or flower growing
wild, which one only sees in England and New England
in a state of cultivation.

At the end of our route down the mountain, we went
to the Botanical Gardens, situated on the lowest slope,
and there our eyes were feasted indeed with more beautiful growing things than I could describe in a small
volume. Some of the trees which impressed me most were
the Australian " silky oak " (which has no apparent
affinity with our oak). The silky, green leaves, which are
five or six inches long, are notched and split so as to
have the effect of a fringe, and are very exquisite. The
flame tree was another, very tall and wide spreading,
the leaves formed like that of the most delicate acacia,
only very large, like a mammoth fern — ten inches
long. When you look up to it you see the sky as through
a veil of pale green lace work. The effect is indescribably
beautiful! I suppose it bears a scarlet blossom in season,
from the name, and I am almost sure that I saw it at
Honolulu, with clusters of something resembling scarlet
geranium all over it.

Then there was the coffin-wood tree, and some wonderful banyans. These have the peculiarity of sending
out from the upper branches pendant shoots which
finally reach the ground and take firm root in the earth.
One banyan that we saw today looked at first sight like
a group of about nine trees, but it was really all one tree,
each trunk having descended from an upper branch.
It is among trees a veritable clown! There are whole
avenues of banyans in Hong Kong. It grows there as
freely as the elm does with us, but they lop off pendant
shoots as they come, as otherwise the trees would fill

HONGKONG: Typical Street Scene

up the entire streets, whereas this one, in the public gardens, was permitted to grow as it pleased.

I wish I could have ascertained the names of many of the strange trees which held our attention, but no one seemed to know what they were called. When I asked our Chinese guide, "What you call that tree?" his answer was invariably, "That Chinese tree." What would you think of a poinsettia as big as an apple tree, its huge crimson flowers as large as plates? Yet we saw several of these in gardens as we passed along. Then the cactus plants of all kinds, the century plants, the royal palms, and others, were a feast to the eye. I had no idea that the flowers of China were so varied and so beautiful; but, according to report, the azaleas — pink, yellow, red, and purple — which grow wild on the mountains, up to the Yangtze River, outrival those of Japan. But may be the Chinese do not make so much of them, nor have festivals in their honour, and therein lies the difference. But the streets of Hong Kong are full of flower vendors with exquisite chrysanthemums and flowers of all kinds in their season. There are also beautiful song birds of gay plumage. In the public gardens there was a perfect concert of them. All of these things, somehow, one has never associated with China, and they have come upon me with genuine surprise and delight.

After we had explored the public gardens, we made our way gradually towards the Hong Kong Hotel, where we were to dine, passing through a number of native Chinese streets instead of the European quarter. These differ altogether from those of Shanghai. They are not so narrow, and the buildings are a story higher, but the effect of colour produced by the balconies and *loggia* supports, which are often of green bamboo, and the really gorgeous Chinese lanterns of which several hang outside each shop door and window, is very rich and picturesque. The hotel is imposing and pretentious, the dinner and service rather bad. At about nine we took the ferry again, and returned to the protection of our ship for the night.

November 25th

As WE found that our ship was not to leave the harbour till noon today we went on shore again after breakfast and remained till eleven. Both Mrs. H. and Harry had to do some calling, and transact some business, so Marie and I moused about the town and poked in and out of shops till it was time to return on board. The weather is still splendid.

On board, Nov. 27th

WE ARE now in the South China Sea, and well under way for Singapore, where we are due on Sunday. The temperature is growing higher every moment, and were it not for the roominess and excellent ventilation of this monster ship we should suffer intensely from the heat already, though we must expect to have it a great deal hotter yet. We have put away all our thick clothes and wraps, and are arraying ourselves in the thinnest things we have, and with the electric fans, which are kept in motion in the dining room, library, and in our state-rooms, we manage to keep fairly comfortable. All the officers and stewards have come out in white linen suits, so everything *looks* cool, at least!

November 29th

THE heat is increasing, as we have a right to expect when trespassing on the equator! Yesterday we had several samples of tropical rain storms, which are certainly uncompromising in character. But for these, the weather has been uniformly fair. Today the sky is slightly overcast, for which we are thankful, as we shall land at Singapore this afternoon, where we must fit ourselves out with white pith hats or helmets to avoid sunstroke, as we are told that these are an absolute necessity during our travels in Ceylon and India. The fact that this is Sunday makes no difference in these parts. We are now passing some pretty islands, the name of which no one seems to be sure of. Some say they are some islands in the Malacca Straits.

[*Note by* H. M. R. " We have had a pleasant run down from Hong Kong, 1440 miles away. Everybody who had them, dressed in white clothes and grass cloths and such like, and fans, electric and others, not only in the staterooms and dining saloon, but on the decks in the hands of ladies, or Chinamen, or other passengers. The infinite variety of color and costume, the lying off on deck by day and in the evenings, the evening trumpet before dinner sending us to our staterooms to put on our dinner dress — for we dress for dinner on board for comfort — all are so different from the cold and wraps and general air of discomfort on the Atlantic at this season or even any season of the year.

" The children play about the decks, the younger ones with their Chinese or Indian nurses (aiyas and " things "), bare-legged and in light, summer costume, and everything flavors of a world different from our world. We fairly revel in it! From my *hot* bath, with a cold shower to follow in the A.M., till I throw off my clothes at night, leaving ports and windows open and electric fan started, it is all like a dream of the last five and thirty years."]

Singapore, Nov. 30th, 1903

WE REACHED Singapore yesterday afternoon soon after
four and went ashore. There we were at once approached
by a native guide who spoke English, and who seemed
to be a nice fellow, so we hired him for yesterday evening and today. We tried to get carriages to drive into
town, but there were none, so we had to content ourselves with rickishas, the disadvantage of which is that
as each one rides alone one cannot make remarks to
another, which, of course we are always dying to do in
all these strange and wonderful places!

The approach to Singapore is not in any way grand
or magnificent. The shore line is somewhat flat. Its chief
interest consists in the great variety of races in their
native dress and nakedness (which are in evidence from
the moment one lands on the wharf); the wonderful
trees, and, to us, strange varieties of palms bearing
curious fruits, the branches of the trees covered over —
as with a thick moss — with small orchids and delicate
ferns; the generally rich tropical vegetation, and the
numerous fruits which never reach Europe or America.

Before we had proceeded far from the wharf it came
on to rain. Nevertheless, we were able to get a very good
idea of the Chinese quarter, and compare the shops and
streets with those of the natives, which are much plainer
and simpler in every way. It being the supper time of
the coolies and other low castes, we had a chance to
see them devouring their bowls of rice and questionable
looking condiments at small street-booths by the wayside. I wished more than once that I was artist enough
to reproduce the picturesqueness of these bronzed figures as they sat or reclined in either graceful or grotesque attitudes. Some had turbans, and nothing else

save a short clout round the loins; others wore a printed cotton cloth, draped like a scant skirt, and on the upper part of the body only a cravat or sort of neck handker-chief. But the varied colouring and polish of these hu-man bronzes was the best part of it.

The rain kept growing more violent, and we were glad to take shelter in the Hotel della Pait, where, we had been told, were to be found the best things to eat, while "Raffles," which is the principal and most pretentious hotel, is famous for its bad table and service. As course after course of ill-tasting viands was served, we kept wondering what Raffles could be like if it was worse than this. But perhaps at Raffles they poison you, and here you do escape with your life!

Like all the buildings in the East we found the rooms large, high studded, and airy, with broad *loggias*, which form a splendid protection from both the heat and glare of the sun, besides giving a distinctly interesting indi-viduality to all the architecture of the Orient.

As soon as we had finished what they were pleased to call "dinner" we hired carriages and returned to the ship for the night, quite relieved to find that all the hotels were too full to take in another soul. Some of our fellow-passengers who had secured rooms by tele-graphing from Hong Kong bitterly regretted it, for amongst other things at Raffles they do not provide covering of any sort for the beds, not even a sheet, and the guests, poor souls, who were taken by surprise at this curious custom, were nearly chilled to death. One dainty little Southern lady told us she had to use her white petticoat for a covering, putting it alternately on her stomach and on her chest for protection, and of course sleeping never a wink!

Curiously enough, we did not find it as hot in Singapore as we expected. There have been days in Naples when it was much hotter, so it seems to me. But then, of course, this is the rainy season, which is always the coolest time. Such funny little carriages they have here. Square boxes with tops and shutters where four can sit, drawn by a single pony no bigger than a donkey. They say these native ponies are very strong.

This morning, after breakfast we went ashore again, the weather having cleared, at least temporarily. On the wharf there were men selling parrots and paroquets of rare colours — not in cages, but on perches and guarded by a monkey. There were also hucksters of beautiful shells and corals, and all kinds of silk handkerchiefs, scarves, stuffs, etc. A great many different races and castes were to be seen — Malays, Mohammedans, Madras-Hindus, Cingalese, Parsees, etc. On our way to the postoffice and bank we stopped at the market to see the fish, fruits, and vegetables.

I always love to see the markets of foreign countries. The fish are beautiful in colour, and nearly all strange to me except large prawns, whitebait, and some ugly, gelatinous things which they used to eat in Southern Italy, called "calamaji." We bought a lot of representative fruits to take back to the ship with us, but we were so sorry that the famous mangestan and the duryan are not yet in season. A fortnight later, David, our guide, said there would be plenty. We found lots of mangoes (not half so fine in flavour as those I have bought in Boston) which came from Porto Rico — in fact we did not care for them.

In the square where the postoffice was, and in many other streets, we saw that wonderful tree which I described to you in my last letter from Hong Kong, in full blossom — great scarlet clusters of blossoms with beautiful transparent petals which bestrew the ground all

Singapore: Snake Charmer

about. It is a sight to behold! In the Botanical Gardens
at Hong Kong it was labeled " flame tree," but our guide
called it the Hong Kong cottonwood tree. There was
another tree with a coarser leaf, which bore a crimson
blossom something like a tiger lily. But what I had
never seen before was " the traveller's palm," the leaves
of which fall into line so that it is like an enormous fan,
fifty feet high. Its peculiarity is that if you prick it, or
tap it, it yields a stream of delicious fresh water. What
a wonderful provision of nature for the desert, is it
not?

After we had transacted our business at the bank,
bought photographs, and fitted ourselves out with anti-
sunstroke pith hats and white umbrellas, we were taken
to a very extraordinary Chinese temple, said to be unlike anything else in the world. All the decorations were
made up of small figures done in porcelain or pottery, so
finely glazed that many of them looked like jade images.
For some unaccountable reason, all the clay used for this
purpose was brought from Ireland, so our guide said,
but even the traditional reason for this was unknown to
him. There was a woman prostrate before the altar, behind which an image of Buddha was half concealed, and
soon she took a box from it in which there were some
long sticks. These she rattled as if they were dice, and,
on observing what positions the sticks were in after being shaken, she went to a sort of scribe-priest in the
temple to have him interpret her fate or fortune, which
the sticks were supposed to tell after her prayer. There
was an expression of deep disappointment, almost of
anger, on her face when the fiat was pronounced after
she had paid her fee.

We entered our carriages again to go to an eating
house for tiffin, when suddenly there burst forth a regular tropical storm — thunder, lightning, and rain in

sheets such as I had never beheld. Arrived within the shelter of the eating house, we tried hard to obtain something simple and wholesome for lunch, but in vain. They apparently only know nasty messes in the East, and our little livers will have to adapt themselves to hard service, I suppose. We were soon driven from the spacious *loggia,* where we hoped to dine, by the pouring rain, and had to take refuge in the covered dining room; but even there we were not protected. The rain beat in at the large open spaces abutting on the *loggias,* which elsewhere would be windows, but in the Orient are not. After tiffin we drove up to Raffles Hotel to see if we could get a case of Munich beer for Mrs. Hearst, and then back to the ship, which was supposed to leave port at four, but which did not really start till six.

One of the interesting sights of Singapore is the ox carts which are the only ones used for transports. The oxen are formed quite differently from ours. Also the water-buffalos, which are so much used here as beasts of burden, are decidedly queer looking — great, hulky, humped, mud-coloured things! They sleep in the mud pools, I am told.

I don't know whether our handsome guide, David, is really as well informed as he appears to be. I have suspected more than once that he was drawing on his imagination a bit for the answers to some of our frequent questions. Now we are under way again for Penang, and shall not lose sight of land till we reach port, as we are in the Malacca Straits. There are interesting groups of islands to be seen now on one side, now on the other.

December 1st

THIS morning a large vampire was seen hovering over the deck. Its head and neck were yellow and its heavy wings the colour of the usual bat that we know, but a bat larger than the largest crow is not a pleasant sight! It is 9.15 P.M., and we are in Penang harbour, which is very attractive, much more so than that of Singapore. Here we have our mountains again — not as grand as at Hong Kong, but still very beautiful. I owe the ship a grudge for not getting in sooner, for, as she leaves to-morrow morning at eight, we shall not have a chance to land at all. It is true the guides tell you that there is nothing of particular interest to be seen at Penang, but from my point of view there would be a great deal worth seeing. However, we shall tarry there for a day or two on our return journey, I hope.

[*Note by* H. M. R. " We arrived off Penang and in the stream late at night, and started away early in the morning and did not go ashore — yet we bring away the beauty of the town, the lovely coloring, the hills crowning the place and dignifying the harbor, the charm of the boats and boatmen, all color, each boat, sampan, with varied hues, looking something like the gondolas of Venice but not so fine, but each one with two eyes painted in the bows, on each side to see the way."]

December 3rd
TODAY is Mrs. Hearst's birthday, and we had prepared various little surprises for her in the form of gifts, verses, etc. I took the chief steward into my confidence, and he at once consented to having a birthday cake made, and some extra table decorations, which, however, he preferred to arrange himself, without supervision from anybody. The result was a sight to behold! Fortunately it was bad enough to be funny. Imagine a pot of stunted Chinese palm, with its pineapple body, in the centre of

which was stuck a large bunch of muslin cherry blossoms of the rankest pink, and at each side a large branch
of blue wistaria of a shade that wistaria never was in
its wildest freaks, two sprays of white intertwined, and
then — prepare for a shock — a large American flag
stuck into the pot, swearing at the pink cherry blossoms
in a blue streak! Then there was a little bunch of muslin
lilies of the valley mixed with violets, with tin foil round
the stems, and *in water,* if you please, in a wine glass by
her plate! It is of no use, these Germans are hopeless!

Well, at least, even if our eyes were put out, we got
a laugh over it, and we drank the birthday's health in
Moselle wine, and were very gay. Mrs. H. was delighted
with her presents, which had been very carefully selected by us.

December 4th

THIS morning at breakfast Mr. Guinnes entertained us
with thrilling experiences with cobras, pythons, and
amadriads (the only deadly snake that attacks you
without provocation). Of finding huge snakes coiled up
under one's pillow, or in one's coat at Singapore, Penang, and in Colombo, for which place we are now head-
ing. We expect to anchor there tomorrow sometime, and
there ends our journey on this comfortable boat. We
shall leave it with deep regret, for we dare not expect
to be acquainted with many creature comforts from
now forward. We find the extreme heat very trying at
times, for it seems unnatural to suffer in this way at sea.
When Mr. Egerton describes to us the broad fields of
pineapples at Singapore, which we did not have time
to investigate, and the miles and miles of cocoanut palms
at Ceylon, which we cannot avoid seeing, the heat seems
at least consistent. But here we are in the Bay of Ben-

gal, with nothing but water in sight, and there seems no excuse for melting away!

Galle Face Hotel, Colombo, Ceylon, Dec. 6th, 1903

Our ship anchored off Colombo at 4 a.m., and we landed, after breakfast, in a flatboat, called katamaran, which held ten easily, Gen. Winslow's party of five and our own. On the wharf there were rows of bullock wagons, queer things, waiting for freight, and rickishas and pony carriages waiting for passengers. Everywhere natives and many other Indian races in a variety of picturesque Oriental costumes, and as many again naked but for a turban and a clout; some with their caste marked by a line of ashes on forehead and breast. Just before landing we saw a banana boat, at prow and stern a large growing banana tree laden with fruit, instead of a painted sign to tell what it was. The natives were such fine, picturesque creatures. How I wish I could have made a sketch of that boat in colours!

On our drive home, again were our eyes feasted with monster trees, covered with huge clusters of crimson and scarlet blossoms, the ground red with their fallen petals; and then came groves and groves of King-cocoanut palms, many nearly one hundred feet high, and loaded with fruit which, when not green, are a rich orange colour, and never brown as they look in their fibrous outer shell in the markets.

This is really an imposing looking hotel, and, I fancy, a very comfortable one. Harry and I have two large, high-studded, airy rooms *en suite,* mine with three large windows with sun hoods painted white.

[*Note by* H. M. R. " The beautiful sea comes as near to our windows as the beach at Swampscott to our house, and in front of our window on the second story, and looking upon the sea, cocoanut palms rise up, clean and clear and without foliage say for forty feet, and then bursting out in an umbrella-shaped top, — not quite that either, a half-shut, umbrella-shaped top, with the cocoanuts scattered around, giving a sort of shade to our room without obstructing our view.

" Warm and balmy air, broad sweep of road and open space like a parade ground extending along the sea far as the eye can reach, every part of the house open and having reading rooms and enclosed verandahs, and color both of men and women and children, native and European, everywhere."]

The waves are dashing in across the road, which is of a beautiful Pompeian red (all the roads here are of a red clay, very handsome in colour), and under my windows are large groups of tall cocoanut trees, bending forward at an acute angle, and hanging their heavy heads a bit, as though they would drink the moisture of the ocean if only they could stoop low enough.

There is not supposed to be very much to see at Colombo besides the vegetation and quaint, Oriental streets — no fine temples and things; but there is always so much to be seen, and one must be constantly on the *qui vive*. We are perpetually wishing for a hundred eyes, for we would see what there is on both sides of the streets as well as behind and before! We are off our heads with excitement most of the time, and how long we can bear the strain of it in this climate, heaven knows!

December 7th

I SHALL never have a better chance to study the anatomy of the cocoanut tree than now. Wherever I look from my windows, I see nothing else, except the Pompeian-red road and the sea. The leaves are over twenty feet long, and they are all bunched up together on top, the nuts grouped together in bunches where the stems shoot out. They grow up straight or crooked as may be, but without a branch, a knot, or a flaw on their smooth bark. All sorts of large birds take their recreation in these trees, where they seem to be fumbling among the nuts and stems for flies and grubs. Some of them are a sort of tropical crow — very noisy, very saucy. They come in at my windows and steal all they can get under my very nose — the butter, marmalade, toast, sugar, and fruit left over on the little tray that by custom is brought up early to one's room, and which they call " morning tea." Some of these birds are like " mynahs " — about the size of small jackdaws, and black all over. Then there is one kind, very large with a dark blue body and a greyish-cream, fluffy head and neck. They all seem friendly together, and share their grubs, but keep up a fearful noise the while, cawing and screaming.

Such a view as I have from my window over the sea! And I get the marvelous sunsets! He who has not seen a tropical sunset knows not what *colour* is! Fire and flame, from orange to purple, and every shade in be-tween. Ahi mai! How beauteous it all is! As I lay stretched out on a cane lounge, right up against a bay window looking out over the ocean, and listening to the swash of the waves beneath, I said to myself, " Can this be Ceylon? I think it must be heaven! " But this was while I was waiting for our luggage, and was enjoying a little *dolce far niente,* but as soon as I had to get my things out of my trunks and move about a bit, wasn't it blazing hot! " Good bye heaven," says I. " I must have made a mistake as to the locality."

We went for a fine drive yesterday afternoon through

the park, the suburbs, and the town, gloating on Oriental colour. The high-coloured garments of the natives would seem out of place, perhaps gaudy or tawdry, anywhere else, but here they are so entirely a part of the soil and atmosphere that nothing else would seem to suit. We went through a cinnamon grove, and our driver picked us a branch. It looks something like the orange bush, and the leaves are delicious and full of cinnamon flavour as well as the stems.

The town presented many a sight that was unsavoury — dirt and unwholesomeness were everywhere, though I must own that it did not smell half as bad as either Japan or China. One thing I cannot get out of my head — it keeps rising up before me as a grim picture. There was an unfortunate dog prowling about one of the narrow streets, who, either from mange, canine leprosy, or what not, had not a single hair left on body or head. It was a mass of sores which showed up horribly on its poor naked body, on which one could count every rib. It could hardly walk, but just managed to drag itself along somehow. In our country it would have been the duty of a policeman to put an end to its misery before it came to such a pass, but here, current superstition will not permit any such humane course, for they believe that some sinful soul may thus be working out its *karma*, and that therefore they must not interfere with natural law. So they permit, without hindrance, a poor, diseased creature like that to roam about, poking its nose into their open shops, and fumbling among their grains and vegetables — perhaps breeding heaven knows what infection. The loathsomeness of it all was indescribable. On turning our eyes from such a gruesome sight to the luxuriant foliage, beauteous flowers, the flaming glow of the heavens above, the calm, blue sea, all the generous opulence of nature, it seemed as if such a sight belonged in some other world than this! The saying " only man is vile " jingled in my ears! Yet we noticed quite a number of little Roman Catholic chapels — in fact there was one whole street which our driver called the Catholic quarter. I only hope that their presence may work as a leaven in time; but I cannot help thinking that in their present state of ignorance, perversion, or what not, the natives need taking in hand in the way good old father Moses did with the Orientals in his day, and after they have learned something about sanitation it would be time enough to tell them about the Virgin Mary! Of course I bear in mind the saying, " Cleanliness is next to Godliness," but I should like to change it into, " Cleanliness *leads* to Godliness " — as I feel at present!

December 8th

THIS morning we saw from our window a native, with turban and clout, shinning up a cocoanut palm to cut off a large bunch of ripe nuts. As the bark is smooth, and there is no place for a purchase, the feet have to be tied together by a double string, about a foot apart, and it was really a curious sight to see him pulling himself up with an action much like the inch worm — a simitar in his belt to cut the nuts with.

This afternoon we start for Kandy up in the mountains, and shall sample Ceylon scenery. Harry and I are growing more intelligent every day, and we are now beginning to know which is a man and which is a woman when we see them. You see the Cingalese men wear their long hair gathered up in a knot behind, near the neck, and a sort of shell comb on the top of the head like a diadem, turned hind before, and they wear a kind of divided skirt, so it really is a bit puzzling at first. I have frequently heard Mrs. Hearst and Clara speculating as to the sex even of those who were naked down to the

waist, and I have more than once jeered at them for
their imperfect knowledge of anatomy! We have engaged two native men servants. Harry now is happy in
that he has someone to pack his trunks and put his studs
in his shirts. David, with his white dress and turban,
and rolling black eyes, is a queer specimen of a " valet,"
but he does the business. Our Japanese man Fujii had
a soul above such things, and when I asked him to strap
up my valises, he called seven coolies to do it instead,
all of whom demanded fees!

[*Note by* H. M. R. " I am more and more delighted
with this island and its people. There is beauty everywhere, of mountain and valley and seashore, of verdure
and flowers, radiant trees with great flaming flowers on
them that illuminate the scene. Then the people are so
beautiful to look upon, and the children, bronze statues,
who have left their clothes in the wash. I should like
to stay in this island and spend a few weeks, browsing
around in the country and wherever else chance took me.
    " On our arrival here we were met by our two serv-
ants from Madras — not the two we expected, but two
substitutes, Daniel Ramasawnie being engaged, we have
his substitute, Anthony Butler and another, whose name
I have not yet mastered. We had one or two others whom
we took to Kandy, and so here we have *four* on hand.
One leaves tomorrow, and I retain David, who already
looks upon me as his father, and Mrs. Hearst and Clara
will take the other two.
    " Butler and ' friend ' are *fine*. They have the cos-
tumes on that we sent the money for from San Francisco
— Mrs. Hearst's colors which we chose for them, blue
and yellow. They seem well mannered and efficient fellows, and are evidently well trained. My David is fa-

miliar now with my clothes and my studs and he gets
me dressed all right in the A.M., and prevents my crawling all over the floor looking for studs and sleeve but-
tons at night. He packed up my belongings at Kandy
and delivered them here, and has helped Dorie pack and
fold dresses and things, and all for one and one half
rupees a day, and he finds his food and lodging. He
generally sleeps at my door when he is not at home.
He lives in Colombo, and he has just gone home to leave
his money (20 rupees — $6.40 U. S.) which I have just
advanced him, for his wife and children two.

" We are up against a very unpleasant condition of
affairs just at the minute. Mrs. Hearst has been called
home by cable, repeated twice, I believe, already. She
to reach New York (or London) certainly by March 1.
This knocks spots out of *her* plans certainly and must
modify ours. We have just determined to go forward
as intended, and when Mrs. Hearst has to leave, to take
one of the servants and a courier and go to Bombay,
taking steamer for Marseilles, thence to Paris, etc.,
leaving Dorie and myself to go to Calcutta and thence
back to China and Japan as intended. Clara Anthony
says she will go back with Mrs. Hearst, remain in Paris,
and go home *after* Mrs. Hearst. Dorie and I feel we
have come too far to give up our trip, especially as nobody wants us to do so, and so we shall probably carry
out our original trip as far as Benares, and then separate.
We are all of us greatly disappointed, but we have had
two months together anyway, and hope to get the cream
of India together."]

Kandy, Ceylon, Dec. 9th, 1903
YESTERDAY afternoon at 2.30 we were duly installed in
our first-class compartment — very like an English one,

only upholstered in white linen — on our way to the
mountains. General Winslow and his party were in the
next carriage, and we all met in the refreshment car at
afternoon tea. It was an exciting journey, for though
mountain peaks, ravines, abysses, valleys, rocks, waterfalls, and streams, whether in Japan, China, America,
or any part of Europe are apt to resemble each other
more or less — or rather, to differ more in degree than
in kind, here it is quite different with all this jungle of
tropical vegetation. For twenty-three miles, while in
sight of the river, we saw nothing but cocoanut palms —
millions of them; but as soon as we began to get well
up among the hills the cocoanuts gave place to all sorts
of other kinds of palm trees and great trees of yak-fruit,
bread fruit, papaya, mangoes, flambeau trees, bananas,
banyans, cane trees, bamboo, and heaven knows what
all. Such a wealth of everything that is splendid and
beautiful!

Then we saw something to us quite new — terraced
rice plantations. Picture to yourself a mountain slope
terraced as in Switzerland or Germany for vineyards,
and then imagine these terraces all flooded with water
and sown with rice, or " paddy " as they call it, the
sun and sky mirrored in each terrace, and you have a
wondrous sight when you see it for the first time. At
one time, on our way, there was a coffee plantation on
one side of the road, and a tea plantation on the other.
We reached this charming place in time to dress for
dinner. Mr. and Mrs. Van Vleaht, a very nice couple
from Memphis, with whom we travelled from Hong
Kong, were there to welcome us, they having come here
the day before, and after dinner Mr. V. persuaded us to
ride round the lake in rickishas and see it by moonlight.
It was a beautiful sight to go to bed and dream on!

CINGALESE TYPE: Low Country

This morning we got up at six, and, after taking morning tea in our rooms, started off to see the sights of Kandy before the sun should be too high in the heavens. First we went to the Botanical Gardens, which are considered, I think, the finest in the world, and no wonder! To attempt to tell you of all the tropical luxury, the unthinkable variety of form and freak, the splendour and magnificence of it all, would be vain! It was delight to be shown round by a nice old Cingalese, who had been in charge there for twenty years, and who knew all the trees by heart. As he spoke some English he could tell us so much that we wanted to know. Clara and I have been perfectly desperate at not being able to find out the names of all these marvelous flower- and fruit-bearing trees. There are dozens and dozens of fruits which we have never heard of before. We saw the mangosteen and the far-famed Duryan, but the latter was not bearing at present. There was also the deadly " upas tree," from the sap of which the natives used to poison their arrows. The orchid tree (*Amherstia Noblis*), with its heavy clusters of crimson, orchid-like sprays of blossoms.

Then the India rubber trees. They are the most curious as well as the most imposing things I ever saw. They are of the banyan family, which accounts for the extraordinary freakiness of trunk, branches, and roots. We were taken into a nutmeg grove and allowed to pick up some of the nutmegs both in and out of their outer green pod — not unlike the walnut, only much larger. The nutmeg itself, when it is fresh, is smooth and black, and looks very handsome in its pretty, trelaced fibre of bright red (which is sold as mace, and which turns a golden brown). We picked green cloves as well, were introduced to the coca plant, from which cocaine is made, camphor, allspice, pepper, pimento, and every sort of spice-yielding plant and tree. A liberal education, I can assure you!

After tiffin we took a long, circular drive, or series of drives, among the hills, where there were fine vistas of peak and valley. A large monkey was swinging himself in the branches of a yak-tree, the fruit of which is precious to his kind. Then we went to see some elephants, and afterwards to a Buddhist temple, where, in the cloisters, there were very crude pictures of a different King of Hell appointed for each crime. It was growing dusk, and we were followed round by such an army of beggars, who persisted in lighting tiny candles to show us the way, and in thrusting decapitated flowers — for offerings — into our hands, in addition to the temple guides who demanded a fee at almost every corner of the building, that it got on our nerves, and although we went there late because there was to be a service at 6.30, after which the temple jewels and a crystal Buddha were to be shown, Harry and I got so weary of it all that we went home without the show, simply to save having the life plagued out of us.

December 10*th*

TODAY we did not go sight-seeing, because there were no more special sights. We just loafed about — in the market and streets, and after tiffin we went to the Governor's house and garden. The present Governor, Sir Arthur Blake, has not seen it yet, but is expected on the 21st inst. It is fine in spaciousness, but the furniture is uninteresting English stuff of the kind one finds in a Liverpool hotel, instead of the rich, Oriental things they might have so easily if they only would. It made me sick to see the cheap Nottingham curtains in the windows where Indian silks and embroideries naturally belong.

We leave Kandy tomorrow morning at eleven for Colombo again, where we take ship for Tuticorin — a journey of fifteen hours. The passage is a proverbially uncomfortable one, like that across the English Channel, only longer, but as the N. E. Monsoon is on, let us hope it will be bearable. During S. W. Monsoon, they say it is terrible.

Colombo, Dec. 11th, 1903
BEFORE leaving Kandy today we poked around among the jewellers, examining and buying some of the Ceylon precious stones. Moonstones, rubies, emeralds, pearls, tourmalines of all colours are found here, and many people buy and are taken in. Mrs. Hearst knows about stones so well that we dared, what we would not have done otherwise, to make a few purchases on our own account. Mrs. H. bought largely. A fakir accosted us as we were returning to tiffin and offered to do the famous ' mango trick ' and some snake charming. As we had heard so often of the mango trick, but none of us had ever seen it, we engaged him to perform there and then, and, having seated ourselves on a row of chairs brought out to us, on the hotel *loggia,* we saw him, after doing various unsightly things with a large cobra, plant a mango seed in a little heap of soil, cover it up with a cloth, and, in a minute or so, there was a little tree — a seedling. He covered it again and pronounced more incantations, and lo!, there was a big bush when he again removed the cloth. He pulled it up to show that not only was it growing out of the seed, but that the seed itself, which at first was quite smooth and clean, now had long dangling roots. It was very well done, and we did not begrudge him his five rupees for our private entertainment.

We arrived here in time for dinner, but I did not want to dress to go down, so I had a tray sent up to me, and I wish you could have seen the procession of three servants who brought it! First there was one of our two Madras Indian servants to open the door, then our own particular man, David, carrying the tray, and the other Madras Indian following him — for no known purpose that I could discover.

By the way, the two servants that we had written to Madras to secure, and who failed to appear on the appointed day, notified us of their arrival in Colombo after we had engaged two others and taken them with us to Kandy. On our return, as the tardy ones, engaged for us by Judge H. looked very fine in their liveries, Mrs. H. concluded to retain them both in addition to our man David, who has already made himself indispensable to Harry. The other man we discharged, as he was of little use. You would laugh to hear the way our turbaned slave addresses us. He speaks of Harry as " the Master," but to his face he often calls him " Pappa " —with the accent on the first syllable as in America. He is perfectly devoted already, and when the news reached us of the belated arrival of the two other men, he came to my room, and, pressing his hands to his forehead while bending low, he cried: " Lady, ask Master to take me with him to Madras, I so unhappy not to go with Lady and Master! " They are a queer lot, these Indians. They sleep anywhere and nowhere in particular. On the mat outside one's door, or under the table if there happens to be one in the hotel corridor.

December 12th
This morning Clara had an experience which caused her great agitation. She had taken off her diamond and

KANDY: Travellers' Palms

pearl rings and other jewellery, and put the little case containing them on the dressing table, prior to packing them in her valise. She happened to turn away for a moment, and that was enough for a thief of a crow which pounced on it and flew out of the window with his prize. Poor Clara, as white as a sheet, called frantically for the servants, who ran aimlessly hither and yon. The alarm was given, however, and every one was on the look-out for the crow thief. When the rogue found, however, that a case of jewels was neither good to eat nor to build a nest, he dropped the case in a garden near the hotel, where it was found by a native boy, who, hearing what had happened, brought it up to Clara, panting and trembling with agitation, crying, " I honest boy, I no keep, I bring back to lady. Lady give me sovereign, I honest boy! " Clara was so relieved that she was only too glad to give him a sovereign with her blessing, but it took her some hours to recover from the shock. The fear was that the crow would either hide it in a cocoanut tree or drop it into the sea. So you see that the " Gazza Ladra " is not a myth.

Madura, India, Dec. 14th, 1903
OUR anticipations of terrible discomfort on the passage from Colombo to Tuticorin were happily not realized. The sea was calm, the boat was decent, and the staterooms comfortable. We set foot on Indian ground for the first time at about 7 A.M., when we went from the wharf direct to the train bound for Madura, as Tuticorin offers no special attraction. Harry had written to the superintendent of the railway, to whom he had a letter, asking him to reserve for us a car for our private use for our journeyings between Tuticorin and Madras. As neither at Madura, Trichinopoli, or Tanjore is there

any hotel, we thought it safer to be prepared to spend the night in our railway carriage, or at least to have our carriage to fall back on in the event of not being able to find beds for our party of five in a Dak Bungalow or at the station, where they mostly have two or three rooms for the accommodation of travellers. There is always so much uncertainty however, about finding these rooms unoccupied that we were glad to have our sleeping compartments to fall back on, especially as we are a party of five, which complicates matters considerably. By paying for eight first-class fares instead of five we have the exclusive use of this very good double car, with four sofa beds in each, a toilet for each, and a small compartment between the two cars for our three native servants. This car is shunted off to a side track on our arrival anywhere, and hitched on to whatever train we choose to take next. Convenient, isn't it? But we have to carry our bedding along with us, and our servants make up the beds for us, and pack it up afterwards.

It is a queer life this in India! At Madura we found that there was just one room over the station unoccupied, so Mrs. Hearst and Clara took that, and Harry and I had our first experience of sleeping in a side-tracked car. I confess I should not ever do it from choice! There were mosquitoes and all the noises that a railway station can muster galore! However, that is passed, and today we have had a fine time sight-seeing. Also yesterday we lost no time on arriving, but started out immediately after tiffin at the station, accompanied by the city guide. There were curious wayside temples to be seen, one where women go to pray for safe delivery, and, when the child is born, they make offerings of the most hideous and grotesque figures in pottery, gaudily

painted. These are all arranged in rows on the top of
the rather low-studded temple, and look about as barbaric as anything well can look. Our guide persisted in
calling them " potted babies," much to our delight, and
when he said to Mrs. Hearst, " Lady like to take a
potted baby back to America? " we exploded! She did
like to take one, however, for her museum — the chamber of horrors I hope! and so a native climbed up and
secured one for her for the modest sum of four rupees.
The thing turned out to be about eighteen inches long,
to Marie's horror, a nice easy thing to pack! But Mrs.
Hearst is nothing if not enterprising. It struck me also
as queer that they were so ready to rob the temple of
its trophies — for a consideration.

We saw many interesting things, but the cream of it
all was the palace of the ancient King Tirumala Nayak,
the greatest of all the rulers of Madura, and who
seems to have been responsible for all sorts of beautiful
things in the way of architectural feats. His palace is
one of the most imposing, grand, and massive structures I have ever seen; we could hardly tear ourselves
away from it, and nothing but the sinking sun and
sudden darkness could have driven us away so grandly
impressive was it. We were also taken to see a banyan
tree, which is, or ought to be, one of the wonders of the
world. It stands in the compound of the judge's house,
and has thrown out such an enormous number of trunks
from its branches, which in their turn have rooted and
thrown out as many others, it has the appearance of a
whole grove of banyans. There are a hundred and five
self-created trees in one, and the main trunk — such
a weird, rugged looking thing — is seventy feet in circumference. I never saw anything so extraordinary in
my life.

There are some very magnificent jewels in the great temple, and our guide told us that by sending fifteen rupees, ($5.00) to the temple the priest would have them taken out of their cases and shown to us on private view, so we sent the money and the time appointed to see them was this morning at eight o'clock. The temple is superb in its way, and the series of gopuras, or gateways, which form the characteristic of all the temples in Southern India, tall, pagoda-like structures, are marvelous tangle webs of ornamentation. It would take days to make out what the elaborate stone carvings represent. There was the hall of the thousand columns, there were horses and lions of mammoth size, of gold and of silver, on which " Vishnu " and his family are placed on festival days and worshipped; there were some fine monoliths, and there were the sacred elephants who guard the temple and the jewels.

We were pestered by minor priests and hangers-on of the temple throwing necklaces of offering-flowers round our necks, whether we would or no, and demanding several rupees in return. On some of us proving restive, our guide sternly cried, " You must not reject, it is to bring you luck." So we were victimized all along the line. Even the sacred elephants were made to perform salaams to us, and we were invited to see how they would pick up the smallest silver coin and hand it up, I mean trunk it up, to the keeper.

The showing of the jewels was quite a serious function. They were all laid out on a large, low table in one of the broad aisles, which was roped off on either side. Six priests were in attendance, a bench was placed for us to sit on, and the jewels, the jewelled head-pieces and breast-pieces, necklaces and girdles, were handed to us one at a time to examine. There were monster rubies,

MADURA: The Lily Tank

sapphires, diamonds, pearls, and emeralds, all of them uncut, very roughly set in massive gold, and very badly cared for. Many of the stones were cracked, some were missing, and all were dirty — as dirty as could be. It is true they were over two thousand years old, which may be some excuse. But still everything else is also badly cared for, untidy and down at heel. The " Hall of the Thousand Pillars " was full of rubbish — a veritable storehouse for trash, and it seems to be the same everywhere. It was the same at that gorgeous, dignified Palace of Tirumala, which we saw yesterday. The people here seem to have no sense of fitness or propriety whatever.

We drove through avenues of tamarind, male banyan, and an occasional teakwood tree, and there seem to be all the same trees here which grow at Ceylon, although everything here looks different, and, I am bound to say, not as attractive. On our way from Madura the vegetation presented a different aspect, on account of the miles and miles of century plants, very large ones, which form hedges or fences to the fields, some in bud and some having blossomed and died of their bloom. They are all-pervading, and do not yield even to the cactus which grows everywhere, while it has a chance. We leave for Trichinopoli this afternoon at 5 P.M.

Trichinopoli, Dec. 15th, 1903
WE REACHED here last evening at seven, and were met by a famous old local guide named Daniel — a picturesque old chap, to whom we had telegraphed, and he laid out a programme for today as follows. Trichinopoli being the hottest place in Southern India, it is necessary to get up at six, take morning tea and start to the Rock Temple, six hundred and fifty feet high, and ascended by four hundred and fifty granite steps. Finish our sight

seeing by eleven, go home and rest while the sun holds sway, and at four P.M. start out again and see the rest. This we did, and found the advice good. Clara at starting declared she would not attempt the four hundred and fifty steps, but old Daniel took us up so gently and gradually, stopping so long at each section to explain things about Siva and his nasty son, Ganesh, who is in evidence everywhere carved in stone, and dripping with oil (for they smear their images with it all the time till the stone carvings look like bronze), that we were on top of the Rock and looking at the fine, comprehensive view it commanded before we knew it.

When we came down we were taken to Bishop Heber's house and bath where he was found drowned, and where the Prince of Wales had a monument erected in his memory. It was much to his credit that he was indignant at the place having been neglected, and allowed to choke up with vegetation, and that he gave orders to have it cleared out and kept in order for the future. In the afternoon we went to the largest temple in Southern India, " Sri Rangan." It is more like a city of temples than a temple, and within its precincts there are many streets where people live and have their little shops and stalls. The crowds of human beings, more or less degraded, that were huddled together in every nook and corner, did their best to render our visit to the temple a hard task and spoil our enjoyment of the wonderful stone work of the numerous gopuras and the imposing monoliths, which seem to be so numerous in these parts.

I must confess that while the magnificence of all these structures impresses me in one way, it makes me at the same time feel an infinite sadness to find such splendour and such squalor cheek by jowl. One feels that India is more dead than an excavated city where life has ceased to be for thousands of years. Nor can one see how a change can be wrought among a people ridden with such hideous superstitions. There seems to be no place for an entering wedge of enlightenment. And yet our guide said that here, in Trichinopoli alone, there are two thousand Christians — converts — twelve hundred of which are Roman Catholics and eight hundred Protestants. To me it has been a shock to find the same barbaric customs rampant that existed two thousand years ago, perhaps even increased rather than mitigated. As we drove along the river Canvery today, which is the sacred river of Southern India, and saw the people bathing therein, washing their clothes and drinking the water — dirty as it could well be, while they told their prayer beads, and went through all sorts of weird antics, remembering at the same time all the bare-faced lies and cheating which they indulge in and of which they are not ashamed, I felt doubly repelled at the sight of the grotesque and greasy gods with which one is confronted at every step. I wish to heaven that a God of Truth could be invented for their benefit! If only I had time to write it, I could a tale unfold! It is a curious fact that while they are so shameless and lacking in all the essentials from our point of view, I have never been anywhere where the religion of the people, such as it is, is taken more seriously, and is more in evidence, more all-pervading and permeating.

The Vishnu worshippers all have a large V painted from the top of the forehead to the bridge of the nose, the two outer rims of the V being white and the middle line red. The followers of Siva have a different mark, but most of them are daubed in some form or other. Then the women are such frights, with from one to three sets of nose ornaments screwed into the outside of each nostril, and a long pendant in the septum, besides usually a large pearl, which, in effect, is unpleasantly suggestive of a running influenza. Then they wear, in many cases, two sets of ear ornaments, one kind screwed into the top of the ear, and the other — a very large and heavy pendant — from the bottom flap in which a large hole has been cut, so that only a thin outer border of flesh remains, forming a loop. The longer this lump of flesh is, the more beautiful it is considered! But enough of the Hindu charms for the present.

[*Note by* H. M. R. " Trichinopoli is said to be the *hottest place in Southern India,* yet here we are, with a delicious June breeze blowing through our apartments, and we had a delightful outing from 6.45 to 10.30 this A.M., and are going out again at 4 P.M. for two or three hours more. I write these things because I am convinced more and more as I travel that people are sensational, or nervous or fidgety, always anticipating troubles and generally finding them. The meat is not very good here, rather tough. Chickens are *sometimes* young and born with only two legs and one neck. Mrs. Hearst tells of Mr. Hearst and herself asking to have lunch put up in Indiana, and when they opened the package they found they had *nine* necks of chicken and nothing else. We find the eggs good, bread fairly good, toast fair, biscuits (Huntley's, etc.), to be had; marmalade good; bananas and oranges and papaya excellent everywhere. We find ample for our needs and many luxuries. We *pass* butter and milk, being a little skeptical.

" The first striking thing to one landing is to see the religious marks on the forehead of the followers of Vishnu — a trident, representing the trinity of Brahm: Brahma the Creator; Siva the Destroyer (by death and decay, I suppose), and the Restorer (from death and

TANJORE: The Great Temple

decay), and Vishnu the Preserver — three incarnations of Brahm. Now this mark is put on every A.M. after the bath, and the wife of one of them will not supply him with food unless the mark be on the forehead.

" Then the followers of Siva with the bars of ashes on the forehead, also sometimes on the arms and elsewhere. Everywhere these marks in evidence.

" The women carrying their babies on the left hip — the little ones astride the hip, give an entirely different impression from the Japanese women or the Chinese women. The children go around as they came into the world, as a rule, and it is not without a feeling of delight that you see a little tot going around with a string for a breech clout, to the middle of which is suspended a key, or a small medal; a showy, but useless appendage in the cause of modesty. There is little clothing worn, but there is an entire covering over the women, almost without exception, bosom by a scarf and below by a skirt."]

We have secured very good rooms over the station, with good baths and everything, and we make an early start tomorrow at six thirty for Tanjore, which is only a couple of hours from here. We are going to take our nice old guide, Daniel, along with us, as he can put us through the sights in less time than another. Mrs. Hearst will, I think, decide to take him on to Madras also.

Tanjore, Dec. 17th, 1903
WE ARRIVED here this morning at 8.30, breakfasted, and then went off a-templing. We had a victoria and a bullock cart to ride in, as only one carriage could be hired. Mrs. H. insisted on riding in the bullock cart for a while, but she soon had enough of it, and we turned it over to our retinue. It was a grand temple that we visited in the

morning. Again we were glutted with magnificence and monstrosities. This time it was Siva's Temple, and there were many things we saw which were too nasty and indecent to describe. But, after all, when one contemplates these wonderful structures, and considers the ardor of belief that must have produced all those immense monoliths, Halls of a Thousand Pillars and such, one cannot help thinking what would not these people who take their religion in such dead earnest be if only they had a good religion?

Again we met with sacred elephants, and were shown sacred flower and fruit-trees of various kinds, but, best of all, a gorgeous sacred peacock, which was disporting itself on the platform of a monolith, came up to us and followed us about like a dog. At last it attempted to mount on Harry's shoulder, and, on his objecting, it grew very angry and offended, and promptly left us. Daniel says that every day at sunrise and at sunset the peacock "makes a beautiful dance," all of its own accord. The only other thing we saw at Tanjore was a Rajah's palace, very beautiful, but, as usual, out of repair. It is owned by one of the surviving wives of said Rajah. There was a most interesting library of Sanscrit and other writings, many of them wrapped up in fine old brocades and other fine tissues. I saw that the librarian, a native Hindu, was an educated and intelligent man, so I began reciting, as if to myself, some lines of a Sanscrit poem which Mohini had taught me. He pricked up his ears and looked surprised. I said, " You recognise that poem? " " Yes," said he; " but we never recite it, we always chant it thus." Then he gave me a line or two with all the queer musical frills and ruffles which Orientals seem to think indispensable. Seeing that I was interested in the chant, he hunted for the written words, and chanted the whole poem for us. I was delighted to hear it *au naturel*.

We are just going to our private car for the night, as the train to which we are to be hitched starts in half an hour — that is, at 9 P.M.

Madras, Dec. 18th, 1903

We reached Madras yesterday at 8 A.M. Finding the Hotel Connemara, which is considered the *best of the bad,* full to overflowing, we had to take refuge at the Buckingham, which is number 2, nominally — but I am thinking, in gruesome vein, " What must No. 3 be like? " This one is painfully dirty, down at heel, and out of repair — panes of glass missing from the windows, and not a bolt or fastening anywhere in working condition. Yet the proprietor, a native, seems anxious to please, and is rather kindly.

The weather is overcast and cool. We expected to expire with heat in Madras, in fact, all over Southern India — but we have not suffered at all so far. The houses are constructed so as to ward off the rays of the sun most effectually — that is the reason, I suppose. Then one regulates one's life according to the requirements of the climate, which also helps, and between the hours of twelve and three we are mostly to be found in the native costume — as nearly as possible.

Madras, as we drove here from the station, made a poor impression on us, and we found it so unattractive that we concluded unanimously to curtail our stay, leaving this evening instead of tomorrow for Bombay. The whole city looks suburban. You see here and there a large European emporium, a shabby shadow of White-ley's, but there is not a single handsome street of any sort, as at Shanghai or Hong Kong. This hotel stands in

rather a fine old garden, and near our apartment there is
a large tree laden with fruit like large, brownish oranges
called wood-apples. The natives use the inside of the
fruit mixed with milk as a cure for dysentery.

At tiffin yesterday we were introduced to a new fruit.
On the table there was a dish of green, soft things looking like large, misshapen pine cones. They proved to be
custard-apples, and we found the delicate, white flaky
meat quite delicious. It was a new and pleasant
sensation.

We have driven about, but there is little to be seen.
The Museum has the reputation of being very fine, and
we planned to devote the morning to it, but alas! when
we got there we found that on Fridays it is closed to the
public, and that even the promise of a fee would not
prove an open sesame. We saw the library, however,
which is a very dignified structure.

We are to leave here for Bombay — a railway journey of thirty hours — this afternoon at six, and shall be
glad to escape from all the bothersome merchants of embroideries, brasses, photos — and fortune tellers, that in-
fest the hotel, and who come actually to the doors of our
rooms and lay down their boxes and bundles, insisting
on spreading out their wares over every table, chair, and
sofa. In an instant the room is transformed into an
Oriental art store. It is useless to say you don't want to
buy anything. They hold up an object, " Look, lady, only
twenty rupees! " " I do not want it! " " How much will
lady give? " " I do not want it at any price! " "Lady
give me fifteen rupees, I pay more for it! " " I tell you I
don't want to buy it at all." " There, lady, take it for ten
rupees! " And so they go on until you are so weary that
to get rid of them you buy it! If, however, you chance to
see something you like, of course a fabulous price is

asked, which you laugh to scorn, and then the bargaining
begins all over again, and you realize the full meaning of
the Hindu saying, " It takes a hundred lies to make a
bargain." Another tiresome custom is the perpetual demand for *testimonials*. Every one, from your local guide
to the dealer from whom you purchase a few trifles, or
even the refreshment-room manager where you take a
meal, brings you a book and asks you to write a
testimonial.

Now we must to the station, as our train leaves at
6.45 P.M. We are glad to turn our faces northward, not
because of the heat, but because there is something de-
pressing and hopelessly sad about Southern India. I
think I have seen all I want to of it. We wanted to sample
it, but I should not care to repeat the visit. My present
memory of it will suffice.

[*Note by* H. M. R. " The south of India has made a deep
impression upon me and I think it is shared by all of us,
of a country sunk to the lips in a religious atmosphere
that is coarse, degrading, and hopeless. A constant attempt at appeasing gods and demons, by offerings at
shrines so hideous, that the mind of man can hardly conceive them. Yet there must be somewhere in the *pure and
real* religion — of which we see no sign, but only symbols
of a grotesque, brutal or hideous character — there must
be somewhere something we do not see that appeals to
the good and pure and true of the south India as well as
to the good and pure everywhere. What it is I do not
know.

" There is doubtless reverence, awe, in the shrines and
temples felt by some poor struggling soul, but when,
where, and how we do not see nor know. The man of
Vishnu worship goes abroad with the trident mark on his

forehead, but that is an outward and visible sign and seemingly *not* of spiritual grace. It is a tremendous puzzle. And then the teeming millions of people — millions and tens of millions and hundreds of millions — at least three hundred millions of them, pushing and crowding for a bare existence and not getting it. If every inch of India were cultivated to the extreme limit with all modern improvements, it is said it could not feed its people. Think of that! You cannot avoid thinking when you get into India. The problems face you every minute.

" I am glad I do not live in Madras. The city has some beautiful things in it, but that south India look on everybody and everything gets on your nerves. The swarming multitudes half naked, toiling at all sorts of work for their pittance. It is as if you were facing whole mountains of superstitions and idolatries and poverties and squalors. Your hotel has so many servants and coolies around that you fairly tumble over them, and, when you leave, the outstretched hands for fees are seemingly without end.

" Well, we were glad to leave Madras and then came thirty-six hours in the train banging and rumbling and swaying on a rough road to Bombay. The train reminded one of the trains South in the old days, when it was said you only knew that a train was off the track from the fact that it then ran much easier than when on the rails. To me the joy of it all is the railroad stations where hundreds and thousands of people, dressed in all sorts of wonderful colors and costumes, and their faces as varied as their costumes, holla and chatter and jabber and laugh and fight and scold in every kind of language and with every degree of intensity. Read Kipling's ' Kim ' if you want to get at the vivid impression of the scene."]

On train between Madras and Bombay, Dec. 19th, 1903
WE HAVE had a very comfortable private car allotted to us for this trip, much more spacious than our last. When I looked out of one of our eight windows this morning at daybreak, after a good night's sleep, I beheld a broad expanse of flat country, a river with large boulders scattered over its bed, and, wading in the stream, groups of picturesque natives with herds of water buffalo, whose backs they were scrubbing. The century plant has almost disappeared from the landscape, and the cactus, the Ficho d'India variety, laden with its bright red fruit, has taken its place, growing in the greatest profusion in large clumps and hedges everywhere. Starting up from the plains here and there are very curious high mounds of loose rock and stones, completely devoid of vegetation. On two of them were fine old forts with massive walls. These mounds or stone hills make a curious impression on one, as of being put there like pyramids, rather than of being a freak of nature. We also passed some Mohammedan mosques, and many quaint villages and wayside temples. We have a long day and another night of travel before us, and expect to reach Bombay tomorrow morning at six.

Bombay, Hotel " Great Western," Dec. 20th, 1903
BOMBAY is fine! We are delighted with it! Madras can't compare with it! The streets, squares, and buildings are imposing and good to look at. The style of architecture adopted by the Europeans is thoroughly in keeping with the conditions and surroundings. Here you see people of every nationality, and all the different castes and races are represented. The variety of costumes and the ab-

sence of raiment you see as you drive through the streets is something extraordinary. Parsees seem to be more in evidence here than in any place we have visited so far. Mahometans also are in full force. I cannot describe to you the perennial interest there is in trying to make out from the costumes and the painted marks on the forehead what race the different people belong to. We are continually asking questions of every one we can get hold of, and I suppose that in this way we gain a good deal of incorrect information. No one confesses he does not know when asked a question, but he thinks it his duty to invent something to satisfy the demand.

This hotel is really not half bad. The rooms are very spacious and at least clean, having been recently renovated, and nice porcelain floors are laid everywhere. After tiffin we drove up Malabar Hill, past the " Tower of Silence," where the Parsees dispose of their dead by exposing their naked bodies in an arena, in order that the vultures may pick their bones clean, as neither air nor earth may be defiled by the impurities of a human corpse. The Parsees, who once were fire worshippers only, now worship all the elements. It is interesting to hear in detail all the methods of purification at the Towers of Silence, and to note how carefully the matter has, from first to last, been thought out. The vultures, of which there were hundreds, had evidently finished their gruesome meal for the day, had flown from the Towers, where they habitually perch awaiting the next corpse, and had betaken themselves to the tops of some palm trees lazily to digest their horrible food. On one tree we noted as many as twelve or more. Their place on the Towers was filled by crows on the lookout for small pickings, now that the vultures had eaten their fill. It ceased for the time being to be " Tower of Silence," for

BOMBAY: View of City and Harbor

the crows kept up a terrible noise; but the vultures make no sound while they are engaged with their prey.

We drove afterwards to Monte Rosa, the bungalow of the American Consul, Mr. Meyer, to whom we had letters, and, as luck would have it, Mrs. Meyer came forward to greet us as we entered the driveway. She was just on the point of going out for a drive with her husband, but instead she insisted on our going in and taking tea on the *loggia*. It is a heavenly place, looking out first on a beautiful garden, and beyond on the ocean and Bombay Islands. Mr. and Mrs. Meyer were most cordial, also Mr. Meyer's sister. We found them charming — so intelligent, refined, well-travelled, and also sympathetic. Mrs. M. must be a woman of great taste, to judge from the exquisite things she has collected and which make of the bungalow something quite unique. We are invited to dinner there tomorrow evening in spite of our protests that we did not want to be entertained, it being so near Christmas time, when every one is so busy. As we sat on the *loggia* I noticed that several tall palm trees had lost all their leaves, and were now only bare poles — sixty feet high. On asking Mr. Meyer how it happened, he told me it was the work of the vultures; that every tree on which they take to perching must die on account of their tremendous weight and their filthiness. Oh! they are dreadful birds when you see them in all their warpaint, by the hundreds! Mrs. M. is going to get a permit for us to visit the Towers of Silence.

[*Note by* H. M. R. " The permit says: ' N.B. Visitors are requested to keep themselves at a distance of thirty yards at least from the Towers, and to withdraw from the compound when the funeral and other religious ceremonies are performed. Visitors will not be allowed to

enter the compound on the day of *Faverdeen* (New
Year's Day — September); visitors are requested not to
smoke and not to carry any camera with them within
the compound. This permit is issued free of charge.
Nothing to be paid at the Towers. The general hours of
visit are from seven to eight-thirty A.M. and two to four-
thirty P.M.'

" The Parsees, formerly inhabitants of Persia, are the
modern followers of Zoroaster. They are very rich and
very influential in Bombay."]

December 22nd

WE SPENT a most delightful evening with the Meyers
yesterday. We like them better and better the more we
see of them. Miss Meyer, who is a fine specimen of a
good, wholesome American woman, has a very good
mezzo-soprano voice, and she and I had some Franz,
Schumann, and Brahms together. I confess it was a surprise to find any one in Bombay who cared for such good
things, the musical taste and understanding in these
parts being usually null, as I am told. Mrs. Hearst had
quite a feast over Mrs. Meyer's splendid collection of
Burmese silver, old brasses, old jewels, and wonderful
old embroidered Parsee robes, which every one is wild to
get, because there are so few left now of the old kind.
Mrs. M. put Mrs. Hearst in the way of getting some
valuable things for her Museum, so she went home very
well satisfied with the way she had spent her evening.

The Meyers invited us to tea at the Yacht Club this
afternoon, which was also a pleasant experience, as we
saw all the *élite* of Bombay in full force, it being band
day. Several very nice barristers and a Chief Justice
joined our party and made themselves very agreeable.
We bade good bye to our kind friends with real regret.

Mrs. Hearst and Clara will see them again when they return to Bombay in January *en route* for England, but we shall not, I think, as we shall be going to Calcutta and up North.

[*Note by* H. M. R. " At the Yacht Club we met a lot of very pleasant people, and took our tea in the open garden, looking towards the sea and surrounded by many of the most agreeable ' society ' in Bombay. The Yacht Club has a large membership, and belonging to it or not has a social significance of its own. Mr. and Mrs. Meyer both belong (it is for both sexes), and as we sat at the table, and took our tea and cake, many people came up to them, and so we were introduced to some people, who, had we stayed in Bombay, would have made it pleasant for us.

" Mr. Meyer wanted me to stay to give me a lunch at the ' Byculla Club,' the swell club of India, to introduce me to some of the men — judges, lawyers, and others, whom it would be agreeable to know, but, unfortunately, our time was too limited to permit it.

" Mr. Meyer is a most agreeable man, of broad outlook, fine equipment, sympathetic, well informed, and a real good fellow besides. We became friends at once. Mr. Meyer is a husband Mrs. Meyer may be proud of, and I think she *is;* and he may, on his part, feel that he has an exceptional woman for a wife."]

Everything is beginning to look festive for Christmas week. The market which we visited yesterday was full of floral decorations and flower chains, which are used here instead of evergreens. I suppose that in a country where verdure is always rampant, there would seem to be nothing festive in green decorations. We have had to put off visiting the Towers of Silence until tomorrow morning. We must start at 7 A.M., as it is a three-mile drive, and no one is allowed within the grounds of the Towers after 8.30 A.M. except funeral folk; everything is done so secretly and mysteriously by the Parsees.

We made a very pleasant acquaintance here at the hotel of an officer in the British army — a Captain Watt. He has been stationed in China, in many parts of India, and is now on his way to Thibet. He gave us lots of interesting information about the Orient, and told us much of the unwritten history of the uprising in China, of the South African war, and threw some light on the present position of Russia and Japan. He seems to think that they will come to blows pretty soon.

In the train en route *for Agra, Dec. 23rd,* 1903
OUR VISIT to the Towers of Silence was most interesting this morning. The site is the most beautiful in Bombay, on the top of Malabar Hill, looking out on the Back Bay and Islands, and a walk through the grounds alone would have repaid us for the early matutinal ride. We simply looked into the arena, for no one is ever allowed to enter except the men who carry the bodies — a calling which is handed down from father to son. It is regarded as one of defilement — properly carried out by outcasts, whose fate it is. There is a sacred fire kept perpetually burning in the temple, where the services are held, guarded by four priests. But no one may see these either, no outsider, that is. There are three towers, one large one for the people, one for outsiders, and one which belongs to a private family. There were hundreds of vultures sitting up expectant on each of the towers. They say that the corpse bearers, after stripping the dead of their clothes and laying them on the grating of the arena,

always wait to see which eye the vultures tear out first, as on that depends the subsequent fate of the departed soul. We were shown a model of the interior of the towers, and all the *modus operandi* was explained to us, but there it ended, of course.

We left Bombay after tiffin, at three o'clock, with a railway journey of eight hundred and thirty-nine miles before us. But the car is comfortable, the heat not excessive, and we are all as jolly as sandboys! We selected Agra as the place where we should like to spend Christmas Day. There was some rather interesting scenery on leaving Bombay. First we had a very good view of some of the Islands, and then there were some very extraordinary looking mountains, suggesting the Dolemites. Soon it will be getting dark, and heaven knows what sort of scenery we may be rushing past during the night!

December 24th

THIS morning when we looked out we found ourselves travelling on plains, studded here and there with queer, classic-looking hills of strange and weird shapes, and as we approached Sonagir there were some grand-looking forts, ruins, and Mohammedan mosques in sight. As we go farther north the people are beginning to wear some clothes — scant, if you please, but still more of their nakedness is covered than in the south. We have not yet reached the shoe-belt, however. I doubt if they wear shoes anywhere in India. But I am getting so used to bare feet, naked bodies with light — very light — draperies, that our mode of dress is beginning to seem to me terribly out of place and even ridiculous, if not vulgar! I cannot describe to you how beautiful the general effect of all these rich, graceful draperies is, and how it feeds the eye with colour.

Our train was delayed during the night, owing to a large influx of travellers at wayside stations, which necessitated putting on new cars, and we shall not reach Agra till after dark this evening, instead of at four, as we should have done.

Agra, Laurie's Hotel, Christmas Day, 1903

CHRISTMAS DAY at Agra! That is what we wished for, that is what we have had! We shall never forget it. This is the India we have dreamed of. This is the wonderland of the East. It is more Eastern than anything we have seen so far in all its characteristics, from the rusty looking camels that wander through the streets, laden with merchandise, or that squat on dried mud in the open spaces near by, to the bright-green parrots and parrakeets which are as plentiful as crows, and which one sees sitting in rows on the telegraph wires, just as sparrows do with us. Then, when you drive through one of the native streets and see huge apes, as big as St. Bernard dogs, tumbling about and frolicking over the roof tops, playing at hide and seek with each other, and occasionally carrying a young monkey pick-a-back, you realize that you are neither in Europe nor America.

I was awakened this morning by some very barbaric music. There were drums, cymbals, and some bagpipish-sounding instruments, the drum beating a tone which had no relation whatever to the key of the tune, or top pattern. So I got up and proceeded to take my bath and dress, which gave me considerable exercise on account of the spaciousness of our apartments. First there is my bed-chamber, with an abnormally high ceiling (it looks like two stories knocked into one), then a large alcove room with an archway, and then the bathroom, which leads out into a street along side of a common. Harry's room, which joins mine, is nearly as large as Steinway Hall, and looks very much like it. Space seems cheap in Agra.

This is a queer hotel, but very interesting in its construction; it suggests an old Spanish mansion. It is all on one floor, the walls are very massive, and there are no windows except high up near the ceiling, and very small ones at that. My room has only a sort of skylight. In Harry's room there is an arched niche in the wall which looks as if it were intended for a shrine. In the dining room birds fly about at their own sweet will; they come in at the ceiling windows, and no one molests them. We were much astonished at seeing a fire in the sitting room when we arrived. A fire in India! But it is really chilly here in the evening and early morning, and only hot in the sun.

This morning after breakfast we drove to the Fort accompanied by a very interesting local guide named Karam Tchahi, a picturesque person who wears a beautiful blue-grey, camels'-hair long coat like all the Mohammedans here, and a fine, apricot cashmere shawl slung over his shoulder. He always addresses us as " Lady-shies," and the peculiar use he makes of our mother tongue is delicious sometimes, but you can't help getting your historic facts a little mixed when he tells you that Mumtaz-i-Mahal, wife of Shah Jehan, for whom the Taj Mahal was built, " died travelling," and you discover by cross questioning that he meant " died in child-birth " (in travail)!

We were positively affected at the beauty of the buildings we went through today. It was the sensation of a lifetime. The magnificent, massive, noble fort, a mile and a quarter in circumference, and all of huge blocks of a rich, red stone, which stands on the right bank of the river Jumna, is the frame which contains an array of splendid Mogul buildings which could hardly be conceived of. How under the sun they ever came to be conceived and executed passes my understanding! First, there was the Pearl Mosque, where the three hundred and sixty wives of Shah Jehan had a private division for them to pray in, to the left of the central division. It is all of white marble, with *such* carvings, such exquisite marble fretwork screens! It is impossible to convey any of the nobility, the chasteness of it all. And how restful to the spirit to gaze upon this beautiful structure without any nasty gods to disturb the poetry of its atmosphere!

We went all over Shah Jehan's palace, into the apartments of the ladies of the harem, into their playgrounds, where they used to play hide-and-seek, and the mosaic platform where they played chess with living figures; into the underground apartments, where they used to take refuge and amuse themselves during the unbearable summer heat; their luxurious bathing tanks, and ponds where they used to fish. Then the apartments of Shah Jehan himself, overlooking the three sides of the square court, occupied by the ladies. The bathroom must have come out of the Arabian Nights! The walls and ceilings glittering and sparkling as though set with diamonds and rubies, the effect being produced by small, convex medallions of mirror glass, beautifully set into the marble like stones in a ring.

Then it was no mean sight to see a flight of green parrots from the surrounding trees, or the brown hawks soaring above, or the splendid bird who is a red brown when he is still and light blue when he flies, a sacred bird, whose name has escaped me — about as large as a crow. Our guide, who is a true enthusiast and loves every

DELHI: Audience Hall in Shah Jehan's Palace

stone of the buildings he took us through, would not let us see everything within the Fort today, as he said we could not possibly take in so much, so we are to return there tomorrow and go over the Diwan-i Khas, a hall of private audience, and the Saman Burj, or Jasmine Tower, where the chief Sultana lived.

After tiffin we were taken to get our first impression of the far-famed Taj Mahal, the wonderful mausoleum which Shah Jehan built in memory of his beloved Queen, Mumtaz-i-Mahal, which means "the Pride of the Palace," who died before she was thirty at the birth of her eighth child. It is a marvel of beauty — of inexpressible exquisiteness — of poetry! A thing never to be forgotten! The approach, the surroundings, everything is marvelous beyond words. I can only *feel* it just now! What a glorious, soul-filling way to spend Christmas, instead of tying up and untying packages, and scribbling notes of thanks! Of course I suppose the latter performance is more virtuous because it involves sacrifice and is unselfish, but oh! it is good to be bad and have a feast like this once in a lifetime at least!

After dinner we did have a sort of Christmas celebration, though. We had each of us bought gifts for the other, and we had a grand display on the table of our sitting room of the handicrafts of India. I wish you could see the beautiful apricot Indian cashmere shawl which Mrs. Hearst gave me, and the finely carved sandal-wood box that Clara gave me, besides other sundries. We have just bidden each other good night, with full hearts.

[*Note by* H. M. R. " It is Christmas evening — the end of our first day in Agra, and it will ever stand alone in memory as the day when I first looked upon the Pearl

Mosque, on the great Fort which embraces it, and on the Taj Mahal. No pen can describe the wonders of this glorious city of the Great Moguls. You hear the stories of the rulers, of Akbar (Akbar means ' the great,' as I learn from our guide, so when we read of ' Akbar the Great ' it would seem to be the superlative Great), Jehangir, Shah Jehan, and Aurangzib, and they become very real as you trace their works through the 16th and 17th centuries, and you say they have left monuments of their greatness and of their appreciation of beauty such as the whole world besides cannot offer, up to this very day of our Lord, and these marvels of beauty of design, structure, and environment, thanks to the climate and to the perfectness of detail in finish and thoroughness of workmanship, stand today to gladden your eyes and to enrich your soul as if they had just left the master's hand.

" Such a Christmas Day as never was — so different from anything before or that will ever be again. We left the Taj Mahal this afternoon as the setting sun was on it — as the reflection of it was mirrored in the water of the garden beneath — and in that same water the young moon was displaying itself, promising us that if we would only be good and patient chilluns and wait for a few days, we should see the Taj by the glamour light of that very moon."]

Agra, India, Dec. 26th, 1903
TODAY, after breakfast, we returned to the Fort and began by going all over the ground again. Then we explored the Jasmine Tower, the golden pavilion which is roofed with gilded plates of copper, where there were some of the ladies' bedrooms, and our attention was called to certain deep holes in the wall into which they

used to slip their jewels. The Jasmine Tower is un-speakably exquisite! The marble walls are inlaid with jasmine blossoms and sprays in coloured stones in every conceivable manner. A fitting abiding place indeed for the chief Sultana of a Shah Jehan, the Pride of the Palace. There is a fountain, which was always charged with rose water, for which Agra is famous.

As one contemplates the splendour of these buildings, and learns of the luxury, the untold wealth and mag-nificence of display, one wonders what can have become of it all. Where are all those pearls, monster rubies, emeralds, and diamonds? Where the vases of jade with insets of precious stones? The squalor and poverty, which are always painfully in evidence everywhere in India, make all this luxury of the past seem like a thing of enchantment, which, with a wave of the wand would disappear! Yet there are the bare walls to tell the tale, the carvings, the flowers inlaid on marble with precious stones, and all the other wonders.

I peopled the palace in imagination with beautiful Zenanas richly attired, flitting to and fro, at their games or reclining on divans. I pictured the merchants spread-ing out their gorgeous brocades and jewels in the court to tempt them, and I saw them eagerly leaning over the terrace and watching a fight between an elephant and a tiger in the enclosure beneath. We sat on the huge slabs of black marble which was once the throne, and looked towards the white slab opposite, where the court jester used to sit. After all, it was not so difficult to people it all over again in one's own mind's eye!

December 27th
YESTERDAY we went again to the Taj Mahal to explore the interior as well as the exterior. The sight of so much

exquisiteness quite beggars description. The whole thing is a dream of loveliness. How aptly it has been described as a work " conceived by Titans and finished by Jewellers! " Such grandeur and such delicacy in combination could be nothing short of an inspired concept. No one could regard it without being possessed with an entirely new sense of purity and beauty.

This morning we went to Sikandarah — five miles away — to see the tomb of the great Akbar, famous for the broadness of his views, his religious tolerance, and his wise statesmanship. In this same mausoleum the wonderful Kohinoor diamond was to be seen for over seventy years — until it was seized by the Shah of Persia in 1730. We were shown the marble pedestal on which it was exposed to the public gaze in the open court.

One can hardly take in the fact that such a superb edifice should exist for the sole purpose of sheltering the remains of even so great a ruler as Akbar and his Portuguese Christian wife, also interred there. There is a magnificent gateway to the garden in which it stands, of red sandstone inlaid with white marble, and over the archway a splendid large scroll of Tughra writing, than which no design, especially thought out, could be more decorative. The garden itself is superb, and the huge tamarind trees were the finest we have seen.

[*Note by* H. M. R. " Akbar, the greatest of the Moguls — head and shoulders above all the others — died at Agra in 1605. He was a ' three decker ' — a soldier, statesman, jurist (his law is administered today), and though he had some 353 ladies in his or their apartments in the palace, think why, among other reasons, he had them.

" He had each of the great chiefs, rajahs, and what not, send a daughter of the house to his palace, whether Mohammedan, Hindu, or what not. How could the fathers fight him when their children were in his palace? They were rich themselves, but, if I recollect aright, he made an ample allowance to each of them besides, and their separate apartments in the palace, with amusements, fish ponds, summer apartments where they could look out and avoid the sun, with fountains, fish ponds, etc., showed he tried to make them comfortable.

" To be sure, he *did* keep a dungeon or two, and when any lady misbehaved he had a *carved beam* below stairs to which he hanged her, or had her hanged, and dropped into the Jumna River, to prevent too much levity among the girls. They would sometimes get into the clothes of the eunuchs and go sight-seeing in the city, and otherwise disport themselves, and *if not caught* they had a very pleasant memory of it.

" Now the mogul emperors of Hindustan whom we care to know about are Akbar 1556, Jehangir 1605, Shah Jehan 1628, Aurangzih 1658, and the greatest of these was *Akbar*. Now today we went to his tomb, which he began in his life time and it is certainly worthy of him, as it is also characteristic of him."]

We passed many interesting old tombs and landmarks, and as we returned we met a band of pilgrims on their way to Muttra, a sacred city, because Krishnu, as our guide informed us, " had his borning there." This afternoon we went across the pontoon bridge to the tomb of I'timadu-daulah, a Persian, who became high treasurer of Jehangir. It is quite different in style from the Taj, but in its way it also is extraordinarily beautiful. It is a square structure with an octagonal tower at each corner, and a raised pavilion in the centre. The window recesses are of exquisite marble lattice-work, the rest of the interior being inlaid with half-precious stones. It is a veritable jewel box. Dainty, exquisite, and distinguished!

[*Note by* H. M. R. " I'timadu-daulah was the father of Jehangir's wife and grandfather of the lady buried in the Taj Mahal. This mausoleum was built by Nur Jehan, his daughter, in memory of her father, and being built before the Taj Mahal may have and probably did furnish ideas for that structure."]

Agra is indeed a city of palatial creations! It can boast of no natural scenery to speak of, but the streets are more interesting and picturesque than any one can imagine who has not seen the like. As you drive through one of the native streets this is what you see: shops like enlarged pigeon holes raised a few feet from the street, and in these tiny spaces all the business of the town is done. The merchants squat on the floor, and each shop resembles a gypsy camp on a small scale. The tradesmen are very noisy, and make as much clatter over selling three turnips as though they were jewels.

Above these mean looking shops there is always another story, and this is as beautiful as the lower one is mean and dirty. There is generally a balcony, mostly enclosed, with pillars of beautiful stone carving, and often lattice work worthy of a mosque. No family seems too poor to have a bit of artistic work somewhere about the outside of their dwelling. I wonder that painters do not flock to India for their subjects, instead of perpetually frothing around Holland and Venice. There is such a wealth of colour, quaintness, and picturesqueness everywhere!

AGRA: The Taj Mahal

We have been somewhat puzzled during our travels in India at being treated as if we were grandees, but the mystery has now been solved. I must tell you about it as it is rather a good joke: before leaving San Francisco Harry sent a cheque to Chief Justice White, at Madras, requesting him to hand over the sum to the servants we had — on advice of the Bridgewaters — asked him to engage for us, for the purchase of suitable liveries. Accordingly the men went to a first-class tailor and asked him to fit them out. " Some grand Sahibs from America named Rogers (which he pronounced Rahjahs). " All right," said the tailor, " I'll make the regular Rajah's livery for you. Of what country is your master the Prince? " " I don't know," replied our men. The result of this interview was a long, dark-blue cloth coat, bordered with gold braid half an inch wide, and white-silk, gauze turbans interlaced with gold cord — a style adopted by Indian princes for their servants.

So now, wherever we go, our men are asked what Prince they serve, to which they doubtless reply, " We serve Sahib Rahgers; his kingdom is America! I need hardly add that we are charged accordingly. These dignified gentlemen sleep on a mat outside our doors. It takes some time for a stranger to get used to seeing people sleeping all over the floors of the hotel corridors, rolled in a blanket or a sheet according to climate. They all sleep this way, also in the open porticoes of their little shops, and those who have no shop curl up by the wayside. They sleep anywhere — just like dogs! It is odd, too, to see a man being shaved in the open street, and the other day we saw a man cleaning his teeth in the street. He had a sort of wooden tooth brush which he dipped in the dust of the road, and after brushing his teeth with this, he rinsed his mouth with water. Another

queer sight in Agra was a woman kneading horse dung
to make dung cakes which are used here as fuel. She was
kneading it just like bread, and her arms meanwhile,
were covered with braclets — there were nine or ten on
each arm! Have you ever read " Kim "? If not, do. He
is brought to my mind at every turn here, and I must
say that Kipling's knowledge of the Hindu nature and
modus operandi is simply wonderful.

December 28th
TODAY we called a halt from sight seeing for a while and
attended to other matters. This evening was our climax
at Agra. We have been nursing a new moon in the hope
of its growing up in time to let us see the Taj Mahal by
moonlight before we leave tomorrow. Well, there was
only half of it, but it sufficed to shed a most beautiful
light on the Taj, and the effect was heavenly! No words
can describe it! We went inside, and the keeper chanted
some of the Koran for us, the reverberation being something extraordinary. We bade adieu to the Taj with
deep emotion. I could hardly keep the tears back at the
thought that we might never look upon it again! We
were all greatly moved. We leave here for Delhi tomorrow at one o'clock.

[*Note by* H. M. R. " Think of looking from the height
of the chamber in the Castle, or Fort of Agra, wherein
Shah Jehan died, and from which he saw the exquisite
Taj Mahal rising like a glorified poem, his lasting memorial to his beloved wife, who had died thirty years before
him, and whose place he had never sought to fill. Think
too, that all of this was the memorial of a man who died
in 1665, when Charles II was come to the throne, for a
beloved woman! What was Charles II doing those days?

Honoring women — by the score — and leaving no memorial behind! This ' barbarian,' in the estimation of the England of that day, building the finest thing that the eye of man has yet seen in marble, even to this very day, and as glorious in its wondrous and touching beauty this afternoon as we left it as when the dying eye of Shah Jehan looked upon it for the last time. What was Louis XIV doing about these days?

" The Taj Mahal (Crown Palace), properly Taj-bibike Roza (the Crown Lady's tomb), was commenced A.D. 1630, finished 1647, and cost from 18 to 32 millions of rupees (a rupee is now 32 cents). Let me quote a few words from Murray's guide book. ' Built by Shah Jehan as a tomb for his favorite queen Arjmand Banu, entitled " Mumtaz-i-Mahal, the Chosen of the Palace," or, more freely, Pride of the Palace. She married Shah Jehan in 1615, had seven children by him, and died in childbirth of the eighth child in 1629 at Burhanpur in the Deccan. Her body was brought to Agra and laid in the garden where the Taj stands until the mausoleum was built.' I merely note these facts for future reference.

" I love the streets of this place, with the living life, with everything Eastern, the parrots in hundreds in some of the trees — parrakeets more properly; with monkeys ' skiting ' around the roofs and running along the balustrades; with the wonderful carts, wagons, bullocks, donkeys, camels, and every variety of noise, color, costume, I have sat in the carriage an hour at a time seeing this instead of going to see the carpets, shawls, draperies, jewels, etc.

" I love the carved balconies overhanging these dusty, crowded, narrow streets, and nearly touching because the street is hardly wide enough to get a carriage through, and when you do go through you are almost *into* the

shops where the people are squatting, barefooted or not
as the case may be, smoking their hookahs and gabbling
all the time, and the beggars shout, and the people hurry
and scurry, and there is food to be looked at and purchased, and there are all sorts of deadly looking sweetmeats for sale that might taste good ' if you knew the
woman as made 'em,' and color, color, color, and powdered dust on the clothes of every mortal soul who goes
along, and slim, bare legs or legs in close fitting garments
in evidence everywhere. It is such a sight so crammed
full of motion and noise and confusion and people and
people and people that I seem to live hours of picture
books in sixty minutes."]

On the train bound for Delhi, Dec. 29th, 1903
IT WAS really very hard to tear ourselves away from
Agra today, and the real friendliness and demonstrations
of affection we received from two or three of the natives
made it still harder. The Meyers, in Bombay, advised us
to go to a merchant in Agra named Sargee Lall, who has
a most wonderful collection of rare, and almost priceless
things — old Burmese silver, old embroideries, magnificent cashmere shawls, superb old jewels that have belonged to rahjahs from time immemorial, and ultimately
sacrificed to raise money to buy the wedding silver for
the daughters of the house. Also such rare boxes and cups
of jade, set with emeralds and rubies. He has a large
tent opposite our hotel, where he sells, by proxy, brasses
and modern enamels, embroideries, wrought silver, etc.,
but he took us to see his private collection of beautiful
things in a house in one of the principal native streets.
Our appreciation of the artistic side of the work, and
Mrs. Hearst's real, expert knowledge of the intrinsic

CINGALESE TYPE: Up Country

value of his possessions, quite won his heart, and the instincts of the canny merchant seemed at times almost overcome by his enthusiastic delight in finding sympathetic souls. Mrs. Hearst bought a number of things from him, but not to any very considerable amount, because, in the present uncertain state of the money market, she did not feel justified in so doing. Clara and I also made only a very few, humble purchases, but Sargee Lall is, I feel sure, our friend for life!

It has been a very interesting feature of our stay in Agra to see so much of him (for he was in constant attendance when we were at the hotel), and as he let himself go quite a good deal, we felt that we were really getting at some of the true inwardness of a better class. I think he was more impressed than he knew by Mrs. Hearst's altruism, which revealed itself to him little by little — for altruism is a virtue unknown, not to say, foreign to the Orientals. They know the emotion of kindness, of pity, and of generosity, but to work for or sacrifice for the interest and welfare of others — that is to them an unknown quantity, and friend Sargee seemed to be touched by it. He brought us gifts of attar of roses and oil of sandal-wood, and of the fruits of India, and came to accompany us to the station in his beautiful carriage with a pair of fine horses and two liveried servants dressed in green and gold. He looked so handsome and distinguished as he stood there on the platform with his fine, blue cashmere shawl thrown carelessly over one shoulder, that I wondered whether Shah Jehan himself could have made a better appearance. Our guide, Karam Tlahu, was there also to see us off, and several others, so that we felt that we were really leaving friendly hearts behind.

[*Note by* H. M. R. " Sargee Lall was an interesting man. He belonged to a strict sect of religionists, and I had some interesting talks with him. He is a splendid look-ing man, and the way he wears his shawl and the beauty of his face, clothes and all, make him ' a feature ' in our Agra experience.

" His sect — caste — forbids his going onto the sea, or, at any rate, eating any food there not cooked by the undefiled. He would like to go to England and to the United States, but cannot, because if he did he would become defiled, and would lose his place in his caste. Some of his fellow religionists, as I have learned, have separated, gone to England, been educated, and re-turned, and, though out of their caste, have, so to speak, made a caste of their own, and marry and give in mar-riage in this ' seceding ' caste, if I may so call it.

" I have been talking with one of his sect — Chattee, I believe is the name — here in Delhi, and he tells me curious things. He showed me a string he always wears. I looked at it, and examined it, and took it in my hand quite unconsciously. He told me he would have to take that off and get another (if he followed strictly his caste), as I had defiled it by my touch. He said, too, he would take an orange or a banana from my hand and eat it (he doing his own peeling, I suppose), but he would not eat bread or biscuit I gave him. By the way, this gentleman worships at the Monkey Temple on Tues-days, to which crowds go on that day. The monkey is one of the holy animals, and there are lots of them in Delhi."]

The scenery we are passing through is somewhat mo-notonous. It is very flat, and after a while hedges of cactus and miles of aloes become tiresome.

Laurie's Hotel, Delhi, Dec. 30th, 1903

HERE we are in the ancient, historic walled city, or rather series of cities, called Delhi. In it are the ruins of seven different forts and cities, built by different kings before it was conquered by the Mohammedans in 1193. But very few of the ancient Hindu landmarks remain to tell the tale.

We started off this morning in two very gorgeous looking carriages, so lofty in their build that there are three long steps to mount before one can get in. For some reason unknown, both here and in Agra, we are furnished with two native footmen besides the coachman. The former stand at the back of the carriage, and when an ox-cart or a group of people seem to be coming our way, they jump down and run, one on either side of the conveyance, shouting " Get out of the way " in Bengali, at the top of their voices. They go it even one better than in Japan!

We were taken to the Palace, then through an arcade like a huge cathedral, with shops on either side, to the Nakar Khana, beyond which is the Diwan-i-'Am, or Hall of Public Audience, a fine structure, supported by rows of red, sandstone pillars. Behind the throne, which we mounted, the walls are covered with mosaics in precious stones, representing bright, plumaged birds, fruits, and flowers of Hindustan. Then we passed on to the Diwan-i-khas, or private Hall of Audience, which is very beautiful and rich with the most exquisite inlaid work, some of which is done also in precious stones. We were then taken to a mosque in carved white marble, which, though it has been called the " Pearl Mosque," does not compare with that of Agra of the same name. This impressed me as being much too ornate for its size.

After we had done the Palace, we went to the Jumma Musjid, one of the largest and most imposing mosques in the world. It was one o'clock when we got there, and the "muezzins" were calling the people to prayer, shouting the call — in which the sound of Allah predominated — from all the four sides of the temple to the streets below. It sounded very weird, and seemed a wild substitute for a bell. We were shown some writing on parchment of Mahomet, a hair of his head, and his slippers, all kept locked in a sacred shrine. In the centre of the open court was a huge tank of sacred water where numbers of worshippers were bathing their feet and arms, and drinking the water at the same time! After this performance they prostrated themselves many times in front of the mosque, laying their foreheads on the bare pavement. They seemed very genuinely devout. That was all we could get of sight-seeing before tiffin, but on the way there were little side shows, such as dozens of monkeys frisking about on the walls of a low bridge, doing all sorts of funny things, and then we passed through the " Chaudni Chank," or silver square, where all the jewellers congregate.

After tiffin we started forth again, and drove all round the Ridge, where many objects of interest were pointed out to us in connection with the mutiny and siege of Delhi. We saw the " Lat," or Asoka pillar which has such a chequered history. It was originally a monolith of pink sandstone, erected at Meerut in the third century before Christ by King Asoka. It was removed and set up in the Rushak Shikar's palace near by in 1356, and later, in 1713, it was broken into five pieces by the explosion of a powder magazine, and finally it was put together and set up again by the British Government in 1867. The poor thing is now broken at the top in a jagged

way, but it stands as a monument of the fact that there
has always existed a reverence for a thing of beauty in
this benighted country. And this same reverence always
seems to be a saving grace in a people whose ways are so
unlovely. It was delightful to see how many of the
natives took the trouble to go a couple of miles or more
out of town to look at the Taj Mahal in Agra by moonlight! We visited the grave of Nicholson, and the exact
spot on the city walls where he was shot and mortally
wounded. We drove through the fine old garden of a
Begam, and through the Queen's gardens.

I noticed a number of very large, heavy-looking birds
poking about in the hotel grounds this morning. They
looked something like vultures, but they had a queer,
white, whiskery growth all round their heads. Some were
brown, others white with a few brown patches. On en-
quiry I found that they were kites. I wish you might
see the wonderful birds of this country! There are so
many, to me, nameless ones. Birds that one only sees
in royal aviaries as a rule. Then the mynah birds. Hundreds, thousands of them hopping about in all directions,
and so tame and independent that they will hardly get
out of the way of our carriage.

[*Note by* H. M. R. " Here we have not only the great
Palace, Castle, Audience Chambers, and the greatest
mosque in India, but the place is crowded with memo-
rials of the great mutiny of 1857 and the evidences of
British valor — made necessary by what must seem to
any student of history the gross stupidity, overweening
confidence, and utter disregard of every ordinary precaution in dealing with a conquered people, full of caste
prejudices and as utterly unlike Englishmen as any peoples could be made or imagined.

" The siege of Delhi in 1857 and its capture are matters of history. When I was sick two years ago I got absorbed in reading General Roberts' book, ' Forty-one Years in India,' and the siege of Delhi, the assault on the Kashmir Gate, and the death of General John Nicholson, who led the assault, nearly overcame me, and I had to send the book back to the library unfinished, and to wait for stronger nerves and for less feverish conditions.

" Well, yesterday I went over the ground of the story here, and stood by the grave of John Nicholson, the most superb man, physically, mentally and morally, from all accounts that you can find amongst all those heroes of '57. He led the assault on the Kashmir Cabul Gate, while on the walls of Delhi (they are like the walls of Chester, some five feet wide along the side within the outer battlements) calling to his men to follow him. His body rests not far from the walls in the beautiful cemetery, and over his body is a slab with this inscription:

THE GRAVE OF BRIGADIER GENERAL JOHN NICHOLSON, WHO LED THE ASSAULT OF DELHI, BUT FELL IN THE HOUR OF VICTORY, MORTALLY WOUNDED, AND DIED 23RD SEPTEMBER, 1857, AGED 35 YEARS

" I stood on the wall over the tablet which records the spot where he was wounded, and I thought back how he had impressed me and become one of my heroes two years before in Boston. Little did I think then that I should feel so near to him as I did yesterday!

" India as a country is flat, brown, bare, parched, and uninteresting physically. It is poverty stricken, and seemingly almost a hopeless conglomeration of hundreds of races, speaking hundreds of languages, and with

DELHI: The Kashmir Gate

thousands and tens of thousands of gods. It is an impossible chaos of atoms — called men and women — with
caste ruling and with little hope for the individual man,
so far as an onlooker can judge.

"I have no doubt myself that if the English were out
of India absolutely it would not be twenty years before
every vestige of them disappeared from the lives, conditions, and knowledge of at least 300,000,000 people,
and those who then had any part or lot with English
ideas or traditions could be counted by the thousands
and not millions — so little impression do I believe England has made on the body of the people.

"When will the next uprising come? Who will lead
the people? Will it be a religious war? Will a prophet
arise who is likewise priest and soldier and a natural
leader, and combine the heterogeneous elements so they
will cohere and be filled with a grand fanaticism to ele-
vate the people themselves and drive out those who are
merely administrators? When that time does come, the
world will stand aghast at the possibilities of daring that
can animate clods. I cannot describe how overwhelming
all this mass of teeming life, with its dust of ages settled
upon it, becomes to one who is simply looking at what
he does not understand. In vain to attempt the solution
of the meaning of it all, and what our God is working out
in the scheme of the world."]

December 31st
THIS has been a great day of tomb-ing, temple-ing, for-
tress-ing and mosque-ing. We started this morning at
ten on a whole day excursion, taking a lunch basket
with us, as we had to cover eleven miles each way. We
went to explore the ruined cities and forts of Delhi.
There are nine Delhis in all, and this one where we are

stopping is No. 9. The first we visited was No. 5, Ferozabad, of which little more than the ruins of the fort
remains, and a remarkable pillar, a monolith of pink
sandstone, called the Lat. On it there is an inscription
in Pali that no one has ever been able to read. From the
hill or mound on which it stands we had a good view of
some of the other ruined cities, of Humayu's tomb, and
especially of Indrapat, a wonderful old fort, in a much
better state of preservation than Ferozabad.

As we walked through the crumbling old gate towards
the fine old Killa Kona Mosque, I happened to spy a
couple of rusty looking old camels, which looked as if
their hides were so worn out that they had been patched
in several places, and with the usual camel sneer on their
mouths. It only wanted that note to complete the picture, a very epitome of all that was ancient, Eastern, and
defunct. The mosque though, was really beautiful still,
for Humayu had restored it in fifteen hundred and
something. He did so many good things of that kind
that he deserved the noble tomb erected by his widow,
which took sixteen years to build, and which was the
next thing we visited.

Then we drove five miles to the enclosure where
stands the wonderful Kutt Minar, or Tower of Victory,
an extraordinary structure in red sandstone 240 feet
high, the base being over 47 feet in diameter, and the
top nine feet. It is simply overpowering in its impres-
siveness! We did not attack it, however, till we had
taken our luncheon in a Dak bungalow near by. I think
we should have died of it on an empty stomach! Then
there was the famous Iron Pillar to be seen in the same
enclosure, a series of beautiful tombs, a Jain Mosque, a
Mahomedan and a Hindu, all of which must have been
superb once! They are still beautiful. Then we drove

home in clouds of dust from Delhi No. 1., through uninteresting country, redeemed occasionally, however, by
the sight of a flock of beautiful peacocks, or a bunch of
buffalo, parrots, mynahs, and other birds.

It is now midnight, and five guns have just been fired
to announce the advent of 1904. Harry has drawn the
noisy bolts of his communicating door, and entered to
wish me a Happy New Year, and Clara, who has the
adjoining room on the other side, has tapped at my door
and I have drawn the bolts for a New Year's kiss.

[*Note by* H. M. R. " Here we are, about as far from all
of those who have made our year what it has been as
we can well be. It is not places and peoples that make
our years after all, but the home thoughts, the heart
thoughts, the recollections of our beloved, and what they
have been and are to us, and so places and peoples in
our real lives, the part that makes us ' we ' and nobody
else, play the secondary part.

" All the same, we are in the midst of a world of
people so different from all the world beside, and in the
midst of history, ancient and modern, of such stirring and
interesting character, that we cannot help feeling that
in being here we are getting new draughts of energies
to make the years to come fuller, higher, better, and
more crowded with reasons for gratitude and thanks-
giving than we have ever known before.

" David — ' my David ' — came to my room as usual
at 7.30 this morning bringing chota hazari (tea and
toast and early breakfast before dressing, and for us hot
water to drink) and also a bouquet of beautiful flowers
for ' the lady,' and also one for ' the master' and a
Happy New Year.

" I do not know what I shall do without David. He is

a little fellow, homely and not well put together, with liquid eyes, and he is dressed in the suit I gave him for cold weather — a blue, ministerial button at the neck, coat trimmed at the collar with two rows of gold braid and a line of gold braid down the front to the skirts, and two rows of gold braid on the sleeves and trousers. He has a pair of shoes belonging to the suit — tan shoes — and he also wears a white turban.

"When around my room he is barefooted. He packs everything; keeps the run of everything; gets out my underclothing and shirt for the day, and my evening dress for dinner; sees that my bed is properly made; that there is hot water to shave with, and he puts out my razors; that my bath tub is filled with hot water. He puts my night dress and underclothing by the fire to warm; puts a hot-water bottle in my bed; sleeps in my dressing room, and is always on the alert, locking doors, putting away clothes, and attending to every mortal thing; getting a ' dobe man ' — washerman, counting my linen.

"We pay for washing by the *hundred* pieces in most places. The prices vary. Here, David says, the price is 5 rupees ($1.60) a hundred. When we travel David packs my trunk, gets all our hand bags, packs them and then assembles them and sees they are in our compartment on the train. He makes our beds at night on the train. We travel everywhere with our own bedding. Even at hotels they do not supply anything but a mattress.

"The hotel is all one story, with rooms having a dressing room and a bathroom out of them; a single window lets in light. You do not look out that window as it is a foot below *the ceiling*, and the room is eighteen or twenty feet high. The bathrooms have stone floors, and

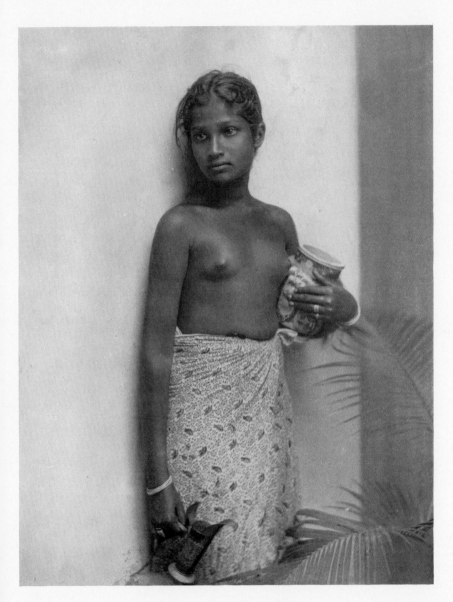

CEYLON: Low Caste Girl

the dressing room, too, although the latter has a matting on it. Of course the house is built to keep out sun and to be kept cool.

" Here I wear my thick Scotch suit in the daytime, with a light overcoat when riding and at nightfall put on my ulster when riding. The crowds in the streets in the evening, sitting around fires, selling wares of all kinds, and the moon throwing its light over all beside and around the buildings, whether hovel or mosque, giving to each a weirdness of its own, make this the land of the Arabian Nights where anything may be."]

January 1st, 1904

THE NEW YEAR opened out brightly for us today, with the usual wealth of sunshine. We continued our explorations of Delhi and saw many interesting sights. There was the " Black Mosque," right down in the heart of things, the Jain Temple also. To reach the latter we had to dismount from the carriage, as the streets leading to it were only wide enough for foot passengers. One of them resembled the narrowest *calle* in Venice. Nevertheless, every now and then, as we walked through, we came upon a splendid bit of architecture — a house with a court inside, and with fine stone carving and lattice-work over door and windows, and a most beautiful projecting covered veranda of carved stone. These houses we learned were inhabited by high caste Hindus. It is needless to say that they were, nevertheless, in an utterly tumble-down condition, as though no repairs had ever been made since they were first built, and no dirt ever removed. It is a curious fact that all the native streets impress Europeans as slums, so, when one sees dwellings like the one I have just described, in such narrow, dirty streets, cheek by jowl with dirty little shops and stalls, it is almost impossible to take in the fact that the aristocracy of the town live there.

At one o'clock we went to see the Mahometans worship in the great Jumma Musjid, the mosque we visited on the first day of our sight-seeing here — when we saw the hand writing on parchment of the great prophet himself, a hair of his head, and his slippers in the sacred shrine! Friday is the only day that special service is held there, and thousands of people pour into it when the muezzin calls are heard from the terrace. Of course we were not allowed to go near the worshippers, but they let us go up into a little recess in the wall above the great Court of the Mosque, where we could look down and see the show. It was indeed well worth seeing, if only as an orgy of colour.

But to watch the people in their devotions was intensely interesting even without the colour. In the interior of the mosque, which is all open to the view of the spectator, the worshippers were as thick as flies on a cake, and, in spite of its enormous size, a thousand or more spilled over into the Court, where there was a rough pulpit erected, on the top of which stood two priests, one in yellow and the other in brown. These declaimed in a loud, metallic voice, while the worshippers, with their faces kissing the earth and turned towards Mecca, presented to our view nothing but a wonderful array of upturned fundaments, draped in every colour of the rainbow. It was the funniest sight I ever beheld! But this was not all, for every minute a couple of men entered the Court, and, instead of joining the masses, remained in the middle of the Court, and, after whisking the dust from the stone pavement with a white cloth, they made a prayer, first erect on their feet, then in a stooping position, and, finally, sinking on their knees, with their foreheads touching the pavement. This they repeated at least three times, then they got up and walked away. Meanwhile the tank in the middle of the Court was in great demand. Every inch of its stone margin was taken up by devotees who sat there washing their feet and their arms, and throwing the slimy, green water over their heads and into their faces and mouths, after which, being purified (?), they joined the other worshippers. It seemed strange to see no women among them, but women are supposed not to have any souls to save! As we entered the mosque, however, we saw five or six women entirely enveloped in white muslin, worshipping in a corner of the passage leading to the court, in an humble, unobtrusive way. From their draperies I should judge them to be of the aristocracy.

As we descended the steps of the mosque we saw a funeral procession, or rather a body being carried to the burning Ghat on the Jumna River for cremation (the Jumna being a sacred river like the Ganges). The body was simply tied up in a white sheet and laid on a sort of open bier, with just a few flowers scattered over it. It was a low-caste funeral. The bearers and followers chanted a little and talked and chattered a great deal among themselves.

Apropos of the Hindu attitude towards the dying and dead, they have a superstition about anybody dying in the house, so, as soon as they suspect that a member of the family is in danger, they carry him or her out in the open, no matter how cold it may happen to be, and, placing a mat for them to lie on, leave them there to die. Some one has an eye on them to see that they are not molested by birds or monkeys. As we passed the hospital this afternoon there was a woman lying outside, covered with a red cloth, either dying or dead.

Both in the morning and the afternoon we broke the monotony of mosqueing by going into the shops of some of the jewellers and embroidery merchants, who have been tormenting the lives out of us since we have been here, dogging our steps wherever we go, poking their large books of testimonials under our noses, and shouting after us, " Come, see my things. There are no others in India same like mine — that other man — he no good, he ask big prices — see my testimonials — Lord Northwick write he buy of me 25 per cent less than others — ladishies please come — now I show you fine things! " And so forth *ad infinitum*. Their persistence and their patience is something prodigious. Mrs. Hearst says that if she remains in India much longer she shall take to swearing. She gets perfectly furious with these men, while I remonstrate mildly with them, and whisper confidentially, " Lady no go near you if you bother. Go away, be quiet, perhaps she buy."

We are going to see some nautch girls this evening. As there are no public places where they perform, we have to engage them for a special entertainment for us four. Their keeper, manager, or what not, is the manager of the Turkish baths, and on our way home we stopped there to make the necessary arrangements. We are to pay 35 rupees for the show.

January 2nd

THE NAUTCH girl entertainment last night was decidedly queer! At nine o'clock, after dinner, we betook ourselves to the Turkish bath establishment, a very down-at-heel, smelly place, and there, in an upper room, were already assembled the orchestra, consisting of four stringed instruments called " sarungi," two sets of kettle drums, queer little things that look like bean pots, and

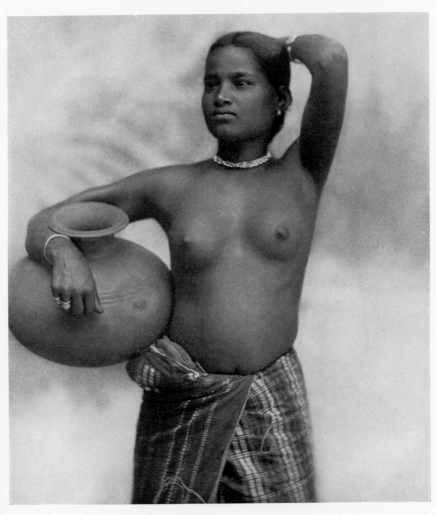

CEYLON (KANDY): Low Caste Girl

are called " tabla," and two sets of tiny cymbals, called
" majura." A buxom nautch girl, all dressed in red and
tinsel, with gold filigree ear-rings four inches long, a
bangle in her nose and otherwise covered with jewels,
and a very young girl, dressed in the same way, completed the material for the entertainment. They all
salaamed as we entered the room, and seated themselves on the divan. Then they began.

There were curious dances, so called, one in which
the postures represent a peacock with spread tail, the
tinselled skirt spread out and gathered up. There was
one which represented snake charming, done with a
little brass image of a cobra on the floor. The cobra is
supposed to bite the charmer at last, and some significant
writhings followed. Then there were dances that were
simply movements of the wrists, elbows, and shoulders,
and other hip movements, but very little leg or foot
work, and scarcely any quick motions. There were songs
— descriptive songs, with a great many words almost
like patter songs, which were sung and played with a
great deal of spirit. The music surprised us by being real
ordinary *tunes*, the barbaric quality being supplied by
the instruments, especially by the drums, which were
always in a foreign key to the melody, and which played
a strange, rapid figure, the drummers growing tremendously excited over it. The sarungi players bowed away
on their eight or ten strings (there were both kinds),
following the tune with variations and all sorts of dis-
turbing flourishes. It was not pretty, and I doubt if even
Loeffler could have found material for a new scheme
of harmony! On the whole it was a disappointment, and
the game was not worth the candle.

The fact is, a thing of that kind needs a proper background — a proper setting. A palace, marble floors, rich

hangings, and, above all, an audience, might make it seem intoxicating, perhaps, but in a room with just four sahibs it doesn't work. The principal nautch girl was chewing betel nuts all the time, and once she raised a brass spittoon from the floor and . . . ! She offered us betel nuts from her silver box, the constant companion of the Hindus, but we could not bring ourselves to follow their example and make our teeth red. The expression on her face was somewhat scornful and defiant throughout, and the minute she had finished, and we stood up to go, she cried out in a loud, imperious voice, " Bakshish! " upon which every member of the orchestra followed suit, and pressed forward with extended hands.

This evening at 8.30 we leave for Jeypore, one of the most thrillingly interesting cities of India, it is said. We meant to leave it out of our itinerary on account of its long distance from any of our chosen centres, but we feel really obliged to take the time for it because it must be so very much worth while. This morning we rode about the city, only taking in the sights of the streets. We saw great, lumbering, roofed wagons drawn by camels, which are not often harnessed in that way, and we were much entertained by seeing men shaved in the open street, yes, and having their heads shampooed, too. Everything takes place in the streets here. We have not yet seen any one actually *born* in the streets, but we shall, no doubt! Many of the men here, when it is cool, wear for outer garment just an ordinary quilted, cotton bed-quilt or comforter. How it does simplify life to make the same covering serve for both day and night! to walk round with your bedding on your back, so to speak! Besides, your bedding gets well aired in that way! Oh, surely the Hindus are a great people!

Rustom Hotel, Jeypore, Jan. 3rd, 1904

IT WAS a good scheme to go to bed on the train last night at Delhi and find ourselves at Jeypore this morning at daybreak — to be transported to a distant city without losing any time. As we drove up to the hotel the first thing that attracted our attention was a large panther, which a boy had charge of. There was only a rope round its neck, and it was just tied to a wooden stake. It was so near the hotel — just round the corner — that we all of us expressed the hope that he was well fed, especially when our rooms were consigned to us on the ground floor, and we discovered that, as usual, all the bolts were out of order, and none of the doors could be kept closed. All the hotels in these parts seem to be built only one story high, bungalow fashion.

As soon as we had put ourselves to rights and breakfasted we engaged a local guide and sallied forth. Jeypore is unlike any city we have visited so far. It is, I believe, the only city in India built on a regular plan. Here the streets bisect each other at right angles, and are very wide. The city gates and almost all the houses are of a faded, Pompeian red, almost pink, decorated with elaborate designs in white. The effect is very gay, if at times just a bit tawdry, but, as we looked up the fine, broad streets, swarming with natives in their gay turbans and draperies, and saw bevy after bevy of supercilious-looking camels passing by, some with a proud and richly dressed rider, some with two on their backs, others carrying loads of stones, grain, cotton, or what not, then some queer-looking chariots, or else some quaint bullock carts, the impression was gorgeously Oriental.

I suppose that the reason everything seems more vivid and bright in Jeypore than elsewhere is because it is the residence of the Maharajah, it being the Capital of the most prosperous independent states of the Rajputana. The walls which surround the city are very handsome. They are crenellated, and there are seven fine gates. The town is framed in rugged hills crowned with forts, one of which is particularly imposing, namely the Nahargarh, or Tiger Fort. The first interesting building which we passed was the Hall of the Winds, which has a curious and extremely ornate *façade*. It is in the heart of the town, and gets its name, " Hawa Mahal," on account of being so constructed as to ensure a cool breeze from its terraces at all times. The Maharajah often goes there to cool off in times of extreme heat.

We were taken to see the Maharajah's really fine collection of chariots, and all the different conveyances used by him on festive occasions. Then we went to see his elephant stables. I do not dare to say how many there are, but one monster in evidence made the memory of Jumbo sink into nothingness! The royal elephants are all painted with gorgeous colours and designs over the head and trunk, and their tusks are bound with three ornate brass rings. They are truly grand creatures! Then we went to see his collection of Bengal tigers. There were six of them, royal beasts! besides his herds of elephants, camels, and his three hundred horses.

The Maharajah has three wives and twenty concubines. He must be, in many ways, a fine fellow and a good ruler, even though his favourite amusement is pigsticking. He has done a great deal for his people, however, and seems intent on helping them to enlightenment. He has built a splendid museum for them, which he calls " Albert Hall," and of which the then Prince of Wales laid the corner stone in 1876, and, moreover, he has stocked it with a fine collection of things. After tiffin

INDIA: Fakirs at Work

we visited the interior of the Palace, the grounds, and the really wonderful observatory constructed by the royal astronomer, Jey Sing, in 1740. It is an open court-yard, full of curious instruments by which Jey Sing him-self used to make the most accurate measurements and calculations of the positions of the constellations, with results which stagger the astronomers of today.

Of course we did not go over the private apartments of the Maharajah or his ladies, but only to the public and private Halls of Audience, and over his garden and fernery. We saw two youths rehearsing some fine sword play in the garden for an ultimate performance before his Royal Highness. There are three hundred servants and retainers in the Palace, but none of them seemed to think it their business to sweep out, or clear up the dead leaves from the garden. Such a lazy set of noisy gossips as they are! I don't know whether the Maharajah saw us from behind his window screens or not, but if he did he could not have been impressed with our appearance for he did not invite us in to afternoon tea! There is a beautiful house in his courtyard where he entertains his friends — called the Guest House. It is exquisite in structure and decoration. I wish we had had an introduc-tion to *him* instead of the other Rajah who lives so far away in the interior that I don't believe we shall take the trouble to go there.

After doing the Palace and Observatory, we were taken to the large enclosure where his three hundred magnificent horses are kept. It was a fine sight! There were many pure-blooded, Arabian steeds, which were good to look upon. Some of the keepers, under the direc-tion of the master of the horse, were training a bunch of horses to chase the wild boar, ready for His Highness' next pig-sticking game. They had one of these poor beasts with a rope round its throat, and one of the men was dragging him round and round at full tilt at the rope's end, while another, mounted on a horse, chased him, and tumbled up against him. This was done to train fresh horses not to be afraid of the boar. The poor beast was thoroughly worn out and exhausted by the time a fourth horse had been trained, and I can assure you it was a grisly sight — this dress rehearsal, and all my sympathies were with the boar. Only man is vile!

January 4th

WE STARTED bright and early on an excursion to the ruined city of Amber, or Amer, as it is sometimes called. It was formerly the Capital and residence of the Maharajahs, but as these gentlemen had a time-honoured superstition that it was unlucky to make headquarters of any city for more than five hundred years, it was deliberately abandoned towards the end of that period (195 years ago), and Jeypore was built and made the Capital instead. What fools! To think of their leaving such a place in all its beauty! It is sublime even now, ruined as it is. The Palace is superb, and the outlook from the terraces is enchanting. The ruined town of Amber lies at the mouth of a rocky mountain gorge, in which there is a lake, and on it the remains of a terraced garden, which must have been very beautiful once. In the town there are Hindu temples and all sorts of interesting landmarks.

We drove for the first three miles (Amber being only five miles away from Jeypore), and, at Chandrabagh, where the hills become too steep for a carriage, we were met by and transferred to an elephant. Oh, that you could have seen us four mount the ladder and install ourselves in the howdah on that pre-historic-looking back! The elephant was trained to kneel down when we mounted or dismounted, and, as it rose to its full height when we had all taken our seats on its back, there was such a shouting for us to hold on firmly that we thought we must be in danger of our lives.

It was rather a long elephant ride (two miles), but not uncomfortable except once or twice when the path was very steep and rough; then we were sorely jolted. I do not object at all to riding on an elephant for my part, but it is not exactly a lightning express way of travelling. We passed another elephant on the road returning from the Palace, with one of our fellow guests at the hotel lounging on the howdah, which he and his guide had all to themselves, and I couldn't help thinking what a fine note it was in that particular landscape. It forms just the right background for elephants and camels! The latter were very plentiful among the ruins and on the winding, hilly roads. The hills are covered with a luxuriant growth of cacti of several varieties. These grow thick and very tall, like trees. The soil, which is like dried mud, seems to favour them particularly, while the other trees looked poor and badly nourished. But how harmonious it all was! Cactus trees and camels — moth-eaten and thread-bare-looking camels, who hold their heads up like decayed gentlefolk, who feel the pride of what they once were; ruined palaces, temples, tombs, elephants, and turbaned Orientals — they all seem to belong together!

Talking of temples, we went into one within the palace enclosure, dedicated to the Goddess Kali, whose specialty is war and destruction. In olden times a human being was sacrificed every day on her altar, and as the victims were chosen one out of each family in Amber, the people decamped from the town as fast as they could, until one of the Maharajahs, fearing that it would become depopulated, began to substitute goats for human victims. Our guide told us that now, every morning at seven, a goat is slain there. The head is given to Kali (I wonder what she does with it), and the body is consumed by the priests. It occurred to me that it was rather an ingenious way for the priests to get a good square meal every day free of cost — a free lunch, so to speak, out of the Goddess Kali's leavings! — and such a good excuse for a Hindu to eat meat! After all, one might do worse for a profession than be the proxy or understudy of a Goddess of Destruction!

An indignant exclamation from Clara at the cruelty practised, elicited from our guide a protest that it was " the will of the Deity." " Pooh," said she, " God has nothing to do with any of these things; they are of the ignorance and vileness of man! " This was a challenge, and the Hindu, who was an intelligent fellow, and very earnest in his belief, appealed to me afterwards to explain what the lady meant. So we sat on the ramparts and talked religion awhile, for I saw that he was sorely puzzled, and it resulted in his regaining his equanimity and expressing great gratitude and admiration " for my great and profound knowledge, and wonderful interpretation of the holy scriptures! "

To return to the Maharajah and his palace; he has a great regard for Kali, and on her birthday he always goes to the Palace of Amber and spends the night there with a number of his household, his object being to sacrifice twenty bullocks in her honour. You see we are still in the bible, " And they set up their idols in the high places, and sacrificed unto them, and were an abomination in the sight of the Lord." Those are not the precise words I know, but they are near enough. I could run on a great deal longer extolling the beauties of Amber, and describing all the different halls, some parts of which have been judiciously restored to show what they looked like in their former splendour, but I must refrain from too prolonged ecstasies.

Our elephant was waiting patiently for us in the palace court, and was in a good humour, Mrs. Hearst having sent a coolie to buy twelve pounds of the coarse sugar of the country to feed him with. He knelt, we mounted, and passed through the stately gate, looking up to the fort four hundred feet above, and wended our way back to Chandrabragh, where our carriage awaited us to take us back to Jeypore. We saw numbers of large monkeys on our way. On two trees by the roadside, there were as many as eight or nine monkeys in each, jumping about from branch to branch — large grey ones. There were also numerous peacocks all over everywhere — beautiful, majestic creatures with the sunshine glittering in their tails.

We came home in time for a late tiffin, and rested till 4 P.M. Then we drove to the public gardens to visit the Albert Museum, with which we were delighted, and to listen to the native band, which always plays there on Mondays. The musicians were indeed natives, but alas! their instruments and their music were European. It was interesting to see the native grandees of the place, however, in their gay equipages. Afterwards we drove to a famous manufacturer of enameled brass — a specialty of Jeypore, where Mrs. Hearst wished to make some purchases. His name was Zoroaster, nothing less! At the same place in the courtyard they were also making the fine Indian carpets and rugs we prize so highly. There were over a dozen huge frames, from ten to twenty feet high and very wide. In front of each one of these frames

there sat a long row of children on stools, weaving, with
their deft little hands, the pattern which a boy of about
ten read from a painted design on a scroll of paper. This
he did in a sort of chant at the top of his voice. It was
getting dark, and another boy held up a miserable oil
lamp over the part of the frame where they were working. Poor little chaps! No wonder their eyes give out, and
their voices grow raucus. Let us tread softly on our Indian rugs! We little know all that goes to the making
of them! Yet the little fellows seemed merry. How little
it takes to make some folk happy! These children are
paid from one anna to five annas a day for their work,
an anna being a penny. We found the brass work fascinating, and all of us came away with more brass and
less money than when we entered. Jeypore is likewise a
great place for precious stones. Garnets, topaz, and car-
buncles are found here in quantities, and are in evidence
everywhere. It is needless to say that we bought chains
and necklaces galore.

Delhi, Laurie's Hotel, Jan. 6th, 1904
WE LEFT Jeypore last night to return here for the day.
Tonight we leave at 8.40 for Lahore. We have been
flying through the Orient at such a rate that it seems
an age since we were in Japan — and shall we be able
to go there again? That is the question. Things look
very critical there at present, and if war with Russia is
declared we shall have to go home *via* Europe. And there
will be no more China for us and no cherry blossoms!
However, I won't borrow trouble, and it is useless to
give it a thought till the time for deciding approaches.

Our last day in Jeypore was spent not in sight seeing,
for we had finished with that, but in driving about and
steeping ourselves in " Orientalism." What a place Jey-

pore would be for a pageant, with its broad streets and splendid background! The street scenes are a perennial joy to us. One sees such funny sights. One was a " hunting bee." The hunt took place in five little black forests on five little black heads. One hunted in the other's forest, while another hunted in his, and so on! There were about thirty people squatting outside a house, singing and playing on native instruments. We were told it was the celebrating of a child-marriage, and that was the house of the child-bride. The friends keep that kind of celebration up for three days. A little farther on about a dozen people were squatting outside another house. It was the house of the groom, and they were his relatives, who were likewise making merry. Then we saw a procession of people carrying on their heads baskets of sweetmeats and cakes, which were wedding offerings. The people all seem gay in spite of their poverty.

I think that strangers feel the depression and sadness of the situation a great deal more than they do. They are used to dirt, dinginess, and starvation, and nobody seems ashamed to beg. Not to spend money, when they have it, seems to the Hindu a folly, when he can get what he wants by trumping up a pathetic story and begging of some soft-hearted green-horn! In this respect, and in the way the merchants follow you up and almost force you to take their stuff, they are utterly shameless.

We visited Zoroaster's factory again, and also we went to the School of Art, where all sorts of native industries and arts are taught. The showrooms were well filled with all sorts of specimens of brass enameling — some of it very fine, and the designs, taken from some of the beautiful old things in the temples, beautifully reproduced. We bought many of their things, Mrs. H. of course, being chief purchaser. The house of one of the Maharajah's ministers, now defunct, was given up to it, and a beautiful old house it is, with a fine cortile and some good stone carving. We left Jeypore with regret, precious glad that we didn't miss it! Our train left at 10.30 P.M., but as our special private car was on one of the side tracks all ready for us, we boarded it at nine and went promptly to bed. This morning at eight found us at Delhi. I have been quiet here today, giving myself up to correspondence and generally putting things in order instead of gallivanting.

Charing Cross Hotel, Lahore, Jan. 8th, 1904
WE ARRIVED here yesterday at 12.30, hungry as hunters, so the first thing to be done after taking possession of our rooms was to get some ballast aboard. A half hour after tiffin, however, we were in front of the famous old gun " Jamzamah," or " Hummer," the cannon of the Bhangi Confederacy, and picturing " Kim " and the " Red Lama " sitting there. We afterwards drove through the old native city, which is very curious and interesting. The streets are narrow, and there is a wealth of fine wood-carving in the overhanging balconies and oriel windows, many of which are charming in construction.

The city does not resemble Agra, nor Delhi, nor Jeypore, nor any of the other towns we have been in so far, but it has quite an individuality of its own. Every now and then a vista through some of the streets and squares suggests pictures I have seen of Jerusalem. The mud walls, with thick hedges of cactus on top, and the frequent high mounds of dried mud, together with the dung cakes which are stuck up against the sides of the

INDIA: Procession of Naked Fakirs

houses in hundreds to dry in the sun, serve to give the old city a dingy, sad-coloured appearance. We went through the old fort and the Palace of Jehangir, the armoury, where we saw a lot of the swords and other arms used in the mutiny, the mosque of Vagir Khan, the Jumma Musjid, and the Shish Mahal, or Palace of Mirrors. We have seen nothing here, however, in the way of mosques and palaces to compare with those of Agra, Delhi, or Jeypore. But I suspect that what we shall see in future will be more or less replicas of the great and famous ones we have already explored. I feel that I am beginning to lose my zest for mosques and temples partly in ruins. They have become anti-climaxes!

Outside of the old city, Lahore is rather good looking. The avenues are broad and shaded with fine trees, and there are many handsome private bungalows with fine grounds. One feature is the quantity of large, king-orange trees, laden with splendid fruit, that one sees everywhere. The orange is shaped like a pear, with a rough, loose skin, and the inside is like a Mandarin, only very juicy and large. The oranges are better here than in any part of India where we have been. The climate is like that of Italy in winter — quite cold and chilly in the evening and early morning, and fairly warm in the midday sun. The natives have to wear clothes here, and the only really naked person I have seen was a fakir covered with ashes, sitting cross-legged in one of the streets, with a few sticks burning in front of him. Near him was a tiny calf, almost a baby, which had been attracted by the warmth of the burning sticks. It stood gazing into the fakir's face as if transfixed, and never budged an inch for full five minutes while we were buying some silver articles at a bazaar hard by. It seemed as if the fakir had hypnotized it.

This morning we went to the Museum and saw many good specimens of native industries, old and new, admirably grouped and assorted. Lahore is the capital of the Punjab and headquarters of the Punjab Government. I have been trying to get some one to explain to me just what Punjab means, and I have at last learned that it means " the place where five rivers meet." To-morrow we are to make an excursion to Amritsar, only an hour's journey from here by rail, and shall spend the day there, returning here in the evening.

I am sitting in my room with a blazing wood fire, and have drawn my writing table up near it, glad to get the full blast of it even though this is India. And yet we passed acres of roses the day before yesterday, cultivated, I suppose, for rose attar, and the song birds are as vociferous as in spring. In the summer, they say, it is insufferably hot, never less than 105 in the shade. Of course the bungalows and hotels are constructed with a view of defending one from the intense heat in summer, and therefore one has to pay for it in winter. The rooms are large and terribly high-studded, and none of the windows have direct connection with the sunshine. There is always a very broad *loggia,* which not only keeps the sun at a respectful distance but excludes the light also. They are not comfortable, these hotel rooms in India! They are dreary and damp, no better than barns in appearance, and not so attractive as are most stables. The doors and windows, when they are not in the roof, close with heavy bolts, and these are seldom in order, so that when we are out our servant has to keep watch over our apartment to guard it from the natives attached to the hotel, who seem to spend their entire time squatting or lying on the floor in the corridors, and who are proverbial pilferers.

It takes more men to do nothing in this country than it does in any other to accomplish great things! Then the " bakshish " system makes it as much as your life or fortune is worth to come to India at all! If a man salaams as you pass, he expects bakshish, and as everybody lays his hand reverentially on his head, and bows low when he sees a "sahib," who to him represents simply a money bag and nothing else, you can well imagine that a sahib and his purse, well stocked with small coin, must never be separated! If, in paying a fee for any small service performed by coolies, your heart melts at their half-starved appearance, and you follow your impulse to give them twice as much as the regulation fee, then your troubles begin. Instead of the grateful smile and respectful salute which you naturally look for, the gentle coolie, being persuaded that you are a fool of a European, and don't know anything of their customs, starts to play a part, and does it well. He begins to talk in a loud and excited voice, faster than you can listen, and tells you that he is being defrauded of his rights — that he is entitled to twice as much as you have given, and he calls all the coolies to witness that he is downtrodden and maltreated. If you know enough to shout " Jao! " (which means " get out! "), in a stentorian voice, he subsides at once, and walks away smiling and contented, hugging his coin as if it were a treasure trove! They are accustomed to being treated like dogs, and if you treat them like human beings they turn and rend you.

A scene at the Delhi Hotel the other day was quite amusing. We were about to leave, and Harry ordered our man, David, to assemble the servants who had done anything for us that he might fee them all at one time and have done with it. This he did in self defence because we had found that some of those who had already received fees came around again, swearing that they were not the ones we had paid, while our own man, who knew them all and was versed in their tricks, told us that they were only " trying it on." Well, the coolies all put in an appearance, and stood in the entry salaaming humbly. There were about eighteen of them in all, and Harry began his catechism, " Who are you? " Four of them spoke up, " We all of us waited on your table." " No, you didn't, these two only were our waiters." " No, Sahib, I pass something to lady one day." " And who are you? " turning to some naked creatures with matted hair. Then came a chorus, " I am the man who brings water for bath," " I am the slop-emptier," " I trim the lamps," " I sweep the stairs," and so forth. Well, Harry gave something to each one, even to one who said he took care of our room (though we knew he had never been inside of it with broom or duster during our stay), and then, turning to our guide who was standing by, he said, " Now I have paid every one? " in a determined voice! " Yes," replied the guide, " every one except the poor cook — he is so unfortunate as not to be present! This was nearly the end, but not quite. When we reached the station, we found our guide there to see us off. He was most obsequious, but, after many flowery expressions, such as, " May you be the father of many kings " (the wish was a shade late, I thought — for Harry!), he brought a strange man up to our car window, and said in an insinuating voice, " This is the hotel runner." " What's that? " asked Harry. " Oh, the man who goes to meet the hotel guests; he would like a present." " He never did anything for me, did he? " " No, sir; but I thought the Sahib would like to give him a present! " That was the last straw for me — I laughed long and loud in derision. The fellow got the present, though!

January 9th

OUR excursion to Amritsar today was not particularly exciting. We left here at eleven and reached there at about one, the train being much behindhand. We drove at once through the native city to the famous Golden Temple, where we were forced to take off our shoes and wear some queer, soft-soled slippers of velvet, embroidered heavily with gilt, before they would allow us even to walk around the large tank in the open court. In the court there were natives, with a low bench before them, making and selling little, wooden tooth-combs, a suggestive, but very necessary article both in and out of the temples. The Golden Temple, or " Darbar," stands in the centre of the tank on a high, raised platform, about 60 or 70 feet square. It is entirely of gilded copper with the exception of the lower part of the walls, about three feet, which are of white marble, decorated with modern inlaid work in *pietre dure*. It is entered by four doorways, one on each side.

We found the effect of both exterior and interior extremely tawdry, and could not get up a particle of enthusiasm over it. It was a Sikh temple, and, though the Sikhs' religion is Hindu, they worship no gods, but keep to the dignified simplicity of the " Granth " or scriptures, " the book " as they term it. We stood inside the temple for a while as there was some kind of service going on. On the east side was seated the high priest, either reading from a copy of the Granth, or waving a " chauri," whilst pilgrims entered now and again, throwing offerings of Cowry shells, pice, and decapitated flowers onto a sheet spread on the floor to receive them, and then sat around chanting verses from the Granth to the music (?) of discordant stringed instruments. They mostly present cups of sugar to visitors, but we escaped before they had a chance at us. The view of the houses round the tank, outside the temple precincts, was attractive, its irregularities making a beautiful sky line. The native streets too, were picturesque, but quite on the same lines as those of Lahore. We visited a large factory of Indian carpets, and saw hundreds of small boys working at them in the little stalls allotted to a dozen or more at a time. The stalls extend over a quarter of a mile. It is an enormous business. Most of the Indian carpets sold in London and New York are made by this firm.

We returned to Lahore in time for dinner, and tomorrow at twelve or thereabouts we leave here for Lucknow. We had Cawnpore also on our itinerary, but the plague is very bad there, and we have concluded to do no more than stop there over a train. There is not much to be seen there anyhow, except the Ghat, where that dreadful massacre took place.

Wurtzler's Hotel, Lucknow, Jan. 11th, 1904
HERE we are at Lucknow, where we arrived today at noon after a long night's journey. As we had to wait for an hour and a half at Cawnpore, which we reached soon after 7 A.M., Harry and I determined on utilizing the time to visit the sites and landmarks of the mutiny and massacre of 1857, which it still makes one's blood freeze to think of! Mrs. Hearst and Clara had had a bad night on the cars and did not feel able to make the effort. Harry and I got a carriage and a good guide at the station and started forth after a rapid breakfast at the refreshment rooms. Our guide, who happened to be a Welshman (and what a relief it was to have an English-tongued creature!), had been a soldier in the British army, and was an eye witness of the horrors. He knew every nook and corner by heart, and showed us every

stick and stone of interest in connection with the terrible event: the little church into which the women and
children crept for safety, but where they were slaugh-
tered one and all; the ravine through which our people
were led on the pretext of safe conduct, and where they
were confronted by the enemy who were lying in wait
for them; the well where hundreds of bodies were cast
and over which a monument now stands; and last, not
least, the Ghat, or steps, leading down to the River
Ganges, with the little Hindu temple on top, where those
that remained took to the boats, but were treacherously
overwhelmed and slain.

The Memorial Garden is very beautiful, and everything has been done by the Government to record ten-
derly and reverentially the cruel sufferings and frightful
slaughter of the victims. How terribly real and vivid it
all seemed as we stood near the little Hindu temple overlooking the Ghat, and got our first sight of the Ganges!
It was low water, and the stream was often interrupted
by strands of mud, which our guide told us in summer
time are a series of blooming gardens, covered with
water melons and other luxurious vegetation. A group of
native women were at the water's edge, washing their
clothes and chanting wildly as they made the motion for
throwing the garments against the stones to cleanse
them.

We got back to the station just in the nick of time, and
found Clara and Mrs. Hearst just getting up. The landscape still continued to be flat, but, as we are not so far
north as at Lahore, the palm trees, of which we had almost lost sight of late, began to show up again here and
there, plus the aloes and cacti which have been our constant followers since we got to Agra.

This afternoon we lost no time in engaging a guide —

a native this time — and going over the Residency, thoroughly exploring every landmark of the mutiny and siege, and thoroughly steeping ourselves in its gruesome memories. Everywhere great gaps in half-ruined walls, made by shells and bullets — everywhere a story of suffering, heroism, and death; everywhere monuments and tombs. In speaking of the " Residency," they always mean the cluster of buildings which were destroyed during the mutiny, and not only the Residency building itself. In front of the Baillie guard is a fine obelisk erected by Lord Northbrook in memory of the native officers and Sepoys who died loyally in the fight. All of the ruins are situated in a beautiful park, and many of the crumbling walls are covered with a most luxuriant growth of bougainvillæa (which in India is not mauve, as in other climes, but a rich, royal purple), and another wonderful vine which I have not seen elsewhere — it has large clusters of orange-coloured blossoms like trumpet flowers in bud. They call it " cheenia " (I am writing it the way it sounds). Then there were peacocks striking attitudes on the fragments of walls, and mynahs, parrots, and enchanting song birds everywhere, mocking at the tragedy of the past.

January 12th
THIS morning we began by going to the Museum, where we saw many things of interest, and afterwards we were taken to what one can only call a city of palaces and mosques. One building after another of passing magnificence. The Machehi Bhawan and Great Imambarah, the Constantinople Gate, the Jumma Musjid, or principal mosque, the second Imambarah, the Moti Mahal, the Shah Najaf, which was built by the first King of Oudh and is now his mausoleum, the Farhat Bakhsh Palace — these and more did we see, and as one hears of the dis-

soluteness and general lack of decency and principle of those ancient princes, and then one contemplates these splendid edifices which they have bequeathed to posterity, one cannot help thinking that perhaps things are mysteriously averaged up in some way! In this day of our Lord, such a plethora of grand buildings in any one city would be an impossibility. No country has money enough to pay for such work where the spirit of altruism compels us to give every working man a man's wages. These buildings were the outcome of oppression and grinding of the poor and the weak. The wages of a skilled workman were a penny a day, and often thousands were compelled to work without any pay at all. And yet, we were told, in the face of this fact, that the great Imambarah was built in 1784, the year of the great famine " to afford relief to the people! " There are many things we cannot understand — this is one of them!

After tiffin we went to see more things — among others, Sikandara Bagh (Alexander Garden). It is surrounded by a very high and solid wall, and during the mutiny a body of Sepoys took refuge there, believing that there was an outlet through which they could escape, but the wall was breached by the Highlanders, and every man within the enclosure was bayoneted. Two thousand people were killed in four hours. We went into the garden, which is now just an orchard of mango trees, and very peaceable it looks, but the hole in the wall, which has been reinforced for safety, is an ugly reminder. Afterwards we drove again to the Residency to get the landmarks well impressed on our minds, and then, our guide having informed us that he had shown us everything of importance in Lucknow, we drove through the native city, after being assured that the plague has not reached here from Cawnpore as yet.

There was nothing to distinguish it from the average

native city. It is all very interesting — everything is, here in India. Some of the streets are extremely narrow and very crowded. These form a powerful contrast with the modern part of the city, where some of the avenues — one in particular, of fine tamarind trees — are superb. We saw two men bearing something which looked just like a small hearse, only it was covered with a red cloth. I asked whether it was a funeral of any kind. " No," said our guide, " it is a lady going to pay a visit."

When we returned to our hotel we found that our friends, General Winslow and his party, had arrived, just now from Benares, where we are going tomorrow. We were mutually glad to meet again, and exchange experiences of travel. They made a long stay in Calcutta, and gave us a very bad account of the hotels there. This hotel is paradise compared with the average one in India. It is actually *clean!* We are so comfortable here that we are quite sorry to have to push on. But Mrs. Hearst's time is very short now — she must leave for Bombay, where she is to sail not later than the 17th inst., and she must see Benares, of course, as we are so near.

Clarke's Hotel, Benares, Jan. 13th, 1904

IN MY longings to go to India, which were very frequent at the time I was engrossed in the study of the Bhagavad-Gita (Hindu Bible) with the young Brahmin, Mohini Chatterji, my thoughts always flew to Benares as the place of all others that contained the most vital interest, and where we would come upon the very essence of Hindu-ism. And now we are actually here in the sacred city, to see and understand it all, as far as we can, for ourselves.

We arrived this afternoon at two, and at the station a Hindu city-guide presented himself, an insufferably conceited and tiresome fellow; but as he seemed fairly intelligent, and speaks English a little better than some of them, we concluded to put up with him. He informed us at once that we were fortunate in arriving here today, as tomorrow is a great religious festival on the Ganges, and if we were willing to get up early, say at six, there would be sights to behold worth the beholding. All the hotels in India are in the suburbs, and all the suburbs of Indian cities look alike. There are attractive bungalows in fine gardens, broad avenues, perhaps one building devoted to English stores, and miles of dusty road, bordered by aloes or cactus, tamarind, and other fine trees. Whether you are in Delhi, Agra, Jeypore, Lahore, Lucknow, or Benares, it is all one till you get into the heart of each city, which is always from two to three miles away — then, and only then, does the individuality of the place assert itself.

You can imagine, therefore, how anxious we all were to get into the midst of things at once. We wanted, one and all, to make straight for the river, but our guide said " No, tomorrow is better. Today I show you the monkey temple and some other interesting things." So we put ourselves in his hands, and to the monkey temple we went. It was rather a shabby little temple, in a crowded thoroughfare, and all that was noteworthy was the swarms of monkeys everywhere. They literally owned the place, and outsiders without tails are evidently only admitted on sufferance. We were informed outside that we must buy a large dish of confections to feed them with, and thus make ourselves *persona grata*, as they were *sacred* monkeys. Here everything seems to be sacred — monkeys, cows, birds, and dirt, especially dirt! There was plenty of this where the monkeys were, and we were so beset with loathsome-looking beggars

that we were glad to hurry back to our carriages after a
very short stay.

Then we were taken to Maharajah Amethi's garden,
where abides a famous " Holy Man," — so holy that no
Maharajah, even, ever sits in his presence! He is a great
sage, and tells people wonderful things when they question him. He has not a penny in the world, he lives in
the garden which is called " Anand Bagh," under a
little stone canopy or shelter. He is scantily clothed in
white drapery, with bare feet, of course, and, wonder
of wonders, he does not accept alms! He was surrounded by quite a little court of adoring Hindus, who
at a glance I took to be a self-constituted syndicate who
were " running " that holy man. The sage himself attracted me, for he was simple, unaffected, very kindly
and gentle in speech — and clean!

He sent some of his followers to gather some roses
from the temple garden, and these he presented to us.
He appeared to be interested in us, and when our guide
told him that we were from America, he showed a desire
to converse. I seemed to be singled out as spokesman,
and so I held a little confab with him, our guide acting as interpreter. He informed me, in a very benevolent
tone, that while our religious belief is very different
from his, yet he respects our belief highly, and that we
are to be commended if we live up to it; that, after all,
there is only one God, and He is intrinsically the same
for all of us. I thought these sentiments pretty liberal
and broad for a Hindu, and I told him so, by proxy,
whereat he smiled most sweetly. He spends a great part
of his time in contemplation or " Sadhu," and he has
been the means of founding a school for the purpose of
strengthening and supporting the Aryan Hindu religion
— the money coming, of course, from his devotees. One

of his followers presented us with a book containing a short biography and portrait of his predecessor, the famous ascetic of Benares — Swami Bhaskara Nand Saraswati, and of the present ascetic, his " chela " — the holy man in question, whose name is Pundit Mati Ram Misra.

Before departing, I asked if we might be permitted to leave a little gift of money to be devoted to the needs of the holy man. The Pundit shook his head deprecatingly, and the syndicate in chorus shouted " On no account; it is our custom to *present* this book to the strangers who visit the Anand Bagh, to confer with the Holy Man." When we reached the outer gate, however, we were approached by two of his " porters," as our guide called them, who were obviously there for blood! They took the rupees with eagerness, which we thought were to be used to procure sustenance for the " Pundit," but as soon as the money was safely in their hands, and the signal given to drive on, our guide leaned down from the box and said, " If you wish to make a present to the Holy Man, I will show you how you can do it — you may give *me* the money, and I will buy fruit and other simple articles of food for him." Then followed a few remarks from Harry and a female chorus, which were not altogether complimentary to the syndicate or to our own crafty guide! Oh, these Hindus! It seems to me that all of their mental energy is directed to scheming and intriguing. This they do with an elaborateness which is simply astounding to the Western mind. In all else they are stupid and dull as cows. Even the most educated and richest of the manufacturers and merchants — and we have had more or less to do with many of them in different places — show an obtuseness and lack of comprehension of the simplest matters of business, and a laboriousness in their methods which are exasperating beyond words.

January 14th

WHAT a day this has been! — our first introduction to the Ganges, its sights and scenes! I can never forget it as long as I live! Our interest was aroused long before we reached the river, for, as we drove through the streets, we passed hundreds and hundreds of people who had already bathed in the sacred river, and were hurrying home with the soul contentment of purification written on their faces. Many of them had tawdry-looking little shrines, or gods, made of gaudily painted clay, which they were taking home to worship in private; and others carried small, brass jars with some of the sacred water, which they were taking to some infirm member of the household who could not go to the river. There were also bands of pilgrims hurrying along as if every moment were a moment lost which separated them from the sacred stream.

Arrived at the river bank we dismounted, and, descending the broad, stone steps, which at intervals are present all along the high river-banks, we got on board a boat, which our guide had ordered yesterday to be in readiness for us. It was like a small river steamboat — without the steam, and rowed by a number of coolies. On the upper deck were cane chairs for us to sit on, and it was quite comfortable. But who could ever describe the colour and the animation of the scene which met our eyes! There were thousands and tens of thousands of people of all ages and of both sexes crowding the flights of steps on the high embankment, and it looked to the casual gazer something like one side of a vast arena crowded from foundation to turret with peo-

ple dressed for a festival. Those on the steps were waiting their opportunity to descend to some of the hundreds of wooden platforms on a level, nearly, with the
water, some of them sheltered from the sun with can-
opies, and others with huge tent-umbrellas made of
straw matting.

From the platform it is only one step into the water,
into which they plunged partly clothed — men, women,
and children, all together. They immersed themselves
again and again, they stood up to their waists in the
water, and poured it over their heads as if they could
not sufficiently saturate themselves with it, they poured
it down their throats and washed their mouths with it,
all the time uttering prayers with hands joined now
above the head and again in front. Imagine thousands
of people huddled together in the water as thick as lily
pads in a pond, and their brilliant-coloured turbans,
clothes, and " saris " hanging from the tops of the shelters and lying about on the platforms! Imagine these
thousands of souls so full of fervour and religious exaltation that each one seemed to ignore the presence or
proximity of any one outside himself, and you have a
sight which is as unique as it is impressive! I don't know
when I have felt more touched! I had never before seen
such a manifestation of living faith. All our ideas of religious worship pale before such abject surrender to an
ancient superstition. One may deprecate their creed as
childish and their manner of worship as loathly and disgusting, as indeed it often is, but the pure, unalloyed,
unalterable faith — the *strength of their conviction* —
must always awaken a certain respect and sympathy,
if not envy! Here were the richest and the poorest, in
spite of the inexorable caste distinctions, all on common
ground where the Ganges flows. Every now and then my

eye would rest on a fine noble specimen of a man — perhaps a pampered, luxurious mortal — winding his magnificent crimson silk and gold " sari " around him after the immersion, and close by, in the water, a group of unsightly creatures of the lowest caste. As we rowed slowly along it was a pretty sight to see hundreds of wreaths of flowers consigned to the river, out of homage to the river god.

But I shall never forget the cry of joy that came from a band of pilgrims who had come from a far distant place to behold the sacred river. They were carrying all their belongings on the two ends of a pole slung over their shoulders — the largest and most important items being the jars to hold the sacred water. They were footsore, covered with dust, and ready to drop with fatigue, but on sight of the river that they had so longed and toiled to reach, they almost sobbed with the emotion of it! One could hear it, one could feel it — it meant " At last! At last! "

Our boat rowed slowly up and down, about twenty feet from the steps and platform where the crowd congregated, each time passing the " burning-ghat," or slope where dead bodies are burned. There were several corpses being brought down, and, as the pyre had just been laid for one of these, and the relatives were bringing down the body, we waited to see the whole process. It was the body of a woman with just a red cotton cloth wound round it, and tied at the ankles, waist, and breast, as is customary here, and it was carried down to the water's edge by two of the relatives, on a light, wooden bier. They set the bier with its burden down at the river's edge, and let the sacred water flow over it, then they opened the folds of the red cloth at the head and poured some Ganges water down the throat of the deceased.

After this they carried the body to the pyre and laid it there. They then piled on top of the body as much wood as there was underneath, entirely enveloping it with the exception of the top of the head. Then the eldest son, whose special office it is to set fire to his parent's pyre, proceeded to get some of the special sacred fire (without which the soul of the deceased cannot take flight in proper order). This fire is provided by one particular person, a Domra, or low caste, who has the monopoly of the sacred fire, so to speak, and who charges what he pleases. A rajah, or even a wealthy man, is often forced to pay thousands of rupees for a light wherewith to set fire to his mother's pyre. A poor man can make better terms. We saw the son, a well built youth of manly bearing, approach the fire man, who was appropriately dressed in yellow, and the bargaining began. It was several minutes before the terms could be agreed on, but at last the fire was given — no more than a handful (it was burning charcoal, I suppose), and the son carried it in triumph to the pyre and lighted it. It was fanned and coaxed into a flame, powdered sandal wood was thrown in, also butter, and soon the flames rose high and bright. The son remained near the pyre to keep watch over it, while a couple of the nearest relatives assisted by giving it an occasional poke or adding a little butter, or a bit of sandal wood.

[*Note by* H. M. R. " I want to tell you of the Sudra class, the lowest class man, supplying the fire to light the funeral pile, an inherited calling. The reason for this is that when a body is burned it is believed that there still remains — or that there may remain — some unholy taint, some unwashed sin. The Sudra furnishes the fire, and agrees for a certain price to take that sin, if there be one, on himself, and he, being of 'no account,' is the selected receptacle of the sins of others. That clears up the whole account of the corpse. Then for ten days the spirit is afield, and so water and food have been given, and during the ten days milk from the sacred cows is poured into the river, and when the ten days are up, there is a feast, the eldest son, who has performed the rites and who having touched the body is unclean for that ten days, and has eaten only rice, I believe, eats with his friends, or has dishes with his friends, and the priests have incantations and things, and the food is thrown into the Ganges (presumably) and then I suppose all feast."]

Meanwhile other bodies were being brought down, one of a man, tied up in a white cloth, and similar proceedings followed. There was on the slope a body nearly consumed — it had been burning perhaps for an hour, and in the river, up to their knees, were two coolies — sweepers of the ghat, as they are called, sifting the ashes of a yesterday's corpse in a large straw sieve, to see if there were any silver coins to be found, as is frequently the case. We remarked a priest pouring milk into the river from a brass jar, and were told that this is ordered by those who can afford it, the day after a body has been burned; it is an offering to the river or to Brahm, I don't know which.

The river has many gifts bestowed on it. Numberless wreaths and chains of yellow and white flowers are thrown in, and whole patches of the river look golden with the accumulation. These flowers are sold on the steps, and those who cannot afford a wreath buy a small, straw plate filled with the decapitated blossoms, which look like French marigolds. The sacred cows, which are all over the place, reposing on the upper steps and slopes,

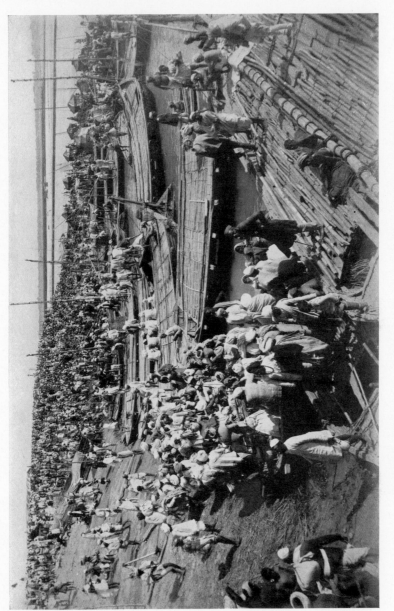

INDIA: Religious Festival at Balahad, where the Ganges and the Jumna Meet

get hold of these yellow flowers and eat them whenever they get a chance, for even the sacred cows are thieves in India!

On the deck of a battered old boat, which lay there by the burning-ghat, there sat an old " Sadhu," in the regulation position, making his toilette for the day. He had already rubbed ashes all over his body and taken the shine out of it, and he was now engaged in making a paste out of dirt and grease, mixed together, with which he was carefully marking his forehead and smearing his face. Then he commenced some Yoga breathing exercises, and mumbled some prayers, telling his beads meanwhile. When he had finished he blew a prolonged blast into a conch shell — a long, sustained note of tremendous carrying power, followed by another an octave higher; this he did several times, and then he settled down into " contemplation," with eyes upturned into his head, and quasi cessation of breathing. He was a nasty sight to behold! However, afterwards I saw so many others of these Sadhus who were still worse (for one of them had smeared himself all over with dung) that this one seemed a perfect gentleman by comparison! It was a sad sight to see the poor little widows, dressed in white, and bereft of all their ornaments, creeping down to the river in some secluded spot, with the patient consciousness of being pariahs.

After one has seen the proceedings of a festival day in the Ganges at Benares, one must come to the conclusion that this is the place where religious superstition as well as religious fervour culminates. The priests seem to be a bad lot, and are the chief oppressors and bloodsuckers of the people. There is no part of the world where reform is more needed, but an attempt to make Christians of them seems to me rank foolishness! To teach them their own religion in its purity, eliminating the gross perversions and corruptions, brushing away the loathsome and poisonous superstitions, would be far better, and surely that might be attempted. Brahminism in its essence is a fine religion untainted by the horrible superstructures invented and kept alive by the priests, who are a set of unmitigated rascals, who believe in nothing themselves except their own interests and comfort. Their unprincipled rapacity is manifest in its most hideous form in India, and in Benares it is more shamelessly in evidence than in any other part. I should like to see the whole band of them exterminated! It would be the saving of the people!

January 15th

THIS morning, as we were driving down to the city to see some of the temples and sacred wells with which Benares abounds, we were hailed by our quondam travelling companions on the " Hamburg," Miss Booth and Miss Leighton. Our carriages stopped and we talked nineteen to the dozen for the next five minutes, when we parted with the understanding that we were to meet at our hotel at three and talk over our respective experiences. We then went to a sacred well, or tank, where people flock to be cured of all sorts of diseases.

One can hardly conceive of anything more sickening than to see the people rush down the steps into some of these tanks and plunge into the filthy water; but when they gather some of it in the palms of their hands and pour it down their throats with an ecstatic expression, that is the climax! Seeing that the water is as thick as pea soup, that it is stagnant and full of rotting flowers that have been cast in as offerings to the presiding Deity, and that people with all kinds of sores and loathsome

diseases bathe in it — even lepers, you feel that credu-
lousness and superstition have reached a point beyond
which it would be impossible to go.

We went also to the Golden Temple, which is right
in the heart of the crowded city, to be reached only on
foot by walking through little alleys, too narrow for an
elephant to pass without grazing his sides. We had more
than once occasion to regret that we did not have on
short skirts up to our knees, and storm rubbers, so wet
and sloppy were the temple and the immediate surroundings of the sacred well. Another one — called Inan Kup,
or " Well of Knowledge " — was situated in the quad-
rangle between the temple and the mosque. Nothing can
exceed the filthiness and the wetness of it all, for the people, believing that Siva resides in the well, throw water
in as well as ladle it out, perhaps in the belief that Siva
may like to change his liquor (and no wonder), but the
result is that every one who draws near is besprinkled
with the loathsome, fetid-smelling water, which, like that
of all the other wells, is filled with rotting flowers and
other putrid vegetable matter. There were four vulgar,
rascally looking priests in different corners of the quad-
rangle reading aloud from the sacred books, who, as soon
as they caught sight of us, sent some of their satellites to
follow us about and officiously give us information in
order to extract money from us. What with these nui-
sances, the hum and buzz of hundreds and hundreds of
voices, the din of gongs and being jostled alike by men
and cows — sacred ones, of course, it was like pande-
monium let loose.

And yet, withal, I would not have missed it for anything! For, even if we were standing in a puddle of dirty
water most of the time, after all, we were getting at the
heart of the people and seeing them as they are, and that

is what we came to Benares for. Besides, it was interesting to be there and note the strange mixture of beauty and barbarism, for really some of the stone pillars and cupolas, and a gate here and there, were of most exquisite design and workmanship.

From the Golden Temple and its adjuncts we proceeded to explore some of the numerous " ghats," or sections of steps alongside the river, where there are more temples and shrines and wells. One leprous well, which was more disgusting than the rest, was supposed to be filled with the sweat of Siva — it is called the Pilpilla Tirth. Pilgrims bathe in it before bathing in the Ganges, and the water is highly prized for drinking! A pilgrim plunged in as we were standing over it, and, as he displaced the water with his body, oh, the stench! But he seemed to like it, for he drank a lot of it.

The question naturally suggests itself, if the waters of these wells are saturated with leper pus and all sorts of impurities, why can these people continue to drink it and bathe in it without being infected with leprosy and other diseases? One answer is that the strength of their faith in its curative qualities renders them immune; the other is that it is such a conglomerate of poisons of various kinds that no microbe can exist in it for a moment. Some scientists in Agra have been making an analysis of Ganges water to find out why it does not kill everybody who drinks it or bathes in it, seeing that all the sewage of the city drains into it, to say nothing of the half-consumed bodies of those whose relatives are too poor to buy wood enough to finish the process of cremation, and which are seen floating about. On trying experiments in germ culture, they found that all disease germs when put in Ganges water promptly died, whereas when put in pure spring water they bred and mustered right merrily!

One of the ghats, called Sindia's, which was evidently

constructed with the intention of being something very massive and imposing by Baiza Bai, though it was never completed, has sunk several feet from the action of the river on a foundation unfit to bear such a weight of stone masonry. The effect is very curious, for the stone stairs are all awry, some projections look like a series of leaning towers of Pisa not quite grown up, and the temple on the left of the south turret is rent from top to bottom.

After tiffin our friends called on us, and we stayed chatting about our mutual experiences so long that there was no time to carry out our plan of spending a few hours on the river. However, we drove down and took a boat for a twilight acquaintance with the Ganges, which was quite a new sensation. There was a beautiful, soft, aftermath from the sunset, and the dim light of the stars lent a glamour to the water and made us forget what might be floating on its surface. The burning-ghat was very active, there were several pyres half burned, and the glowing flames sent forth a lurid light on the water. It was a pretty sight to see one or more floating lamps on the water, offerings made to the river by some pious soul. We made the acquaintance at the hotel of a bright maiden lady who turns out to be a Miss Griffith of Barmouth. Her father was a lawyer. She is a dabbler in archaeology and, being absolutely free-footed and independent, spends a great deal of her time in travel. Benares and Barmouth don't seem to have much in common except the letter B, but in talking with Miss G. our thoughts revert very readily to the Welsh mountains, and I can see them quite plainly at this distance in my mind's eye.

January 17th

YESTERDAY morning we went again to the river and invited Miss Griffith, who is alone, to go with us. It pre-

sented a very different sight from the day before yesterday. There were many people bathing, there were fakirs
and Sadhus, and burning bodies, there were also the
yellow wreaths of flowers floating about, but there was
no crowding, and the ghats looked somewhat bare and
forlorn. These ghats have but little beauty in themselves,
and need to be decorated by the bright garments of the
people. There are also only a few buildings which are
architecturally fine — the observatory, constructed by
Jey Sing, and the famous mosque of Aurangzib with its
tall and graceful minarets. Later on, we went with Mrs.
Hearst to some manufacturers of " kinkobes " — a kind
of cloth, either silk or cotton, with gold or silver threads
woven in. Some of these are perfectly gorgeous — especially the rich, silk brocades, which are immensely
heavy with gold. These kinkobes are made for the
" Saris," and coats worn by rajahs and the wealthy class,
but other nationalities hanker after them when they can
get them. Mrs. Hearst bought some superb specimens.

The merchants have a way here of treating you to all
kinds of things while you are making your selections.
They brought us dishes of nameless Indian confections,
flavoured with saffron and some of cocoanut and sugar,
very greasy and flavoured with sandal-wood oil. Of
course we had to taste everything, but there were moments when we longed for a dark corner and a spittoon!
They also insist on saturating your handkerchief with
some essential oil, either attar of roses, sandal wood, or
lavender, they give you cardamon seeds, and when you
leave they throw necklaces of jasmine blossoms and tinsel chains round your neck.

In the afternoon we went to visit the Maharajah's
Palace, which was not worth the trouble, as it turned
out, for it was a long way up and across the river, the

Palace being on the side opposite the city and all the ghats. The opposite side of the Ganges' banks, with the exception of the Palace, are without habitation. It is supposed to have been cursed by Siva, and no greater misfortune can happen to a human being than to die on that side. The Palace was built there — once upon a time — by the author of the sacred books of the Vedanta to break the spell, and to show that his will could counteract that of Siva, and the Maharajahs of Benares have lived there in succession ever since, but that does not seem to have inspired confidence in the rest of the community, for not a rod of land can yet be sold there, or even given away. It was a long and hard pull for our clumsy, heavy boat, and, finally, when we approached the other side of the river, the coolies tied long strings to the masthead, waded to the shore, and five of them walked along dragging the boat, while one remained to steer and another to push from the back with a long oar. We steered through more sewage than I ever dreamed could accumulate on one river, and passed the unsightly remains of one partially consumed corpse, the lungs and bladder inflated above the water. It was quite dark when we returned, and a heavy mist was rising from the river, millions of gulls were fighting with each other vociferously for the best place to roost on a sandy strand near the banks.

This morning there was another festival on the river. This time it was called " the dumb festival." All the pilgrims assembled from different places remain silent till they have taken their first dip, and then the tongues are unloosed with a vengeance! The scene resembled in all essentials that of our first morning. There was all the life, the vivid colour, the fervour, and the pathetic sadness of the poor widows. We saw a woman *in extremis* brought down and laid on the ghat to die, a group of her relatives in white muslin draperies sitting around her. As she breathed her last, she was at once wrapped in a red cloth and carried to the burning-ghat. It is regarded as a great privilege to die on the banks of the sacred river, and every one who is *in extremis* seeks, if possible, to be conveyed there.

This afternoon we went to another merchant and bought more kinkobes, and were again " treated " and decorated. It was dark when we came away — these Indians are so deadly slow in their operations — and lo! it was raining — the first rain we have seen in India. It will do a lot of good, though, for the dust was inches deep everywhere, and the trees and flowers were beginning to look parched.

This is our last day together. Mrs. Hearst, Clara, and the maid Marie, leave for Bombay tomorrow at 7 A.M. We are all feeling very sorrowful at the impending separation. We have been such good friends, and everything has been so sweet and harmonious in our intercourse. Tonight, the young salesman at the merchant of kinkobes, who spoke a little English, appeared at the hotel " to ask your ladyship for the favour of a testimonial " — " What for, in heaven's name? " cried Mrs. H., who was in the thick of last things to be done. " For my English and my courtesy," replied the man. " I shall do nothing of the kind," said the indignant ladyship. " Then I would ask another favour," said he. " I would like your ladyship to make me a present." I need hardly say that he left without either, but got a piece of her mind sharp and tart for his trouble!

January 18th

A HEAVY rain this morning. Our last day in Benares! I am feeling a bit low in my mind after accompanying our dear travelling companions to the station *en route* for Bombay. It was hard to part, but it couldn't be helped. It would have been a pity for us to give up the Himalayas, especially as we could, in any case, have only been together a fortnight longer, as Mrs. H. must hasten to London and then to New York. Clara will remain in Paris for a few weeks. We leave for Calcutta at 3 A.M. tomorrow, but are going on board the train at nine this evening as we have a special compartment as usual, and we shall have a chance to go to bed quietly.

Grand Hotel, Calcutta, Jan. 20th, 1904

WE SPENT Monday night very comfortably on the train, and now are in Calcutta after a journey of sixteen hours. We arrived here yesterday evening at about seven. In the course of the day, during our travels, we had a view of some interesting ranges of hills for a brief space, to relieve the monotony of the flat landscape which in India has prevailed so far. The palms are in evidence once more, the date, the tallipot, and the cocoanut. It was like a beautiful day in June at home, neither too hot nor too cold, and the country looked so fresh and the vegetation so luxuriant after the rain. We passed many quaint Indian villages, the little houses constructed of mud. The natives appeared in light draperies again, which grew more and more scant as we approached Calcutta. We had got quite used to seeing them dressed up in bed comforters in the north, and it made us realize quickly that we were in warmer climes, even more than did the sight of the palm trees with a gorgeous red and flaming sunset and afterglow behind them.

We had heard of the smells of Calcutta, but as soon as we started to drive from the station I was in a position to diag-nose them. The atmosphere was thick with a sort

of blue smoke, and it became quickly apparent to me
that the odour proceeded from the dung-cakes, which
are so universally used as fuel in India. I had noticed
that every little hut had in front of it a bright fire — for
they build their fires outside instead of inside their dwellings, and thus the atmosphere becomes charged with the
stench as well as the smoke of thousands and thousands
of these cow-dung fires.

So many of our travelling acquaintances had told us
that Calcutta was " a beastly hole, with nothing to see in
it," that we were prepared for the worst, and as usual we
are agreeably surprised. It is a remarkably handsome
city, with fine, broad streets and avenues, plenty of open
spaces dedicated to turf and trees for city lungs, and an
unusual number of imposing buildings, in the construction of which our government has wisely kept to the Indian style of architecture with slight modifications only.

Our chief object of interest here was Mohini. I wrote
him from Benares to say that we were to be here today
and tomorrow, and that we hoped to see him. He answered promptly with a charming letter to say he would
call here this morning. I was sitting out on this spacious
loggia, where I am now writing, and, somewhat dis-
tracted by the noise of the crows and kites mixed in with
the notes of hundreds of beautiful birds that collect in
the mango and magnolia trees in the garden which we
overlook, when I saw, crossing the garden, and being
conducted towards the *loggia* steps, a Brahmin — but
not Mohini, surely! Mohini was slender and ethereal in
appearance, with large, luminous, spiritual-looking eyes,
and a far away look and manner; this was a vigorous,
well-fed-looking, alert, and genial personality, who, with
the most cordial smile and outstretched hand, greeted
me with a warmth which was as foreign to our Mohini

as flesh. But it *was* Mohini all the same, though *not* the same.

Harry was at the bank, so we sat down and had a long, straight talk, beginning with his experiences in Rome, and going minutely into his reasons for holding to the forms of his own religion. He also talked freely of the different states of mind through which he had passed before becoming convinced that to be simply an ascetic was not the way to work for " the higher life " — that there was no strength engendered by living away from all friction with humanity; that the greatest and most difficult thing is to live among men and lead a life of action in their midst without being touched or tainted with their abuses — without being deflected from the dictates of one's own conscience; to remain honest in the midst of thieves, truthful in the midst of liars. So he returned to his family, took up the profession of law for which he had studied, and became in due time the father of six more children, in addition to the son that had already been born to him.

The new Mohini is a fine fellow. He has lost nothing in refinement and dignity, his luminous intelligence is what it always was, his sincerity and wholesouledness of manner are all there too, and yet he is an entirely different creature! All traces of that intense spirituality which was his have disappeared with his beard and mustache (for now he is clean shaven), and in its place you find a broadminded, liberal, and alert man of action, full of kindliness and affection. As Harry expresses it, " He has had all the nonsense knocked out of him," and now his natural, fine qualities of heart and mind have asserted themselves. He was very glad to see Harry again, on whose return from the bank, of course, there was a change in the topic of conversation. The law of the courts was discussed instead of the law of life, and we are to be taken by Mohini tomorrow to the High Court to meet some of the barristers and solicitors of Calcutta, and, perhaps, hear part of a trial.

This afternoon we went for a drive together, and he showed us all the most characteristic streets of Old Calcutta, which were indeed well worth seeing. Then he took us to the house where his sister and father-in-law, brothers-in-law, and a host of relatives all live together in harmony. There are four generations under one roof. He took us there because it was a typical Brahminical family mansion of the old time, whereas his own family mansion is more modern, and also distant, in an opposite direction, likewise through a part of the city which he thought would not interest us. I was much impressed with the dignity, even grandeur of the old family mansion. It lies back from the street in a sort of private park, and covers many acres of ground. The house is built around a large and beautiful garden, in which the lawn, the tall palms, and other trees are truly magnificent. This garden, in relation to the mansion, is that of the *cortile* in the ancient palaces of Italy, and indeed it is as large and extensive as any palace I have seen there or elsewhere. You think at first that what you see there is the whole of it, but not at all. You are taken to the back of it, and there you find another and inner court with buildings all around it.

He took us up to the spacious reception room, which to me looked somewhat cheerless, as all interiors do in India (when you have seen the outside of a house, you have surely seen the best of it). We sat out on the fine, broad *loggia* overlooking the court garden, and there, in slow procession, all the members of the family who were at home were brought in and introduced. They all of

them spoke a little English, but not much. I liked Mohini's sister very much. She had a refined face, and looked
very picturesque in her simple, white muslin gown and
" sari," bordered with gold. She took me all over the
women's apartments, which are separate from those of
the men, and was very friendly, expressing a cordial
desire to have me visit her again. When I admired some
large, brass jars, which here are used for water and which
were standing on one of the terraces, she pressed one of
them on me so that I found it difficult to excuse myself
from accepting it. Our visit there was an interesting experience, the more so as it is very rarely that a
stranger has an opportunity of meeting a large family
of high-caste Brahmins on friendly terms. I confess I
should have liked also to see Mohini's wife and children,
but I did not like to propose it. I saw his eldest son at
his office today when we called for him, a nice-looking
youth of about twenty.

[*Note by* H. M. R. " We have enjoyed especially the re-
newal of our acquaintance with Mohini Chatterji, now
fifteen years older and a little more since we parted from
him in Boston. He spent his last night in Boston with us
at 309 Beacon Street. He was most cordial and heartily
glad to see us. He is no longer the young and spiritual
looking Mohini of his picture, with flowing, black hair,
moustache and beard and a face where the eyes seemed
the one feature because of their brilliancy and changing
expressions as he talked.

" The questions of every-day life here and not of the
life to come probably absorb him in the main, though a
man of his breadth, learning, intelligent appreciation of
the best things, can never wean himself or be weaned
from consideration of the higher questions — but the

attrition of life has affected him as it must all men; they know more than they did, and they cease to be ' like an ill-roasted apple — all on one side.' "]

January 21st

WE SPENT an interesting hour or two at the High Court, and it was a very agreeable experience to meet personally such a number of highly educated Hindus and high-caste Brahmins — the tourist's knowledge of the race being derived chiefly from coolies, hotel keepers, and merchants. You get a very different idea of a race when you come into contact with its more enlightened members. For instance, it is chiefly with the ignorant classes that all that dreadful fetish worship prevails. I noticed in the private temple of the family mansion where Mohini took us yesterday that there were no images. I find, too, in talking with Mohini, that all we are told about the contempt for women and the treatment of widows is vastly exaggerated, and that such things only exist among the ignorant classes.

Harry seemed to produce quite an impression in the court room this morning. All eyes were turned our way, and some of the Hindu bar looked as if they would eat him up with their eyes as he stood telling some of his bar stories to Mohini and an Englishman named Vose. This afternoon we went for a drive to the Eden Gardens, along the banks of the Hooghly River (which is really a branch of the Ganges under another name), and saw a number of large steamers making ready for their journeys in different directions, and all the activities of a great river. We finished up at the Zoölogical Gardens, where we saw a wonderful array of tigers, lions, monkeys, and all sorts of birds and animals.

Talking of monkeys, two of them are disporting themselves in a tree opposite where I am writing, and are up to all sorts of impish tricks! When we reached home, I found standing at my room door a very magnificent-looking servant with turban and gown of black, bordered with silver, and bearing aloft a huge tray, in the centre of which was a large basket of splendid roses, and around it a generous supply of the fruits of the country — a parting gift from Mohini. There were pineapples, pomegranates, plantains, large king oranges, Indian gooseberries — which are quite different from ours and grow on tall trees, and almonds, walnuts, and pistachio nuts in profusion. What to do with them I'm sure I didn't know, but David, Harry's valet, said he should buy a large basket and take them along tomorrow, as we shall be glad of them at Darjeeling and on the journey thither.

We leave here for the Himalayas tomorrow afternoon at 4.30. Had we known sooner that tomorrow was to be a day of festivity, we should have planned to stay over and see the fun, but it was too late to change our arrangements when Mohini told us that on January 22nd they celebrate the first day of spring. Just why it is hard for me to conceive, as, from my point of view, it is like celebrating spring while the summer is on. With roses in profusion, and all sorts of gorgeous flowering shrubs, trees, and vines in bloom, what need of a spring opening?

Woodland's Hotel, Darjeeling, Jan. 23rd, 1904
OH! THE HIMALAYAS! Who would dare attempt to describe them! Picture to yourselves everything that is grandest, most magnificent, most terrific, and you may get some faint idea of them, or rather that portion of them we have seen as yet. The impression they make on one is simply overwhelming! In coming up in the little observation car of the narrow-guage, mountain railway

which we boarded this morning at Silliguri, after a comfortable night in the sleeper, we were kept in a constant state of excitement and wonder, not alone by the scenery — the deep abysses into which we looked, and the lofty peaks towering above, but also by the strange freaks of vegetation. There were trees without a leaf bearing large red blossoms something like tiger lilies, and here and there exquisite purple, flowering almonds, the sight of which made me understand why spring is celebrated at this season. Then there were great bunches of orchids hanging from the branches of some of the big trees, and doing their best to strangle them. Brilliant scarlet poinsettia peeped at us frequently through the jungle, and white spirea was growing in large tufts on the slopes. At one of the stations there was a leopard — such a beauty, that had just been shot in the jungle and was still warm. At Silliguri there were recently twenty-three tigers killed in one month, and we were warned against walking about in the outskirts unarmed. As we made no stay there, an exact connection with the mountain train being made, the warning proved unnecessary.

The mountain railway is a remarkable feat of engineering, and as it was continually describing loops, we could salute our fellow passengers who were at the other end of the train. The engine is not allowed a speed of more than seven miles an hour, and each hour an ascent of one thousand feet is made. Darjeeling is seven thousand feet above the bed of the great Ranjit River, which, as we twisted and turned, often showed up glistening in the sunshine. It was interesting to see specimens of the different mountain tribes, some of which were of a distinctly Mongolian type, others might have been Cossacks, and again others might have been North American Indians as far as their appearance indicated. They are all of a lighter colour than the people of the plains. They are covered with jewellery, some real and some imitation. Men and women alike wear necklaces, bracelets, and ear-rings, but the women have apparently a monopoly of nose-rings. Great quantities of turquoises are worn, and some of the women had long ear-rings set with large pieces of turquoise matrix, three inches long, and also charm boxes, an inch and a half square, of silver, set with turquoises, suspended from the necklace. Quantities of turquoises are found in Thibet, and as the blue stone has some peculiar religious significance, everyone must wear it who can, and if not, imitation ones. As we got up about 5,000 feet we were already in the clouds, the inseparable adjuncts of mountain peaks, and scenery was no more.

We reached Darjeeling in time for tiffin, and just as soon as we had satisfied our mountain appetites, we sallied forth down several inclines into the town, which is a series of streets built on zigzag terraces, no one of which can be reached without trudging up a steep hill. Fortunately the roads are very good. As we walked through the town, we were beset by both men and women from over the mountains, that is, from Thibet and Nepal, who offered for sale old Thibetan " devildaggers," prayer wheels, rosaries of human bones, amber, and coral, silver charm boxes and ear-rings set with turquoises. We had much fun bargaining with them, for they not only are fully aware of the actual value of their antiquities, but also of the foolishness of strangers, which leads them to demand double or treble what they are worth.

One cannot help feeling how much more beautiful Darjeeling would be if it were not so thickly settled. The numerous villas and bungalows scattered around

do not enhance the romance of the Himalayas. The villas
are rather mixed in style, and the bungalows have but
little individuality owing to the use made of corrugated
zinc for roofing instead of the natural thatching, which
would be so much more in keeping with the wild landscape. When we see corrugated zinc roofing on the houses
in Western America we bow down to the inevitable, but
in India, ancient, primitive India — in the heart of the
wildly wonderful Himalayas, corrugated zinc has no
right to be. It is an unpardonable false note!

How I hope it may be clear tomorrow that we may
get the full sweep of the snow mountains!

[*Note by* H. M. R. " It soon became evident we were
leaving the Hindu peculiarities of costume and feature
behind us and the Mongolian, — the Thibetan, — began to show itself, as different from what we had been
seeing as a Chinaman is from a negro almost, only here
there was a sort of blending of the two races, the face
flattening and the cheek bones higher and the eyes
smaller. And then costumes! More picture books! The
high peak to the hat, the long bodied coat, the hair
caught back and ending in a short pigtail and many of
the men carrying knives in their girdles and occasionally
pistols.

" Darjeeling itself is a very pretty place, full of
private villas and having two or three good hotels — a
kind of India-Switzerland town of some 18,000 people,
and is the resort of the Viceroy sometimes, and of all
the people who can come to the hills in summer. The
villas are scattered everywhere, have superb outlooks,
and are built, evidently, for permanency and for comfort.

" While I am writing, the great snowcaps and wonderful mountains are beginning to uncover their heads, and the grandeur of the scene is disclosing itself from our piazza. It is cold here, with the usual mountain cold, I mean, but nothing extreme; much like a clear crisp November with us, nothing more. The nights are rather colder and so are the early mornings, but, if we had American houses and means of heating, there would be nothing the least uncomfortable. Here the small grate, the rather open-work cracks to doors, the bathrooms opening into the *open*, and so on, make things less warm than otherwise would be.

" We have seen today also high poles, to which prayers were attached written, and were thus hoisted part way to the gods. It is all very, very fascinating. We saw similar things to the prayers on poles in Japan. This makes you wonder whether Thibet or at any rate China proper did not originate what we saw in Japan."]

January 24th
WHEN we rose this morning the mountains were still in the clouds, but after breakfast we had a good clear view of Kinchinjunga, 28,156 feet high, Janu, 25,304 feet, Kabru, 24,015 feet, and the rest of the range, all giants, none less than twenty-two thousand feet. The effect of these snow-capped peaks above the clouds was something colossal, but alas! of too short duration. The white clouds settled down on them again jealously, and they were seen no more today. Later in the morning we went through the bazaar in the centre of the town to see the people of all the different tribes who throng the streets. There are to be seen Thibetans, Lepchas, Limbus, Bhutias, and Nipalese as well as Hindus, Kabulis, Cashmeries, and Parsi shopkeepers. Sunday is the great day for the bazaar, and it presents a sight of activity

which is in its way unique. The noisiness of it is indescribable.

This is a nice little hotel — for India, and there are
some pleasant people coming and going. We sit at table
with some Americans whom we met at Kyoto, a Mrs.
Crawford and her daughters, and a friend, Miss Sanborn, from Los Angeles, California. We have not yet
summoned up courage for the famous semi-nocturnal
excursion to Tiger Hill — six miles distant, where people go in " dandies," a sort of carry, to see the sun rise
over Mt. Everest, the highest mountain in the world,
29,002 feet high. You have to start at 4 A.M., in the cold
chill of the anticipated morning, and people say that it
is paying a high price for the little glimpse that one gets
of a mountain which is 150 miles away. But every one
wants to be able to say that he has seen the highest
mountain in the world! Although really, Mt. Kinchinjunga, which we see all the time from our hotel
piazza when it is clear, is a much grander sight, because,
while it is only a few hundred feet less in height than
Mt. Everest, it is only forty-five miles distant, and it
must, therefore, necessarily appear more imposing.
Harry arrived here with a bad cold so I have not suggested going to Tiger Hill yet, but I don't want to leave
Darjeeling without making the trip if I can help it.

January 25th

WE HAVE quite suddenly and impulsively determined
on doing a very unusual thing before saying good bye
to India. Our trip to Darjeeling was to have been both
the climax and the end of our stay in this wonderful
country, but we have changed our plans, and, instead of
returning direct to Calcutta from here as we intended
to do on Thursday or Friday, we have decided to leave

Mount Kinchinjunga: Himalayas from Darjeeling

here tomorrow, making our way from Silliguri to Dhubri, thence go through the Assam Valley on the great
and sacred Brahmaputra River as far as Gauhati, where
we remain through the day, and thence back to Dhubri
and beyond to Goalundo, where we leave the river boat
and take the train for Calcutta. We shall have the
grand snow-range of the Himalayas in view most of the
time, besides the beautiful Garo and Bhutan Hills.

This projected trip is quite off the line of travel. With
the exception of those who go to hunt tigers or elephants, few people go to the Assam Valley. We were
led to it by a very enthusiastic acquaintance at this
hotel, who has been all over the world, and who is keen
to make this particular trip, and in our company. His
name is Dr. Nies, also a good deal of an archaeologist,
and a professor of Semitic languages. His wife is a very
nice woman of English origin, and their home has been
Brooklyn, N. Y., when they lived anywhere in particular, but they have been travelling round the world for
the last six years. I look forward to the trip with the
keenest anticipation of pleasure.

Meanwhile, I am determined to go to Tiger Hill before leaving Darjeeling, and, as my last opportunity
will be tomorrow, I have made up my mind to go without
Harry, in spite of the fact that we are to leave here at
12.30. I can sleep on the journey. A large party of people from the hotel are going, so I have ordered a ' dandy,'
and am to be awakened at 3.30 A.M. I wish you could
see the queer things that we are carried up the mountain
in. Picture to yourself a coffin, deep enough to hold a
little chair at the head of it, with poles at both ends for
the bearers, and you know what a dandy is. There are
six bearers in all, four of which hoist the dandy up on
their shoulders, while the extra ones are to relieve the

others from time to time. Of course one has to go well
bundled up to protect one from the keen air. Tiger Hill
is up two thousand feet above Darjeeling, that is, nine
thousand above the river.

January 26th

JUST returned from Tiger Hill. It was bright starlight
when I got into the coffin, and for the first hour the ride
was weirdly beautiful in the darkness on the brink of
overhanging depths. The glamour of the quasi-darkness
transformed everything, and made it look like something else. I was quite alone on the road the whole way,
my bearers having come to rouse me just as the others
were starting, so there was nothing to disturb the silence
save the rhythmic tread of my Thibetan bearers, little
snatches of song with which they beguiled the time, singing through their noses with closed lips, and the occasional cry or scream of some wild animal. The ascent was
very steep, and it is hard to understand how these men
could keep up a steady trot with such a' weight on their
shoulders for two hours without a single halt, and at
such an altitude, when we know how exhausting quick
motion is. But they were born and bred in the high
mountains, and that explains it I suppose. The roads and
paths were remarkably good, and that helped of course.

We passed many quaint mountain villages, the inhabitants all still asleep, and we passed over roads overshad-
owed by tall cryptomerias which reminded me of Nikko.
At last the stars began to grow dim and a strange half-
light shed itself over the mountains, the birds began to
twitter softly and lazily, and then, to my disgust, a thick
mist began to rise, and the usual all-pervading white
clouds to obtrude themselves. " No see Mt. Everest today, lady; too muchee clouds," said one of my bearers

as we reached the last set of zigzags leading to the top. I felt like uttering three-cornered words all to myself, for I was half frozen, and I fairly ached with stiffness, but when I reached the top, a round plateau overlooking the entire universe, apparently, my artistic soul became all aglow at the sight I saw. The bearers of the party which had preceded me up the mountain, fifty or sixty in number, had made a huge fire of dry sticks, and around this they were all seated or squatting, some few standing, the red light glowing in their faces. Anything more enchantingly picturesque cannot be imagined! All the dandies had been set down in a ring near the fire, some of the occupants preferring to remain in their coffins and get the heat at a little distance. I arose from mine and joined the group of mountaineers at the fire, and one of them (bless him!) pushed over to me a large slab of stone, well heated in the fire, to stand on, and it was not long before my freezing toes were as warm as toast.

Well! It was no use waiting to see Mt. Everest! It was now broad daylight, without any apparent help from the sun, and we were shown the place where Mt. Everest was to be seen *when visible*. Day after day people ascend the mountain with similar results, and yet they go again and again in the hopes of beholding that distant peak. In spite of my disappointment I am not sorry I went, for I experienced many new and interesting sensations, and saw things as I may never see them again. The ride home was fine also, for down in the valleys it was clear, and the quaint mountain villages were all astir, the trees and rich vegetation, the enormous clusters of orchids hanging from the trees, the beauteous roses a-bloom — all was grist to my mill! I reached the hotel in time for breakfast, and David had a nice fire for me in my room. Harry, who was dressing when I got home, was immensely relieved to get me back, for he had some apprehensions that the altitude might affect me.

On board the " Duffla," on the river Brahmaputra
                    [Assam Valley, India, Jan. 27th, 1904

WE ARE experiencing an entirely new sensation! There has been nothing like it during our travels! Here we are on this comfortable mail-boat of the River Steam Navigation Co., steaming along the great river Brahmaputra — sacred of course, as are all rivers that have their source in the Himalayas. We have been sitting here in comfortable cane chairs on this clean, sheltered deck, since early morning, watching the " muggers," or man-eating alligators, which swarm in the river, and looking towards the beautiful ranges of the Zaro and the Bhutan Hills. We are also looking towards the grand snow-range of the Himalayas, but there is a haze in the heavens which veils them. Dr. Nies says that this river reminds him of the Nile, with its high banks of white, sandy dust, or dusty sand, only this is much wider.

January 28th

THIS morning our boat landed at Gauhati, and we were informed that it would remain there till eight this evening, so Dr. Nies immediately set about enquiring what there was to be seen. We engaged two queer old vehicles which they called carriages, drawn by a pair of miserable toy horses, and, taking a well-equipped lunch basket with us, we started off for the day. First we went to a temple, or rather a series of temples on the top of a high hill, to reach which we had to ascend a thousand feet over a steep, winding way of rough, granite blocks, a most exhausting proceeding! But what a weird and

wonderful sequel there was to our climb! All I can think
of is that we found ourselves in one of the " high places "
where the Canaanites used to anger the Lord by worshipping. Here was a temple with pens in the centre for
holding the oxen which were to be sacrificed; at one end a
large, flat, stone altar with a pool of red blood in it which
had flowed from the kid just sacrificed. There were small
bands of pilgrims arriving, one leading a tiny white kid
— the next victim, and other offerings of grain and fruit.
This was the temple of the Hundred Virgins, who dance
at certain religious festivals. We were not allowed to see
the virgins, but, from the abnormal number of children
who swarmed all over the place and perched on the walls,
we judged that there must assuredly be at least a hundred of them, if not more!

There was a huge tank outside the temple, with stone
steps, much in decay, descending to the water. Scattered
all over these steps in groups were native women, men,
and children, principally naked, but some with bright-
coloured draperies. Surrounding the upper walls of the
tank were cocoanut palms in profusion, bending and
swaying in all directions, and through their trunks were
just visible numerous tiny huts, the sides covered with
plaited straw, and the roofs thatched with pampas. Anything more characteristically Indian can not be imagined!

The view from the temple enclosure was enchanting.
You looked towards richly wooded hills and the more
distant mountains, over valleys of matted jungle which
you easily, in imagination, peopled with tigers and elephants. We only entered four or five of the thirty-five
temples which are to be found on this particular " high
place." In each of them, there was a secret hole of some
kind, where we were not allowed to penetrate — God

knows what was in them, but we were allowed just a peep
into some of the holy of holies, and there was generally
either a solitary " lingum " of rough stone, or a puddle
of water brought from the Ganges. Truly India is a most
remarkable instance of arrested development! On nearly
every large boulder of granite, that stood sentinel by the
side of the rough steps by which we ascended and descended, there were hideous gods cut in the solid rock,
and painted red and yellow. Siva, his warlike wife Par-
vati, and their elephant-headed son Ganesh, were all
there in their turn, striking the most grotesque and impossible attitudes. Also the Goddess of Destruction,
Kali, or Durga, as she is often called. Anything more utterly barbaric or primitive can hardly be conceived!

We found the descent from the " high place " even
harder than the ascent, and were glad to rest our weary
limbs in the carriages which awaited us on the main
road. Then we drove back through the village, which I
suppose I should call a town, and started off in the opposite direction, straight toward the hill range. Dr. Nies
had ascertained that there was a curious, old, ruined
temple near a beautiful waterfall to be seen there in the
heart of the jungle, so we started off on a six-mile drive
to explore. It was a long ride, for the miserable, half-
starved, little horses could hardly pull us along at times,
and if a tiger had chosen to spring on us from out the
jungle, through which the road was cut, he would have
had ample time to make his selection of the plumpest of
the lot, which would undoubtedly have been Dr. Nies!

We were told to dismount, finally, at an old, ruined,
stone gate, by the side of which grew tall trees, where
wild monkeys were swinging in the branches, and scam-
pering by the dozens. On walking up the winding and
steep ascent towards the waterfall, we saw a little, dome-

shaped thing, overgrown with mosses, ferns, and other rank vegetation. This was all the temple there was, but picture our surprise when we turned to the left of it, and beheld, in a rough shelter, constructed over some part of the remains of the former temple, right at the side of the stream, two " Sadhus," or Holy Men in comtemplation! Without suspecting it, we had come upon the abiding place of some Brahmin ascetics, who had retired to the seclusion of the jungle to worship Brahm undisturbedly. This was indeed an unlooked-for experience, and my interest was aroused and excited to a white heat. Of course we did not try to attract their attention or disturb them in their devotions, but passed on towards some big rocks overhanging the fall, where we proceeded to spread our luncheon. In a little while, on looking round, we perceived one of the Sadhus (who looked like Perabo!) standing below the rock, gazing at us. He said never a word, but stood there during the whole of our repast. I had a painful feeling that we were intruders on their solitude, and that we were profaning this secluded spot. I doubt if any stranger had ever before penetrated their seclusion.

I have often tried to picture to myself the dwelling places and lives of these holy men who retire from the world and make for themselves an abiding place in the foothills of the Himalayas, or in the mountains themselves, but I never thought that I should actually see one of these hermitages. But what a wonderful spot they had chosen! The waterfall, so called, was in itself nothing more than a stream of water flowing in curves over big rocks, and by no means turbulently. But the surroundings! They must be seen before they can be pictured. Who could describe the wealth of gorgeous vegetation? There were royal palms and cocoanut trees, the former laden with betel nuts, tall orange and pamela trees, wood-apple trees, and others unknown to me, laden with nuts and pods of huge dimensions, and groups of bananas poking out their bright-green, plume-like leaves from the surrounding jungle. The way these tropical trees had ranged themselves about the curving stream, drooping over in one place, tangling each other's branches together in another, forming improvised bowers and arches, was the most picturesque thing in natural scenery I have ever beheld. A more utterly romantic spot cannot be conceived. It was overwhelming!

There is, however, always a false note somewhere in an Indian scene — a something incongruous and out of place to mar the poetry of it. Here the false note was the *débris* of the holy men's repast and utensils floating in the stream, and deposited between the rocks. On the sward, all around their hut, fragments of food were scattered, probably cast out after their last meal, for the benefit of the wild animals. There was some rice and a mess made of the inner bark or skin of the main stem of the banana tree, which looks juicy and succulent, and is of a beautiful, pale-green colour. This was minced very fine, and lay on the ground in a large leaf. I should say that, as food, it would be an improvement on chopped straw! As the one who looked like Perabo continued to hover around, I addressed him, pronouncing the word " Sadhu " interrogatively; whereon he nodded his head eagerly and pointed to a string round his neck indicating the sanctification of his life, as a Brahmin. He was joined later by another Sadhu, and yet another, whose personalities did not impress me as favourably as that of " Perabo." We gave the latter a little silver, which he did not refuse, and left.

We wended our way home slowly, our tired horses

giving us ample opportunity to observe the rich hedges of tree ferns, the orchids, the curious flowering shrubs, and all the wonders of nature which never cease to excite me. We saw a number of small elephants in a field, but no tigers in or out of the jungle made their appearance, which was fortunate, seeing that we were unarmed. We shall long remember our day at Gauhati, with its beautiful scenery — the finest of the Assam Valley, its temples on the " High Place," and its Sadhus in their mysterious seclusion.

This is the farthest point on the river which we make. We leave at eight tonight on our return journey, first to Dhubri, tomorrow, and then to Goalundo, where we take the train direct to Calcutta.

January 29th

THIS life on the Brahmaputra River is simply delightful! There is something interesting to be seen every minute, either in the way of queer craft, the strange conformation of the white mud-banks, an occasional alligator lying on a sand-bar, or sticking its head out of the water, and groups of natives on the river banks, who simply cannot help making pictures for us to revel in. How shall we ever be able to stand getting back to the sight of commonplace clothes again! Our boat reached Dhubri, our original starting point, this morning, and, as it was to stay there three hours, we all went ashore and walked about the native streets. We all of us concluded that Dhubri was one of the most characteristic and essentially " native "-looking Indian settlements we had seen, with its tangle web of palms of various kinds surrounding each little hut, the sides of which were covered with a coarse, brown matting, with its papaya trees laden with its clumsy looking fruit, its large tamarinds, and other pod-bearing trees. The sun was hot, and we were well baked by the time we returned to our boat. On our way we had to cross a bridge made of plaited bamboo, the first we had ever seen.

After leaving Dhubri our ship was stopped at every way-station, and it was great fun seeing the natives get on and off the boat. There are seldom any landing stages, and the boat, after getting as near to the shore as it dares to, throws out just a plank which is balanced on the sandy bank somewhere, and the natives come running down the steep sand-banks and walk across the narrow plank, hanging over deep water with heavy loads on their heads as easily as if it were a fine boulevard. It is a beautiful moonlight night and the sand banks look just like driven snow. The illusion is complete!

January 30th

THIS is our last day on board the " Duffla," and we are very sorry for we have enjoyed every moment of our trip. The Brahmaputra is a perpetual source of surprise! Just now we saw a group of large boats being moved by long oars plied from a very high upper-deck — three oars at either side. Dr. Nies says they are the facsimilies of the ancient Roman galleys. The scenery is quite flat here, but it never ceases to be interesting. The river is very wide, and often suggests a lake in parts. It is five miles across.

Our little party of four was increased today by an Englishman who has been settled on these shores for many years as superintendent of an indigo plantation, and he has given me much information about this part of the country. He says that many of these reptiles which we see about are crocodiles as well as alligators, and he has been entertaining me with stories of wild

CALCUTTA: The Jain Temple

beasts that have been shot close to his bungalow. A leopard knocked one of his men off his horse and made away with him a short time ago, and he often finds cobras inside his room. The other night he was awakened by the barking of his dog in his room, and, on taking up the lantern, he found him in front of a huge cobra with head erect, which the dog was keeping at bay. He hit the cobra a blow with a stick which broke its back, and so ridded himself of it. Harry and I have concluded to see the wild beasts and reptiles of the Assam Valley from a boat!

A large band of pilgrims has just come on board here at Aralia, leaving groups of Hindu women on the banks weeping. They are going to the Ganges for a festival, some of them to die, others to worship. Once on the ship we see nothing more of them till we land, for all these crowds of natives are stowed away in the third-class quarters, where they pay pence for our rupees. The latest news is that our ship has grounded here, and they are making superhuman efforts to get her off. In truth there is something exciting going on all the time! There she goes! They have got her off, and I must put up my writing materials now for this trip. We shall be late in reaching Goalundo this night, as this stick-in-the-mud business will delay us an hour. Tomorrow morning will find us in Calcutta again.

Grand Hotel, Calcutta, Jan. 31st, 1904
WE REACHED our destination this morning before sunrise, very sleepy. Dr. Nies, as soon as we had greeted each other on descending from our cars, commenced holding forth on the origin of the word " calico," which he traced to " Calcutta," and from the Goddess Kali in some round-about way which I was too sleepy to take

in. I'm afraid I gaped and looked at the morning star, which was bright, but not so awfully scintillating as Dr. Nies! I have no use for philology at five o'clock in the morning!

This afternoon Mohini took us for a very interesting excursion down the Hooghly River. We went in a sort of gondola, only there were no seats in the little cabin, and we had to squat, Hindu fashion. He took us to a little monastery (Hindu, of course) founded by Swami Vivekananda, who is now dead. He showed us the place on the river bank within the monastery grounds where his body was cremated, and the enclosure where his ashes were buried in Ganges mud. There were little basil shrubs planted over it, but they were not growing very well. The last time I saw Vivekananda was in Boston, or rather in Cambridge — gorgeous in his yellow turban, and I little thought that a few years later I should be standing over his grave on the banks of the Hooghly!

Mohini took us into the monastery and we were received with great courtesy by the Brahmins, all of whom came to greet us before we left. There was a service going on in the little chapel when we arrived, and they were chanting weirdly. One of the Brahmins, a pupil or chela of Vivekananda, spoke English quite well, and we had a good talk on matters serious. I was much surprised at finding a white man among them, an American, who had followed Vivekananda from New York, and is leading a life of renunciation with his order, being taught the mysteries of contemplation. He was a man of not over thirty-five, I should say, and quite good looking, but he seemed to be taking life very hard! They took me into Vivekananda's room, where everything had been left just as it was when he occupied it, even to his yellow robe hanging over the clothes horse. It was touching to see with what reverence they approached it. They offered us tea, and, on our declining it, brought us Indian fruits, sweets, and a cup of water. Before leaving they gathered for me a bunch of wonderful roses, rare specimens, and, as we went down the steps to the boat, these yellow-robed brothers all came out on the *loggia* to wave us farewell. It was a goodly sight, and I went away with a sense of sweetness and repose which these refined, courteous Brahmins had left with me. A violent storm came up before we reached the landing, but it did not last long.

We leave for Bombay tomorrow, to take a steamer for Egypt. The news from Japan is at this time so threatening that it would be folly to think of carrying out our original plan of returning there. Apart from any danger, which we do not fear, everything would be in an abnormal condition, and there would be no pleasure in it. So it is settled that we leave Bombay on Saturday, February 6th, by the P. and O. steamship " Marmora," a fine new boat — a giant of 10,900 tons, bound for Suez, where we shall have to be quarantined at " Moses' Well " for a day or more, as no one is allowed to enter Egypt from India without having been clear of its shores for ten days, on account of the plague. But, of course, they count the time passed at sea. So, if the " Marmora " crosses in less than ten days, we have to make up the rest of the time in quarantine, and, as she is a fast boat, I suppose we are in for it!

Hotel Taj Mahal, Bombay, Feb. 5th, 1904
WE ARRIVED here the day before yesterday at nine, after two nights and nearly two days on the train. A stretch of 1350 miles is no joke! But, as there were no changes, and we had a private car all the way, so that we could

lie down and sleep whenever we wanted to, discomfort was reduced to a minimum. We found our American friends at this hotel (Miss Booth and Miss Leighton). They also are sailing with us on the " Marmora " to-morrow, and yesterday General Winslow and party arrived, and we had much to tell each other.

Yesterday we went out to the Meyers' bungalow to tea, it being our only chance for a good, long talk. They invited us to dine there tonight, but we had to decline on account of having so many last things to do before sailing for Egypt. We went on board our ship to inspect our staterooms the day we arrived here, as she was still in dock, and I am glad we did, for the stateroom allotted to us on the upper deck was not nearly large enough to hold us bag and baggage, so we selected one below, which is a fine one. The ship is magnificent, and it will not be crowded as it is a fortnight too early for the general exodus from India.

It is pretty hot here already, though! We should have liked to stay longer here, for there are things worth seeing which we have not been able to get in — such as " the caves of Elephanta," an excursion which would spoil a day, and other curious cave-temples, but if we are to go up the Nile we may not delay, as a fortnight after we go it will be no longer navigable.

S. S. " Marmora," Arabian Sea, Feb. 7th, 1904
THIS morning my bath was of the waters of the Arabian Sea. We are well under way for Aden, our first stopping place. The sea is calm and azure blue, the sun hot, but tempered by a delightful soft breeze. The good ship " Marmora " is a palace of comfort, not to say luxury. There is literally everything one can desire, and so much more than one has a right to expect, sandwiched between

sea and sky! We started from Bombay yesterday at
12.30, after a so-called medical examination which was a
mere farce. We had bidden good bye the evening before
to our delightful friends, the Meyers, who came to our
hotel and spent an hour with us, we having had to decline their invitation to dinner, not only for lack of time,
but because our baggage had to be sent on board the
day before sailing, and we had not the wherewithal to
array ourselves properly for a dinner.

February 10*th*
THIS morning early we sighted the first land of the
Arabian Coast — a beautiful, soft line of mountains.
At three this afternoon we saw Aden in the near distance as we steamed up the gulf. We were passed by an
English warship, and violently signaled by the flag code,
which, interpreted, meant, " War is declared in Japan
— the Japanese have sunk a Russian cruiser and taken
six colliers." We all shouted for joy. The next excitement
was anchoring off Aden, where we were to remain four
hours, starting again at 8.15 this evening. A bunch of
Reuter's telegrams were brought on board and read
aloud on the deck, the war news eagerly listened to with
bated breath. I need not say that all our sympathies are
with Japan!

Our ship is flying the yellow flag, which means quarantine, and no one may land. Aden presents to our view
groups of interesting mountains or serrated rocks, on
which not a speck of vegetation is visible from bottom
to top. There is one very conspicuous extinct crater, and
there are many dangerously volcanic-looking peaks in
the neighbourhood. It seems strongly fortified, and you
see towers and tanks on the top of many of the slopes.
The base of the most projecting point is well covered

with long, low, flat buildings with red roofs. Not fair nor interesting to look upon, only queer!

Aden is historically interesting. It was known to the Romans, and was, during a long period, held by the Turks. It has been captured and re-conquered many times, and has been the scene of a deal of bloodshed. There are a number of big ships lying in the harbour, and, near the tug which is bringing on board some passengers, there is a small boat full of natives with some very hideous Swahelis from the coast of East Africa mixed in. We have already made acquaintance with some Arabian mosquitos, who must have had letters of introduction to me, for they promptly found me out!

February 11th

Last night, on leaving Aden, we went into the straits of Bal-El-Mander, and this morning we are in the Red Sea, running alongside the coast of Africa. The shore line is very attractive. It consists of ranges of mountains which are entirely of barren rock, but the colouring is fine, being rich in reds and purples, the drifts of white sand, which have settled in the crevices and ridges, setting off the darker tints to great advantage, and producing a unique effect. There is a strong breeze which we certainly did not expect to find on the Red Sea! We seem now to be leaving the shore line behind; there is only visible the butt end of a big rock with a lighthouse on it, and a small island to finish off. We had been warned of the unbearable heat at this point of our journey, so the freshness of the air is indeed an agreeable surprise. The breeze grows ever stronger and the sea more turbulent than it has been at any time on this trip. It may be that Pharaoh and his hosts are kicking up a rumpus down there!

In Quarantine at Moses' Well, Arabia, Feb. 14th
HERE we are safely ensconced, after some vicissitudes, in a place that, as far as I can make out, is nowhere in particular. Our quarantine consists of a handful of one-storied buildings of wood and plaster on the Arabian desert, planted on the sands close by the sea. Across the water, in the very near distance, is the African coast framed in beautiful though verdureless hills, and, on this side, behind our sheds, are the Arabian hills which frame this particular desert.

The Wells of Moses ("Ain Musa") have by tradition been fixed upon as the spot where Moses and Miriam and the children of Israel sang their song of triumph. These wells are a sort of oasis formed by a collection of springs (brackish ones at that) surrounded by palms and tamarisk bushes. They are only ten minutes' walk from these buildings, but we are not allowed to go near them lest we should infect them with plague! So our walks are confined to that portion of the sand which is near the sea.

The wonder is that we ever got here alive, but not on account of the plague! The P. and O. did their best to have us drowned before we landed here. When we reached Suez this morning, where, of course, we only anchored outside in the gulf, the first thing that happened was the medical examination. An Egyptian doctor and an English lady-doctor came on board, and every passenger had to answer the roll call; but that was all. They did not even go through the form of feeling our pulses. After this, we were to have lunch and then leave the ship, as we had been led to suppose, in a decent steam launch for our quarantine prison. But what was our dismay when we saw a small fleet of very uncom-

fortable and very unseaworthy looking sailboats (such
as they use for fishing) approach our ship, towed by an
equally unseaworthy looking tug! We could hardly believe our eyes, and a general indignation meeting was
held by all the passengers bound for Egypt — about
forty in all. It seemed, however, that that was the only
way we might be landed. On account of our being presumably infected by plague, we could not be allowed to
go on board a launch used by other passengers, so all of
these boats were there to take us, the launch being permitted to tow the whole string of them to avoid the uncertainty and delay of using the sails.

Have you ever been in one of a string of small boats
towed by a small tug in a rough — a very rough sea?
If not, I hope you never may. There were seven strong
miles to make, and we were tossed about with all our
luggage for over an hour, the boats disappearing under
the waves in such wise every now and then that the wonder was they ever came up again. But this was not all,
nor yet the worst of it; for when we approached the
primitive jetty here, and the tug left us to the mercy of
the gale, it seemed as if it would be an impossibility to
land without the boats being dashed to pieces against
the stone props of the breakwater. It was simply horrid,
and we never want to go through such a performance
again!

Our Arab boatmen, picturesque creatures, have to
stay in quarantine here with us till we are taken away
on Tuesday. Let us hope to heaven that on Tuesday
the sea will be calm again! They say it is not often as
rough as it was today. The caterer here is a Greek, and
he has just given us some afternoon tea of the poorest
quality. We ought to be decently fed here, for we have
to pay just the same as at a first-class hotel in England.

The rooms, however, are at least clean, though quite in the rough, but cleanliness in itself is a great comfort after the hotels of India. As this quarantine station was not large enough to put up all the passengers for Egypt, a number of them, principally Cook's tourists, had to go to another station, nearer the canal, for which we were not sorry. So we were only two boatloads, fourteen of us in all. In our boat we managed to keep our spirits up, and we stood the banging and heaving right nobly, but our companion boat had a very hard time, and all the women were deathly sick besides being frightened to death. We have been strolling about with some of our companions who are of various races, but all a good sort. There are Greeks, four Parsees from Bombay, with whom we have grown friendly. The wife of one of them is very intellectual, and they are all of them of a superior brand. There is a Frenchman who looks like an impresario, with a very doleful-looking wife; an English building-contractor and wife, from Calcutta; a genial young English parson, and another ample and jovial Englishman with a waggish tendency, who enters the dining room saying: " Where shall little Willie sit? " They are already beginning to say, " Whatever shall we do with ourselves tomorrow? Go fishing? read aloud? play football on the desert without a ball? " I suggest the appropriateness of telling stories à la Decameron, as we are in seclusion on account of the plague.

February 15th
THIS morning, when we emerged from our cells and looked across the sea of colour towards the African hills, a wondrous-clear, blue sky looked down on the golden sand of the desert and beach in combination, I could not help remarking that but for the feeling that we were

here on compulsion what a charm the place would have
for us, and how we should love to bask in this sunshine
and beauty! Harry and I strolled about the entire morning down near the water's edge. It is very cool and fresh,
and the wind is rather high, so that we have had to resort
to warm clothing, but the air is delicious and invigorating.

We need not have feared that time would hang heavily on our hands! The day has gone like a flash. You
never saw such beautiful shells as you find on these
sands. The kinds that they sell in curio shops, millions
of them! I can hardly help gathering them, they are so
beautiful, and yet I should hardly be able to find a place
for them. But the colour of the water is the greatest
marvel! Imagine the bright, turquoise blue with stripes
of the most intense Nile green, and beyond, the purple
and red hills in the foreground, golden sand in high
waves and hummocks, and you have a scheme of colour
which is an orgy to the eye! I shouldn't mind staying
here for days and days if there were not so many things
we want to see elsewhere in a limited time. We leave here
tomorrow morning at eleven in our wabbly boats (let us
pray for a calm sea!), and we take the five o'clock train
from Suez to Cairo, which we shall reach at eleven P.M.

It rained hard last night — a very unusual thing at
this season, but the wind has blown the clouds away, and
I think it will be fair tomorrow. Two or three of us were
standing on the piazza of the bungalow where we take
our meals, an hour ago, looking towards the exact spot
where Moses and the Children of Israel crossed the Red
Sea, and really there is at that point such a little way to
cross that one could easily imagine such a feat possible
at low tide without any miracle. The trouble with Pharaoh was that he was too late — the tide had risen!

Shepheards Hotel, Cairo, Feb. 17th, 1904
THE fates were kind to us, and the weather was heavenly yesterday when we left Moses' Well. The sea calm as a fishpond, so that the sensation of being towed along by the tug in our small craft was positively delightful. We landed first at Port Tewfik, where the customs inspection took place, and where we lunched, then we drove to Suez — only twenty minutes distant. We had plenty of time, before our train started, to walk about the town of Suez, which does not offer anything of vital interest to any one who is already familiar with the Orient and its everyday sights. The bazaar is lively, and you see a great variety of nationalities — Arabs, Bedouins, Ethiopians, Nubians, and Egyptians, all plying their different trades and making a great noise among themselves. There are some magnificent tamarisk trees and a kind of gigantic acacia bearing long, flat pods in enormous quantities, which, when ripe, take on a fine golden hue; the pepper tree also flourishes in great beauty and its clusters of tiny, scarlet berries were in their glory.

At the station we were pestered by the usual persistent Orientals trying to force on us turquoises, coral, picture cards, and other wares. We were glad when the time came for our train to start. Our way lay parallel with the canal during the first part of our journey on one side, and on the other side we had before us the sand of the desert skirting the sea. Later we passed through miles and miles of sandy desert, in which there were many indentations where a thick deposit of salt had been left by the sea. We saw lots of cormorants perched on buoys and other queer places. Off in the distance there was the Sinai range. I wish we could have seen Mt. Sinai itself, but I am told it is seldom visible at this point. There was a fine sunset, then darkness and a nap which lasted till dinner was served on the cars — a very bad one, and not worth rousing oneself to eat!

We reached our destination finally at eleven, and were fortunate to find good accommodations at this hotel, as Cairo is very crowded at present, and all the principal hotels full. Today we have been prowling about the city, which presents a scene of animation and gaiety which can hardly be surpassed. After India this affects one almost as a European city — a sort of Paris, but for its tropical surroundings. One misses the gorgeous colouring of the native Indian costumes — I mean clouts. The Egyptian long full garment generally of dark blue, brown or black, is somewhat sombre in character, though lighted up in a measure by the tall, scarlet fez.

But the women! They are indescribably queer with their voluminous black silk cloaks and very wide sleeves, the " burko," or veil, which covers the whole face except the eyes, and two strips of black silk over that, which makes them look like huge bats. They tint their eyelashes and eyebrows black, and stain their finger- and toe-nails with henna. Many of them wear on their noses a section of split bamboo about three inches long, which serves to connect the upper part of their veil with the lower. This is a frightful disfigurement, as, by the constant pressure of the bamboo on the nose cartilages, it becomes flattened in the centre, and dreadful excrescences grow out at the sides in many cases.

We found a letter from Dr. Reisner, Mrs. Hearst's archaeologist, awaiting us to say that he should expect us tomorrow at the excavation grounds near the pyramids, to be shown the results of his work up to date, and afterwards to lunch at his camp, so that is to be our first

programme. We went round today to see if we could get
rooms at some quieter hotel than this. Here one is so
much in evidence. It is full of Americans who make
much display of clothes, though there are also many
English here who do the same. It is an interesting place,
in a way, especially for those who have read the numerous novels, the scenes of which are laid in Cairo. There
is a perpetual coming and going, and every nationality
seems to be represented. We found that the only other,
quieter hotel that we would have cared to go to, the
Angleterre, was full, so we must e'en stay where we are
till we have been up the Nile, when we shall seek other
quarters.

Our apartment is beautifully situated, however, and
very large, with four windows looking out on a beautiful
garden, and the long, feathery leaves of three date-palms
hanging over our verandah.

February 18*th*

WHAT a day we have had! A day of desert and pyramids and of wonderful old tombs of over five thousand
years ago!

Dr. Reisner is an enthusiast, and when he saw that
we were genuinely interested in his work he opened wide
the door of his treasure house to us. He gave up the entire
day to us, and took us all over his excavation grounds,
virtually a city of tombs, explaining to us the meaning of
everything, and reading to us the inscriptions in hieroglyphics as easily as if they were the headlines of a newspaper. I may not tell you all that we saw, for he showed
us certain things which nobody has seen yet save his
wife and his assistant, and which nobody is to know
anything about for some time to come. We took lunch
in the camp, where we were to have stayed a month with

Mrs. Hearst, with the wonderful pyramids before us, the desert, with its undulating hills of sand to the right of us, and the Nile to the left of us.

Dr. Reisner did not take in the fact that while we were truly interested in the archaeological side of the pyramid region, we were at the same time tourists, and that we had not yet taken a look at the Sphinx! However, that must be for another time. We shall go out to the desert again before we go up the Nile, and then we won't let the Reisners know, but will haunt just the pyramids and the Sphinx and nothing else. They were so sweet and kind to us, Mrs. R. is a fine, wholesome woman, and they have such a darling baby, six months old. When we return from our trip up the Nile they want us to stay for a few days up at their camp, and be present at the opening of some more of the tombs. We should love to do it above everything, but whether we can manage it or not, with all that we have laid out, remains to be seen.

We are much excited at the war news from Japan. Oh, I do hope the plucky little Japs will end by drawing some of Russia's teeth!

[*Note by* H. M. R. " Today we have seen the pyramids for the first time, and have sat in their presence for hours, at the quarters of Dr. and Mrs. Reisner, and we have looked from their enclosed verandah upon the Great, the Second, and the Third Pyramids, and in the distance have seen eight others, and we have looked, too, on the exquisite green valley of the Nile, and over the brown desert, and have seen camels galore, on our way to the pyramids and palms and a regular picture book of Egyptian sights.

" We have seen, too, the wonderful excavations in progress under the direction of Dr. Reisner, and have

Egypt: The Sphinx

in a way fulfilled the original idea of our trip, which was, as you may remember, to spend some time with Dr. and Mrs. Reisner at the (Hearst) headquarters at the Second Pyramid, where Dr. Reisner promised to make Mrs. Hearst welcome. You may remember how that idea of passing some time there appealed to all of our imaginations and our wishes. To think that our dearest Ladye and Clara could not do it, and that we have had a taste of it gives the only pang.

" Mrs. Hearst reached Port Said on the 3rd of February. Because of the *quarantine* Dr. Reisner could not go on board the ship there, but he stood on the ship's ladder at about eleven P.M., when the ship got to anchor, and talked to our dear Ladye, and crowded into a brief talk all they could say to each other ere the ship left for Marseilles.

" It was so interesting to see what Reisner is doing with his 150 men at work and uncovering day by day tombs built before 2500 B.C., and never yet opened till now. To think that Mrs. Hearst is doing all this, paying for it, pushing it, and giving the Doctor full swing, and he enthusiastic to the very finger tips; and when we saw him this A.M. in his shirt sleeves, his clothes covered with the marks of the fray, the greeting was so warm and hearty, we knew he was worth seeing and knowing.

" He took us around his work, and it is simply astounding what he has accomplished within the last thirty days. He has shown us many things, and has told us many things that will appear in his publications, and every day he is there, as full of life and energy and enthusiasm, and with it all, an attention to details that is simply astounding. He reads the names of the gentlemen buried some 2500 to 3000 years before Christ, and told us as he read one today, ' This man was a judge; there is the sign, a *jackal!* ' I could not help telling him how glad I was I was only a lawyer and not yet on the bench.

" Mrs. Reisner is a very sweet woman and they have a dear little baby girl of some five months old. Dorie insists that the slope of the baby's head, taken in connection with the hair, makes a *pyramid*.

" We lunched and talked and looked at the pyramids, and went again to the excavations, and did not leave till after 6.20 o'clock reaching the hotel at about 7.30. We go to the pyramids by tramway — plain, simple, everyday electrics, and I assure you it is an excellent way to go.

" Things never look as you expect. I expected to see the pyramids on a flat desert — sand all around and nothing else in sight but desolation and the Sphinx. Well, they seem to be on a sort of tableland, overlooking the wonderful green of the Nile Valley and Cairo way beyond, and then, besides, the desert seems more like a rolling country than I thought it would be, and as you took a look at a string of camels, for example, they seemed to be outlined on the landscape as if on a ridge — as they were, so that there does not seem the isolation I expected. I would like to stay at Dr. Reisner's for a few days. He says the quiet of the nights is wonderful. When he is away from his work here for a time he gets such longings that he can hardly control himself. I do not wonder. I should.

" We did not go to see the Sphinx today; we were too busy. We hope to spend next Sunday at the pyramids, and many other days, too. They don't impress you at first as being as high as you expected them to be, and yet they are so massive, and they grow so upon you, that before you have been with them long you *feel* them, and that's a good test of mountains or buildings or works of art."]

February 21st

YESTERDAY we spent the morning in Old Cairo and the Island of Rhoda, famous as being the place where the daughter of Pharaoh discovered Moses floating on the stream among the rushes. There was the ancient palace in an ancient garden where the orange trees, the henna, and the vines all looked sad and rusty. We walked down the little path to the river, where the daughters used to bathe, and examined the old well near which the cradle wedged itself. In fact we saw everything except Moses and the bulrushes and the daughter of Pharaoh! Apart from tradition, true or untrue, it was an interesting and attractive spot — this little island which divides the waters of the Nile.

Old Cairo, from which we were ferried across to Rhoda, is, of course, historically interesting, but it certainly offers no attraction whatever to the eye of the stranger. It is full of the *débris* of buildings, or rather square boxes of stone and plaster, and there are no traces of beauty of form, colour, or ornamentation. The Egyptian houses of the people are ugly in design, and there is nothing to be said except that it all looks very ancient and dead and tumble-down-y. There is no glamour except what is brought about by your own imagination. We also visited an old Coptic church, where there were five interesting early Christian pictures, some good carving and inlaid work added to much that was tawdry.

In the afternoon we went to the mosque Tekiyet-el-Manlawiyeh, where, every Friday, there is a service of whirling dervishes, and afterwards to another mosque for the service of the howling dervishes. Two such extraordinary performances I never thought to see! The whirling dervishes held their service in a rotunda, fenced off from the visitors like the " ring " of a circus. At the end facing Mecca sat the High Priest on a red mat. The dervishes squatted all around the edge of the rotunda, beginning at a short distance from the priest's mat. They were dressed in long, flowing robes — some of navy blue, some grey, and some black, and a cone-shaped fez in tan colour. First there was chanting from a sort of choir up in a gallery to an accompaniment of two fifes and a drum of some sort. The dervishes, meanwhile, looked as if they neither heard nor saw. This lasted a long time, then there was an interminable fife solo — very Oriental in character. Then the High Priest rose and proceeded to walk slowly and solemnly round the rotunda. At his signal the dervishes all rose, and, walking up to the mat where the priest had been sitting, bowed reverently down before it, first on one side of it and then on the other, with a graceful, gliding step. Every dervish (there were about forty of them) followed suit, first bowing in turn to the mat and then following the priest in his slow march around. They went through this three times, going through the whole performance of bowing twice each time, and then the priest returned to his mat.

Some different fife music struck up, upon which the dervishes quickly threw off their long robes, remaining in very full, white-linen skirts and short, white jackets. The dervish nearest the right end of the mat walked towards the priest, reverently kissed his forearm and his hand (his arms being folded), and then immediately began to whirl. And such a whirl! His full, white skirt stood out straight like that of a ballet dancer. Each dervish in his turn did the same until the floor was white and dizzy with these wild, whirling creatures. The two arms were outstretched, the right palm turned upwards (receiving blessing), the left palm downward (bestowing it). They kept the whirling up without intermission for at least half an hour, until one could look no more it became so unbearably painful. There were slight changes in the musical rhythm from time to time, but, while that may have afforded some little relief to the dervishes, the onlookers were wearied to extinction sympathetically. We could not stand more than a half an hour of it, and left to go to the other mosque and hear some howling for a change.

Here the part fenced in was shaped like a horseshoe. The priest at the straight end of it sometimes sat and sometimes stood. First there was chanting, quite in tune, which lasted some time, then there was a curious, monotonous intoning of " Allah " and something else at the end of it. Imagine a chorus of fifty keeping this up for over a hundred times, accompanied by swaying movements of the head and body from the waist upwards. Little by little they grew more excited and changed to a quicker rhythm and higher pitch with occasional ejaculations independent of the set, intonation, and rhythm. Then, instead of musical intonation, they began to make other noises. First a painful sound produced by hard breathing, which in chorus sounded exactly like the puffing of a huge steam engine; another series of sounds followed, which were like a steam saw. I never had any idea that human beings could make so many different kinds of noises with their lungs and throats!

At intervals of about five minutes, the priest came forward and chose from among the dervishes one to lead the chorus of *howlers,* leading him into the centre of the rotunda, away from the chorus. The swaying of the bodies grew ever more violent and rapid, and two of the dervishes, who had heavy shocks of black hair reaching to the waist, were sights to behold when, swaying forward and backward, the entire mass of hair went with it.

When it seemed as if every variety of vocal noise must be exhausted, a number of large tambourines without bells were brought in, and then they all let go with such a howling and snorting as was never dreamed of, even in Erebus! Quicker and quicker, louder and louder, higher and higher, until some of them fell down in convulsions. It was a horrid as well as an astounding spectacle! Again we left before it came quite to an end, as we did not want to see any more epileptic fits!

It was good to get out into God's sunlight again after this weird worship, and we drove up to the Citadel, a fine building on an eminence, built by Saladin in 1166. It overlooks the entire city, three sets of pyramids — Gizeh, Dashur, and Abusir, the Libyan hills and desert. We stood in the courtyard where the massacre of the Mamelukes took place by order of Mohammed Ali, whose magnificent tomb stands in the famous alabaster mosque within the Citadel. This mosque is really splendid! The columns are built of yellow alabaster, and the entire mosque, which is enormous in size, is encrusted with white alabaster. This particular mosque is one of the features of Cairo — its lofty and beautiful minarets are conspicuous everywhere. You might say of it, that it is the eyes of Cairo's face! There are five hundred mosques to be seen here, besides tombs of Kalifs and Mamelukes galore! I wonder how many of them we shall visit before we leave Egypt. Anyway, the rest of them will have to wait till we return from our trip up the Nile, as we start tomorrow.

After leaving the Citadel we drove through the Muski — the native bazaar of Cairo, where you see the real, characteristic bazaar life of Egypt. The little, box-shaped shops where the silver workers, the shoemakers, jewelers, brass workers, etc., ply their trades are much the same

GIZEH: Giant Pyramids near Cairo

as in India, though some of the streets are narrower than anything I have seen even in Benares or in China — there is hardly room to pass, literally! You miss the bright colouring of India. The Egyptian dress is sombre in effect, not to say funereal, but the clatter, the noise, the importunities, — and the cheating, — are the same. It is all intensely interesting, however, and I should have liked to prowl about a great deal longer.

Yesterday we spent the morning in the Museum of Gizeh. It is indeed a wonder house of treasures, and one must return there again and again to get even a bird's eye view of it all. Most of the treasures found in the pyramids and mastabas are there arranged in fine order, so that you really can understand the higher significance of what you are seeing if you care to study it out a bit. You grow to be quite familiar with the countenance of Rameses II and III, and other ancient gentlemen, and 5000 B.C. gets to be as yesterday. One revelation to me was the fine portraits painted on the outside of the mummies. They are really full of life and individuality, and wonderfully executed. Faithful portraiture was considered a necessity by the ancient Egyptians, who believed that the immortality of the soul depended absolutely on the perfect preservation of the lineaments of the " Ka " or physical " double." So, in bending over these mummies, we were actually gazing into the faces of these antique celebrities. We could only give a quick glance at the wonderful collection of scarabees and amulets of all kinds found in the " offering niches " of the tombs. But I cannot begin to tell you how our day with Dr. Reisner at the excavations, with all that he pointed out to us, served to vitalize our interest in all we saw here, and how it stimulated and rendered intelligent our powers of observation.

In the afternoon we went out again to the Pyramid of Gizeh, to take a look at the Sphinx, which we did not see on Thursday. It is indeed an impressive sight — this monster god of the rising sun, hewn out of the living rock. All defaced and broken as it is, it still seems to say to you as you gaze at it, " If only you could understand, what mysteries I could unfold — and I would if you would just try. Why don't you try to understand me? You might — it is not difficult! " We threw ourselves down on a high mound of sand just opposite, and there we remained spellbound for nearly half an hour, gazing from Sphinx to pyramid, from pyramid to Sphinx. Around us were numerous camels and dromedaries with their Arab owners waiting for a job, no, not waiting — clamouring for it! But the clamouring was all done with their mouths, for they were lying about in all sorts of graceful and picturesque groups, both beasts and boys. There were also donkeys galore, with their youthful drivers, and these kept up with the camel and dromedary men a constant play of Arab wit in broken English for our benefit.

We remained until the sun began to sink, and we drank in all the glory of the blood-red, setting sun, with the yellow sand of the Libyan desert in the foreground, the Valley of the Nile, with its fertile plains of tall, blossoming white clover, with here and there a patch of sugar cane, or a field of large white and pink poppies, or of yellow mustard, and grove upon grove of tall date-palms, with their feathery tops. Such a wondrous, clear atmosphere, such softness and mellowness, and such poetry are hard to picture away from the objects themselves, but the impression thereof must stay forever!

I wonder what the Sphinx will say to us next time. I'm afraid there will be reproach in its face! " What, not yet? " it will say. Our Parsee friends arrived on the scene, Mrs. Petit looking very picturesque on a dromedary, with her silk-gauze sari draped from the head. She looked just right in it, all the other tourists looked all wrong. Poor dear, she had lost a diamond worth forty pounds, in the tram, and was much distressed, though she and her husband were commendably philosophical over it. I don't like to think of the pyramids in connection with the tram! I like both to think of them and see them from the desert side, ignoring that convenient and rapid mode of transit. But trams and tourists are enough to take the romance out of anything, and it takes a world of Arabs and scarabs and sand of the desert to bring the romance back!

We spent this morning again in the Museum, and this afternoon has been devoted to packing and writing, for we leave here at 8.30 A.M. for Assiut by train, where we shall catch the express-boat " Nefert-Ari " on the Nile. We could sail directly from Cairo, if we preferred, but we saved four days by going from and back by rail — an eight hours' journey, and we were advised to try it by those who have gone before as the chief interest of the Nile begins at Assiut.

On board the " Nefert-Ari," going up the Nile, Feb. 22nd
SUCH a dusty ride as we had! We were sorry we did not choose the longer route by water. And yet it was most interesting, for we passed through the fertile Valley of the Nile, and with the river in sight most of the time we had a little of everything, but especially of sand and dust! We saw all five groups of pyramids, and some of them were very near. As we passed mile after mile of the desert, which somehow looks as if it was still concealing millions of mastabas and smaller pyramids, to

judge from the peculiar way the sand is heaped up in places, it seemed to me that the desert must be one vast necropolis! The contrast of the desert side of the way to that of the Nile Valley was very striking. Fields of tall and waving sugar cane, of blooming white and pink poppies, and large groves of date-palms everywhere, and here and there groups of flowering apricot scenting the air. We passed many queer Egyptian villages and towns with their curious, straight, square, and oblong mud-houses, with never a curve to be seen. Even the palms refuse to bend over here as the cocoanut-palms do in India and Ceylon. Nature and art alike seem to be in sympathy here in Egypt!

For the first hour or more of our journey there were some fine specimens of high-class Egyptians, who were evidently taking some French ladies for a picnic to do the honours of Egypt to them as strangers. One of the ladies was a Comtesse and one a Baronesse, and one of the Egyptians was addressed as " Pasha " by his friends. They were very lively, and one of them had a nimble wit and seemed very much up to date in every way. We reached Assiut duly at 4 P.M., but our boat, which was due at 2.30, had not arrived and did not get there till 7 P.M. Meanwhile, having deposited our luggage on the little wharf owned by Cook (who likewise owns the Nile, apparently), we took some tea on board a Cook's tourist boat lying at the wharf by courtesy of its manager. Then we took a carriage and a dragoman and drove through the quaint bazaars of Assiut accompanied by an English woman who was stranded like ourselves. Such a sunset as there was! A veritable symphony in flame, golden sand, and palm trees, and added onto that a crescent moon in an azure sky. The boat arrived in time to give us dinner, which was well, for we were fairly famished, no provision for food being made by the railway company, on the way. We have a sizable stateroom, and the boat seems comfortable. It is quite full, and our fellow Nilers are a good sort. We shall sleep without rocking tonight!

February 23rd

THIS express-boat has one advantage over the more pretentious " tourist-boat " in that it stops at a number of way stations to take on natives and freight. The scenery of the river is constantly varying. For a mile or so it may be flat and full of sand bars, then there may loom up massive cliffs and headlands which look as though they were the result of ages and ages of sand drifts and sand storms. We experienced one of these today by way of excitement, and I was glad we were on the water and not in the desert.

When we stopped at Manshieh at noon today some men natives came on board with scarabs and all sorts of curiosities found by them at Abydos — some few genuine ones but most of them false. Thanks to Dr. Reisner I think I can tell the difference nine times out of ten but it is great fun bargaining with them. All the passengers take a hand at it. We spent some of our time munching or sucking sugar cane today. All the time we were in India where sugar cane is in evidence everywhere, I never tasted it because the vendors always looked so dirty, and, after skinning it and cutting it into small pieces, they allowed the flies to swarm on it. But yesterday, in Assiut I saw some which was not skinned, and which looked very fine. I said to our dragoman, " Get me some," whereupon he brought two huge sticks as large as fishing poles, with the foliage on top. So today I have been breaking it up in sections and treating our fellow-passen-

gers. Apparently I have started a passion for it, for at
the last station each party bought a stick for themselves.
I also amused myself by throwing pieces of it to some of
the many young Arabs on the wharf, who were clamouring for bakshish, and they grew so wild with excitement and danced about so violently that at last one of
the ship's servants turned the hose on them! You should
have seen them scamper up the sand banks looking like
wet hens, and kicking up clouds of sand and dust as they
ran! Only one small boy remained, and he, having discovered that the hose proved a cool and convenient
shower bath, simply revelled in it, and scrubbed his face
while he was being showered, until the hose operator became discouraged and stopped the stream. These Arabs
amuse me tremendously. They are full of the devil, and
very humorous.

Here comes another sand storm! And there, on the
other side of the river, is a beauteous plantation of large,
white poppies, extending for at least half a mile, I should
think. I had no idea that Egypt took such a large hand
in the production of opium. There is also a small, cres-
cent-shaped sand bar in the middle of the stream, and
on it six large cranes are disporting themselves. A few
minutes ago a whole flock of vultures were crowding
each other out on the river bank, fighting over the car-
case of some dead beast, I suppose.

February 24th
TODAY, at half past one, we landed at Denderah, where
we took to donkeys and trotted off to the great Temple
of Hathos, about half an hour's ride from the river bank.
It is not one of the very oldest — it dates back, they say,
to the later Ptolemies only, being built in the 1st century B.C., but it occupies the site of an older edifice,

going back traditionally to the earliest periods of Egyptian history. As one enters and stands among its massive and ornate columns, no one can fail to be impressed with its wonderful majesty. When one contemplates such a temple it seems as if all ideas of true magnificence and grandeur had disappeared from the face of the earth, except as preserved in these ancient monuments! The reliefs on the balustrades, the sculptured ornamentations on the ceiling, and the reliefs and paintings in the crypts are in a wonderful state of preservation, and to any one who can read the hieroglyphics reveal their history with perfect clearness. The temple is surrounded with mountains of *débris,* under which all sorts of interesting things are buried, amongst others a large Coptic church and a temple of Isis.

Of course all that the tourist has time for, is a passing glance at these extraordinary relics, but even that passing glance forms an epoch in one's life, and the impression stays.

On our way there and back we were importuned by the usual scores of beggars, scarab-vendors, and saucy young Arabs, some of whom had stripped themselves naked and donned a belt of green clover round the waist and a wreath of it round the head for our especial benefit, in which *al fresco* costume they capered about wildly, and demanded bakshish. My donkey was large and white, and bore the un-Arabian name of Minne-haha, doubtless out of deference to the American invasion. My donkey-man, Abbu, spoke some English, and was therefore quite patronizing when I made use of the few Arabic words I have acquired for convenience sake.

We returned to our boat in time for afternoon tea, and now we are off again and under way for Thebes — now called Luxor, which we shall reach tomorrow morning at eight, and where we are to stay four days to see the sights which are various and famous. We shall have to work hard to do them justice. Then we have booked on another of Cook's boats for Assuan and the First Cataract.

Luxor Hotel, Feb. 25th, 1904

WE BADE good bye to our little steamboat and landed here this morning at 8.30. The hotel is only a few steps from the landing, and is charmingly situated, fronting on the Nile, and backing on to a beautiful garden. As soon as we had settled ourselves in our pleasant apartment, we took a guide and told him to arrange our sightseeing for us so as to let us get in everything of importance before Sunday, when we continue up the Nile. So he conducted us at once to the Luxor Temple, which stands right opposite the garden gate.

It is a wonderful ruin, and has had its vicissitudes. Among other things, a large, roofless court had become so choked up with mud and *débris* that an Arab village had been actually built over it, its inhabitants having no idea that they were on top of some of the most massive and magnificent pillars in the world. What a contrast that squalid village must have been to the buried splendour below, and what a colossal work it must have been to unearth it! It is full of representations referring to the campaign of Rameses II against the Hittites, and it is adorned with a large number of colossal statues of that great personage. There are colonnades, sanctuaries, a bathhouse, a splendid obelisk, and many other grand things to be seen within its walls. One sanctuary, dedicated to Alexander the Great, and practically rebuilt by him, was hardly defaced at all in the inside, the stone reliefs being in a remarkable state of preservation.

On a ridge, above the columns of the temple, there

sat, in front of a private house, a large group of women, robed in black and wailing lustily. I asked the guide what it all meant. He said there had been a funeral yesterday, and these were friends who had come to wail out of respect for the deceased — that this group would be shortly succeeded by another and yet another. This afternoon we are to explore the more distant ruins of the Temple of Karnak — the excavation of which was undertaken at a comparatively recent date — about six years ago.

Luxor, Upper Egypt, Hotel Luxor, Feb. 25th, 1904

THIS afternoon we started off on donkeys to the great Temple of Karnak. After riding for three-quarters of an hour we passed the headless pedestals of a large number of Sphinxes, leading to the granite portal of Philadelphus — a sort of prelude to what was to come, for there were two more avenues of Sphinxes farther on in a better state of preservation, remarkable and weird to behold. The climax of it all is the great Temple of Ammon, approaching the portal of which is yet another row of Sphinxes, erected by Rameses II. On referring to the history of the Temple of Amen, I find that it was not built but evolved, as any number of the rulers of Egypt of different periods had a hack at it. Most of the Pharaohs had a finger in the pie, also Thothmes I and III. Amenophis III, Sethos I, and Rameses I, II, and III. However, the result was certainly magnificent, as each one sought to improve on the other, or outvie with his predecessor. The effect of it is imposing beyond words!

Moreover, as one views this vast array of huge columns, one also feels a reverence for the spirit of science that has caused them to be uncovered at such a colossal expenditure of time, energy, and money. There are two splendid obelisks, one of Sethos II, the largest in the world. Rameses III is almost as much in evidence here as Rameses II is at the Temple of Luxor, which we visited this morning. There were colossal statues of him everywhere. Adjoining were a number of smaller temples dedicated to various ladies and gentlemen, such as Osiris and Opet, Mut, Rameses III, and Khonsu. It would take volumes to describe it all, and months of study to prepare oneself for doing so. We remained there about a couple of hours, and then our guide seemed determined to get us away, rather hurrying us past some of the minor temples and the sacred Lake of Karnak.

The true inwardness of Abdallah's little game became apparent when he announced to us that some native races were to take place at five, at the Sporting Club grounds, and that we must not fail to see them. I also noticed that my donkey, a tall, strong beast, had a tendency to break from a steady trot into a brisk gallop of its own accord. This also explained itself when I found that both Abdallah and my donkey were entered for the races! Do you know, it was quite interesting to see these native sports? Besides the dragomen's and donkey boys' race, there were camel and buffalo races, and horse races, too. It was indeed very novel to see camels, which are always pictured as loping along, disporting themselves in full gallop! And those great, unwieldy buffaloes! As racers they are unthinkable!

There was also a sack race, by some Bishareens, a curious, black race of men, with long, corkscrew curls behind and a topknot in front. They ended with a tug of war, crew of Rameses the Great v. Luxor. Luxor, personified by Cook's Arabs, won of course. It was really amusing, and I am rather glad the wily Abdallah succeeded in trapping us.

Luxor: The Chans Temple

February 26th

THE PROGRAMME for today was to explore Ancient Thebes — or at least some part of it. Our objective this morning was the Tombs of the Kings, which were famous even in olden times. I had always associated Thebes with Greece and not with Egypt, but it seems that besides the one in Greece and this one, there is also one in Asia Minor.

We had first to be ferried across the river; then we took to donkeys, and plunged into deep sand for five or ten minutes, after which we had to walk our donkeys through an arm of the river, which wasn't as bad as it sounds. After a mile or two of long, dusty, but decent roads, we came up to the Libyan hills, and entered a pass which wound in and out and up and down, in a most interesting and enchanting way. The hills include all sorts of queerly shaped cliffs — all equally of a rich yellow, which look wondrous against the azure sky, and every now and then you are deceived into thinking that you have come upon defaced monuments of Colossi and Sphinxes, and you think you detect a resemblance to one of the Rameses; but you are mistaken. It is simply the natural but weird formation of the cliffs, which, having grown up in the company of these gentlemen, have taken on some of their shapes and characteristics. You see, even cliffs cannot associate forever with Sphinxes, mummies, and Colossi without imitating some of their ways.

I shall always remember that long ride through the Libyan range as one of the most poetic things we have experienced. The solitariness of it! The colour of it! There was enough breeze to temper the burning rays of an African sun, so that we suffered no real discomfort except that of backache, which the donkey provided. At last we came to the series of large openings in the cliffs which constitute the Tombs of the Kings. There are forty-one of these tombs which have been opened, but only five or six of them are visited by any except specialists in Egyptology. We went down into three of them, and that was all we had the strength for.

We began with that of Sethos I, 1350 B.C., descending into the bowels of the earth, at least 900 feet, by means of steep, granite steps, with here and there an iron or wooden staircase added by the government. It was like descending into a mine, and, when we reached the bottom, it was so suffocating that I was afraid for a moment that I was going to feel faint, which would have been awkward, to say the least! Every step of the way there was something to hold the eye, every inch of the walls being richly decorated with reliefs, finely coloured, all of which represented incidents in the life of Sethos, mixed up with religious symbols.

One is impressed, however, much more with the elaborateness of Egyptian decorations, whether of temples or tombs, than with their beauty. The conceptions are without the ghost of any poetry, there is no attempt at idealization — on the contrary, everything is barbarously realistic. What strikes one is the massiveness, the ponderousness of all their structures, but one misses the lines of beauty which are always present in the Grecian and Roman designs. I should not say that the ancient Egyptians were an artistic people. Far from it! I should say that with them a sense of the beautiful, as such, was an unknown quantity.

But to return to the tomb of Sethos I. It is a marvel of interest and of vastness. Corridor after corridor, hall after hall, chamber after chamber — there are at least fourteen of them, and all to shelter one mummy! It is

almost impossible to take in the fact that all this structure was cut out of the bowels of the earth. I wonder how
the decorators of old found light enough down there to do
their work. We, who penetrate into its depths just to
take a look at it, would be in danger of breaking our
necks, over and over again, were it not for the electric
lights furnished by the government, which are indeed a
boon.

After exploring the tomb of Sethos we descended into
that of Amenophis II (1400 B.C.), which was not quite
so far down. This last was interesting chiefly because
part of its contents had been left on the spot. In the crypt
stands the sandstone sarcophagus of the King, containing a mummy-shaped coffin with the body of Amenophis
II wrapped in its shroud, and still adorned with garlands.
A bright electric light, with a reflector placed above the
head of the body, brought out the blackened features
with startling distinctness, and it made one feel queer
to think that we were looking on the actual remains of a
king who lived and breathed and built his own tomb
1400 B.C.

In a chamber on one side of the crypt lie three other
mummies — of a man, a woman, and a child. How I wish
that they would leave some of these tombs and temples
just as they find them, instead of carting off all the por-
table monuments to museums, which are already well
enough stocked with such things. It would add a thousand fold to their interest. As it is, all we see at the end
of our pilgrimages is the outer shell of all these, and our
imagination has to supply the rest.

[*Note by* H. M. R. " What a commentary on the auda-
cious spirit of investigation that will neither respect
tomb, nor temple, corpse nor crypt, nor the wishes of the
king, who could once command. Now none so poor to do

him reverence. It is startling and interesting beyond mere morbidness to descend into the bowels of the earth, the walls adorned with the story of the king, perhaps, and the paintings as fresh as if done yesterday; the figures in relief or in intaglio; and down, down, we go, over bridges and through halls, and at last reach the crypt, where the king was to rest forever and forever, so that his body would continue secure and undecayed, and ready to join with his other parts — his image, his double, and what may be called his soul — in the great hereafter; and to feel, that, despite all his precautions, we, nearly thirty-five hundred years later, are looking down upon that five feet eight or ten inches of what was a king — *the* king of that tomb.

" It is not like seeing a mummy in a museum, which without its environment is only a mummy. It is a revelation of the ancient religion, the ancient custom of the time founded on that religion, and you come into the dazzling light of the sun awe-stricken and sobered, and with your heart too full to speak. Waiving the feeling that you are a desecrator of the wishes of the dead, you have a conviction that it was well for you to see this, that you might comprehend how vast is the proportion of influence that religious thought and religious observance have had upon humanity and how every race in its own time and in its own way has sought a resurrection from the dead. It makes one very humble and very charitable, for who shall say, ' I alone am right; I alone am the *only* way.' "]

The other tomb we visited was that of Rameses VI. After this we trudged up to the top of a high hill, too steep to ride the donkeys, where there is a fine view of the plains and surrounding hills, but it hardly repaid us for the fatigue of the climb. On coming down at the other side of the hill, where we were met by our beasts, we found ourselves in front of Cook's " rest house," where we lunched.

It is all very well for us to laugh at Cook for " owning the Nile," but we owe a great many creature-comforts to his enterprise, and he has made many things possible which we would not dare to attempt without the pioneer work that he has done. As we sat in the comfortable little rest house, at long tables covered with clean cloths, eating good cold chicken and tongue, eggs, cheese, sardines, fruit, and excellent Turkish coffee, in company with fifty or sixty other explorers of ancient Thebes, all as hungry as we were, I could not help thinking that Cook deserved a vote of thanks!

After lunch we visited a few temples, and after that we gradually wended our way back over that great necropolis, literally riddled with graves, from numbers of which the mummies have been removed, the holes in the sands and cliffs left gaping wide. We are to come over to Thebes again tomorrow to see the Colossi of Memnon (which we already got a glimpse of today in the distance), and some of the other famous ruins. To see Thebes thoroughly, one ought to pitch one's tent on the west side of the river, up near the site of the ancient city, and stay there a week or ten days. One could then hope to get some clear idea of the lay of the land without half killing oneself with fatigue. We did over fourteen miles of donkey riding today as one item. But there is so much to be seen, and it seems such a shame not to try to see everything even if it kills!

February 27th
ANOTHER day of Thebes has just about finished us up. I ache from turret to foundation! It was much hotter today, for there was no breeze to temper the intense

heat of the sun, and somehow I could not throw myself into the spirit of Thebes with the same amount of enthusiasm as I did yesterday. The Colossi of Memnon are curiously impressive in their alone-ness. They are all that remains of the gateway leading to the great Temple of Amenophis III. Everything else has crumbled away, and these gigantic statues alone keep guard. They are utterly defaced, but somehow you *feel* the majesty of them — perhaps all the more because of the imagination as you gaze at them.

We went all over the Temple of Amenophis itself — what remains of it, that is to say. It must have been very grand and imposing in the days when all the columns and gates between it and the Colossi were standing. A visit to the Ramesseum, a large temple built by Rameses II, and dedicated to Amen, ended our work for the day. I say " work " advisedly, for there is nothing that takes it out of one more than this kind of sight-seeing, and the utter hopelessness of being able to take it all in, or remember half that one has seen, makes it all the harder, for there enters an element of discouragement. I think my tired body is speaking when I say this, for I certainly have had the keenest pleasure in all I have seen up to today, but the vastness of the ruined city and necropolis has been too much for me — in two days!

[*Note by* H. M. R. " Everywhere the people on donkeys; or driving donkeys, loaded with fodder, which swamps the donkeys with envelopment; or leading or riding or driving camels, singly or in strings of two to a dozen, all loaded or burdened in some way; and here and there mounted men on horseback, looking, in their turbans and flowing robes, like Schreyer's paintings.

EGYPT: The Assuan Dam

Everywhere the colors are dark hued, as a whole —
dark blue, dark or black robes, with white or colored
turbans, or with the red fez; a white vest undergarment
often shows, but, as compared to India, there is not a
tithe of the glory and bewildering sensation of color
we have revelled in in Ceylon and India, to say nothing
of other parts. It is fascinating here but with a difference. Here you know you are in Egypt.

" This Egypt is so old and it looks it! Your mind
quite naturally accepts 5000 B.C., and then you know
that some monument may have been 6000 B.C. just as
well as 5000. It is a venerable and hoary Egypt, kept
young by the Nile, which renews it and re-makes it year
by year and wipes out the old and brings in the new."]

S. S. " Amenartas," Feb. 28th, 1904
HERE we are on the Nile once more, bound for Assuan,
which I think will be the limit of our journey. We
thought that we might take another steamer, starting
from the other side of the First Cataract at Assuan, and
go as far as the Second Cataract, which would take us
into the Soudan, but we are beginning to fear that it is
too late in the season to do it with reasonable comfort
on account of the heat, which, of course, increases in
proportion the nearer we approach South Africa. So it
may be as well to put in the time at some cooler clime.
Besides, when we shall have seen Philae, Elephantine,
and the other sights of which Assuan is headquarters,
I think that, unless we call a halt on exploring antiquities, our brains will be in ruins also! It is very hot today,
even on the water, and the Libyan hills are shrouded
in haze.

We came on board at about eleven, but did not start
till after lunch. Our stay at Luxor was very pleasant,

and we were made most comfortable at the hotel, which is admirably kept. Our windows looked out on a beautiful garden filled with oleanders, hibiscus, and roses abloom, besides tamarisks, acacias, and the inevitable date palm — and such a concert of birds of all kinds as we had to gladden our ears! By the way, it always interests me to see the way in which birds take possession of ruins. Every crack and crevice, every hole chiselled by explorers, has its little nest, and is made alive again. Such a chirping and twittering as pervades the stillness!

February 29th
THIS morning our boat moored at Edfu, affording us a couple of hours to visit a fine temple dedicated to Hathos, which took 180 years to build. It was begun in the reign of Ptolemy III, 237 B.C. and finished 57 B.C., so, you see, it is really modern for Egypt! Also this temple had a town on the top of it, and it had to be dug out. It is really quite magnificent in its way, the massive columns being particularly interesting because they are of various designs — some with the lotus pattern, others with the date palm, and again others with the talipot palm, which breaks the heavy monotony of them. The pylons are covered with battle scenes as usual, and the same kind of symbolic designs pervade the whole that one finds in all the temples and tombs. It is a ripping hot day! The farther south we go, the less I want to go to the Second Cataract and the Soudan! I pity some English officers, fellow passengers, who have got to go up to Khartum.

The scenery just at this part of the river is enchanting and full of interest. The Libyan hills are always with us in the near or far distance, and here, for the first time, the water is Nile green! Harry and I have been sitting in the bow in reclining chairs for the last two hours, indulging in the dolce-ist of *dolce far niente*. We reach Assuan tomorrow early.

Grand Hotel, Assuan, March 1st, 1904

HERE we are at the southern limit of Egypt proper, and in the neighbourhood of the First Cataract. We landed this morning after breakfast, but we had to wait till eleven before rooms could be assigned to us, there is such a crowd here, and such a perpetual going and coming as the different boats arrive and depart. We spent the time in walking about the native bazaar, where most of the things for sale are made of beads and shells — Bishareen work, which is distinctly barbaric-African. One finds also many things from the Soudan and Abyssinia, roughly made of crocodile skin, bowls and drums of decorated gourds. Tourists ride through the streets on camels and donkeys, trying hard to look at home and unconcerned on the former. I think I must try one myself!

We like our rooms here. They look out directly on a palm garden, where there are magnificent roses and other flowers also, and to the right we look out on the Nile and its high sand-hills and rocks. The river here is very narrow as it approaches the Cataract. A few miles below it was enormously wide — over two miles across, I should say. We ran into Alice Longfellow today. She is here with a Miss Curtis of Boston.

March 2nd

THIS morning we awoke to a high wind and a regular desert sand-storm, so all idea of excursions must be abandoned for the present. Some of our fellow travellers

who must leave Assuan tomorrow are going to attempt
the trip to Philae, but I pity them, and, moreover, I
think they will come back without seeing it, for there
is nothing to be seen save clouds of sand on a day like
this. This sort of thing seems out of keeping with such
a heavenly climate, where the thermometer registers
something between 80 and 90 all the time, and where,
in spite of it, you do not suffer from heat on account
of the extreme dryness of the atmosphere. The date
palms in front of my window are just beginning to throw
out their large tufts of pith-like blossoms, which later
yield fruit. They are certainly very handsome!

March 3rd

WE HAVE just returned from an excursion to the Island
of Elephantine and some wonderful ancient rock-tombs,
bringing with us as much sand of the desert as my shoes
would conveniently hold. We made it in company
with three charming Englishwomen, with whom we
have struck up a traveller's acquaintance. We look
towards the fertile and palmy Island of Elephantine
from our windows here. We hired a pleasure boat for
the trip, which sailed when the wind was not agin' us,
and was rowed by six Arabs when it was. These boys
were very amusing, and sang all sorts of Arab refrains,
while they were pulling, in lusty tones. Mrs. and Miss
Swan, two of our friends, took with them a tin strainer
and a dustpan for their use in sifting and scraping down
the sand when they were going to hunt for mummy
beads in the waste heaps near some of the minor tombs,
and these gay Arabs used these domestic implements
for musical instruments very effectively when the oars
were still. One of the small boys danced for us also.

Talking of singing, a fellow traveller from the North

of Ireland, of a slightly full-blooded habit, having been thrown twice from his donkey on consecutive excursions, concluded that he would be carried to the sights of Thebes in a chair. The six Arabs who bore him delighted him by singing snatches of wild tunes nearly all the way, and one refrain was repeated so often that he caught the words of it. Later on he asked a native the meaning of the sentence which he had got by heart, and was told in reply that it meant, " Heavy devil, heavy devil! " This was indeed making music out of misery!

But to return to our excursion — the tombs were well worth a visit, going back to 4000 B.C., and hewn out of the solid, sandstone rock. The inside of them were rows of massive columns, also cut out of the solid rock. There were curious decorations in colour — the best being in the tomb of Sarengrut, and every now and then we stumbled up against human bones. All the mummies had been carried away long since, and how these bones came to be there I don't know. We had, on landing, to ascend a high cliff to get to the entrance of the tombs, but the tombs themselves were level with the plateau of rock in which they were cut, so we did not have to descend into the bowels of the earth after our mount, as at Thebes. The Swans, who had visited the tombs before, remained outside hunting for mummy beads while we and a Miss Rantoul explored. We then took to the boat again, and sailed all around the island, stopping to take a look at the famous Nilometer, a sort of well which marks the greatest, least, and mean risings of the Nile; for the water in the well and in the river rises and subsides simultaneously. The rock scenery all round Elephantine and Kitchener's Island adjoining is most weirdly picturesque. It was dark when we got back, and it all looked so wonderful in the evening light.

This morning we walked up to a Bishareen camp in the outskirts of the desert. This African tribe lives far off in the desert, but, during the tourist season, from November to March, they come to the neighbourhood of Assuan to sell their camels and other cattle, and their curious, barbaric, bead ornaments, knives, and sheaths of crocodile skin and gazelle horns.

They are a curious-looking people, immensely tall as a rule, jet black, and naked to the waist. They wear their back hair long and braided into about a hundred little fine braids like string, and at the forehead a wisp of shorter hair standing up straight, like the topknot of a Poland hen. Near the camp there was an Arab cemetery, and after going through that we visited a Soudanese village and an Arab village. The last two were much less squalid than the Bishareen camp, where all the cleanliness and the respectability was kept up by the camels exclusively. It is borne in upon me day by day that there is no Egypt except what lies on the banks of the Nile — all the rest is desert and *débris!* You can imagine nothing more unattractive or uglier than the little villages you come across from time to time in the desert, whether they are Nubian, Arab, or Soudanese. There is absolutely no picturesque element, as such, to be found in them — the lines are all straight, and a village looks like a heap of large packing-cases turned upside down, only made of mud instead of wood, the one redeeming feature being the groups of palm trees which are often present.

We went over to the Cataract Hotel yesterday to see the Morrills — friends from Boston. It is a charming hotel — one of the best in the world Dr. Morrill says,

PHILAE: The Western Colonnade

though it is not quite so central as this one, and any one staying there must have much more regard for dress than here, which is quite an item when one's wardrobe is as utterly depleted as mine. Therefore we did not allow ourselves to be persuaded into changing our quarters. If, however, we do go up to the Second Cataract, the idea of which we have rather taken up again, we shall sample it on our return to Assuan, as it will only be for a couple of days, and I can stand even frills for two days.

March 4th

WE HAD a most superb day for our excursion to Philae and the Barrage and Cataract — the great sight of Assuan, which we left to the last. Philae is an island situated at the head of the First Cataract, about six miles south of Assuan. It was regarded by the ancients as a very holy island, and in one of the old inscriptions it is called " the Interior of Heaven." Its history is interesting, for, after the original shrine of Osiris at Abydos had fallen to decay, Philae became the principal place for the worship of Tais and Osiris, and headquarters for grand ceremonies, and also something of the nature of a miracle play to which crowds used to flock from far and near. The play was a representation of the death and mutilation of the body of Osiris, the gathering up of the scattered limbs, the reconstruction of the body of Tais, and its revivification by means of the words of power taught her by Thoth.

We started on our excursion this morning at 9.30 by train, to avoid the fatigue of crossing the desert both ways on donkeys. Arrived at Shellâl in about a half an hour, we took to a pleasure boat which our dragoman had engaged beforehand for us. We were just about to push off for Philae when there arrived on the scene an excitable little woman who could speak not a work of any language but French. She was trying in vain to make the boatmen understand that she wanted to know the price of the trip round Philae and to the Barrage. We took pity upon her, and told her she might come into our boat on a basis of three in a boat instead of one, for which they would have charged her six shillings. She was very grateful, and grew quite confidential. We soon found that she had made no provision for luncheon (which one must take with one on this trip), and had no permits to enter the temples on the island. In fact, she was doing Egypt by the grace of God, and, with tight purse strings, half starving herself in cheap hotels, and walking long distances to save the hire of donkeys and other modes of conveyance. We thought she showed good pluck to travel alone in Egypt, and get into rows with the clamouring Arabs and Nubians, without being able to make them understand a word! We shared our luncheon and our guide with her, and she had a good time for once anyway. So fortune favours the brave!

But what can I say of Philae and its extraordinary *entourage* that would give any one the least idea of it! I know that after reading, and having various descriptions of it, I had not the remotest idea of it as it really appeared. Imagine a large body of blue water, looking like a lake after a flood, and out of it, at short intervals, appearing the tops of palm trees, or rather the heads and shoulders of whole groves of them, which seem to take kindly to living up to their necks in water; large masses of queer and massive formations of stone cropping up everywhere, and, in the midst of all this, the Temple of Osiris, what is left of it, looming up out of the water. Near it, its colonnades of pillars, more than half sunken in the flood, and a kiosk, the outer shell of which is in a good state of preservation still. Very visible signs of as much more of temple-gates, colonnades, courts, and sanctuaries under water as those which still loom up are also noticeable. We had to be rowed in and out of the temple courts and gates and through the colonnades of magnificent pillars. Only on the main portion of the Temple of Isis were we able to land and inspect the interior, mounting some stone steps to the top, whence we had a fine and comprehensive view of the half-engulfed ruins.

It is indeed impossible mentally to reconstruct the whole, but I tried violently to picture what it was like in the days when it was thronged with people to witness the old miracle plays. What a shame that such interesting ruins should be doomed to perish utterly! For doomed they are, I fear, although the irrigating engineers, who had charge of the construction of the dam, optimistically declare that the foundations of all the main buildings go down to bed rock, and that there is consequently almost as great a depth of masonry below the ground as above it, thus reducing the artistic calamity to a partial submersion instead of a total destruction. It is curious to consider that if at any moment they would open wide the gates of the dam, and let the pent-up waters of the Nile flow back into its old stony bed, the Island of Philae, with all its remains, would once more be exposed in its entirety. As it is, what the tourist at present can see of it is because, during the winter season, to quiet us, they open partially some of the water gates to allow enough of the flood to run off to permit us to see what we now see. During the summer, I am told, they shut the gates again, and the Island is entirely submerged.

Afterwards we were rowed to the naughty dam itself, which, prejudice apart, is a marvelous and a unique feat of engineering. We landed on its steps and mounted on its massive, granite walls, looking out on the bed of what used to be the Cataract, where all the water was wasted which now is used for irrigating lands beyond the reach of cultivation, and which in that way adds between two and three millions of pounds sterling to the wealth of Egypt. Of course it is nearly always a question of expediency versus sentiment, and the former invariably gains the day. Perhaps very properly so! For, after all, when one considers that millions of half-starved Arabs and Nubians, to say nothing of other races, are provided with employment and a chance of future prosperity (ten thousand of them were employed on the work of the Barrage alone) because now their soil is rendered productive, you begin to feel that perhaps human lives ought to count as against columns of stone, particularly in a country where there are so many of them, and where B.C. temples are as thick as blackberries!

On the top of the dam which bridges the river bed is a little hand-trolley on which we were pushed across to the west bank, where there is a navigation canal with four locks. On that side is also the Island of Bigeh — the "Senemet" of the Egyptian texts, on which stand ancient buildings of the Ptolemaic and Roman periods. Within the ruins of a Ptolemaic temple there lies a little Nubian hamlet, and behind the temple there are two headless, seated statues, one of Amenophis I and the other of Thothmes III.

We took our luncheon at the little rest house, in full view of the canal, the Barrage, the rapids, and the river bed — which was once all rapids and cataract, but which now consists of tiny islands composed of polished, black, granite boulders, round and about which flow the streams of water, liberated by the sluices, quietly and harmlessly enough, though quite close up to the sluices from which there is a powerful fall of water. The rapids are quite lively and rampageous. The scene is strikingly unique, as the eye wanders from the rugged bed of the cataract across the gigantic dam (the largest in the world) to the calm, blue waters which surround and also partly submerge Philae, the hills which frame the shores on either side being sometimes of golden sand, and sometimes of brown, earth-coloured sandstone; and all this contrasted with a cloudless and azure sky, of a depth peculiar to Egypt.

Harry and I were too full for utterance, but the woman from Geneva was not, more's the pity. She was uneasy in her mind as to whether she would be able to get a donkey at Shellâl to take her over the desert — six miles — back to Assuan, she having made no provision for that either. If she asked me once how much a donkey would cost, she asked me twenty times — also to point out the exact spot on the other side where we expected to find them. We took to the little trolley again, and were pushed over to the place where the asses were in waiting, and then followed a most exciting canter over the desert. Our beasts sneezed violently at intervals of about a half a minute, their poor noses being all full of sand, and with each sneeze they threatened to shake us off their backs. Their legs were sore, and they stopped now and again to put their heads down and rub the flies off, which also was fatal to equilibrium, and the harnesses were all worn out, broken and tied in rough knots — yet we enjoyed the ride and thought it great fun!

We dismounted once, on coming to a famous granite quarry where there lies a huge, undetached obelisk, measuring 92 feet in length, which never fulfilled its destiny. Many blocks of granite lay there also, just where the old stone cutters had left them when the work stopped. They had a way of finishing their blocks on three sides before they were detached, and statues, sarcophagi, obelisks, etc., used to be roughly worked over by the stone cutters in the quarries in order to lessen the weight for transport. In the south quarry there are still more rough-hewn sculptures ready for removal, amongst others the unfinished colossus of a King, a large, quadrangular block, intended probably for the shrine of a God, and, higher up, a figure of Osiris (which the natives call Rameses) about twenty feet in height. Is it not a weird experience to find in a quarry these unborn works of art!

After leaving the quarry we passed by some Arab cemeteries in the desert. Each grave was marked by a rectangle of stones and a slab bearing an inscription. There were also some small, domed erections, tombs of richer people. On a hill to the left of the road were some large cenotaphs of famous saints, like Shêkh Mahmud and Shêkh Ali, which looked like mosques. We also passed a Greek cemetery, which was enclosed within walls. The rest of our ride, on leaving the desert behind, lay through Bedouin villages and narrow lanes, then came the river front, the shelter and rest of our comfortable hotel. It has been a full day, though not especially a fatiguing one, and this will be our last excursion from Assuan — a goodly climax! We have decided, after all, to continue our journey up the Nile to the Second Cataract, and take a look at the great Temple of Rameses II at Abou Simbel. The heat here has not been such as to scare us, and we may as well do the Nile thoroughly while we are at it.

March 5th

WE HAVE taken today for lying off, writing, and loafing. After lunch we strolled over to the Cataract Hotel to say *Au revoir* to the Morrills. There we had a little talk with Fred Stimson and his young wife. They are staying at Assuan on account of his health. The tourists' boat " Rameses " has just arrived, and our Parsee friends, the Petits from Bombay, are on board, so I'm just going down to see them, as we ourselves leave to-morrow morning at nine. We have to make a half hour's journey by rail to Shellâl to take the boat at the other side of the Cataract. As the company do not wish to be let in for the expense of making use of the canal, they keep the boats running between Assuan and the Soudan at Shellâl above the Cataract.

S. S. " Abbas," on the Nile, between the First and
[Second Cataracts, March 6, 1904

WE ARE now sailing between the shores of Ethiopia or Nubia, having left Shellâl, where our train landed us, at 10.30. The scenery is the most interesting we have yet passed on the Nile. We are still under the rule of the great Barrage, and the numerous groves of date-palms and Düm palms, with their huge bunches of nuts, are still half under water, appearing like gigantic water-plants. The shores on both sides of the river are framed in high and eccentric looking cliffs and rocks which look as if they were the result of some great upheaval, interspersed with ridges of bright, golden sand. Here, there, and everywhere, nestling at the base of the cliffs, are queer little Nubian villages, and near them always a patch of wheat, the green of which is more intense than any I have seen — perhaps by contrast with the yellow cliffs. It is still only a little more than a foot high, although the ear is already formed.

We have an agreeable little party on board, only sixteen of us in all. Amongst them are Rider Haggard (who is evidently taking notes for " copy ") and his fresh-looking daughter, who wields the camera. We are only half acquainted as yet, but they seem very pleasant people. They are travelling in company with some English people named Findlay. Opposite us at table sit Madame la Comtesse Reincourt and her son, the Vicomte de Reincourt. They often speak Greek together, but they also speak both French and English.

After lunch we landed at Kalâbshah to visit two interesting temples, the first, " Bet elwalî " (the house of the Saint), which is a rock-hewn temple, made to commemorate the victories of Rameses II over the Ethiopians. There are some admirably executed sculptures on the walls, and I was at once struck by the difference in design between these and those of the pure Egyptian style. They are much less conventionalized, much freer and more true to nature, and the Ethiopian type is at once recognized.

The other temple, one of the largest in Nubia, considered as a *ruin* is a perfect success. Such a wreck I have never beheld! But there were many interesting features. You should have seen the queer procession of Ethiopians, men, women, and children, who accompanied us. One tall chap with a long coat of many colours, all of quilted cotton, carrying a long spear upright, preceded us in triumph, and about thirty other natives of both sexes, some of the children without a rag on them, brought up the rear. They all came armed with the

" family jewels," some of which they hoped to sell to us for a fortune. There were silver rings and medallions of queer workmanship, and some of gold, very crudely and roughly wrought; they also brought us bunches of the fruit of the Düm palm, and chains of shells and beads strung together with narrow strips of gazelle skin, and necklaces of onyx and carnelian. We are to be landed again at six P.M. to do another temple.

The temple is done! And it was well worth doing and climbing a sandy cliff to do. It was the Rock Temple of Gerf-Husên, called by the Egyptians the "House of Ptah." I found it curiously impressive, supported as it is on columns consisting of colossal statues of Rameses II in the guise of a God under various titles. There are also four recesses, each with the king standing between two deities. This particular temple is quite unlike anything we have seen before. We are now in the land of Cush, and situated on the tropic of Cancer — 24° north of the equator. We are supposed to be able to see the constellation of the Southern Cross from now onward. We are to be dragged out tomorrow before breakfast to see more ruins!

March 7th

WE WERE roused this morning at half past seven to visit the Temple of Dakkeh, which was only a half an hour's journey from the last station where our vessel was moored during the night. It was not bad fun to climb up the high bank of golden sand and clamber over the fallen stones and *débris* of the temple courts; but, *per se,* really the temple was not especially worth the trouble, inasmuch as it had nothing to distinguish it from numbers of others, and would never be likely to stand out in one's memory. We mounted to the top of the pylon, and there we got a fine view of the desert and the strange, black, volcanic mountains that crop up from out of its yellow bed. A group of queer Nubian children were dancing and jumping to a wild, barbaric refrain which they shouted out in shrill tones for our benefit, in hopes of bakshish. Each one had in hand a few beads or a scarab for sale. The fresh, keen air of the early morning was invigorating, and we returned to the ship with a good appetite for breakfast.

At twelve they landed us again at a temple named Wâdi Sabûa, half buried in sand. Its name, which means " The Valley of Lions," was given on account of the dromos of sixteen sphinxes which led up to the temple, and of which only a few remain — ominous and solitary. There are also two colossal statues of the usual Rameses the Great, in a state of dissolution. One lies prone, the torso entirely buried in the sand, and only the gigantic feet and legs visible. These remains of the temple are interesting also from the fact that it was used at one time for Christian worship, which is shown by the figure of a Christian saint holding a key, and an inscription on either side telling that it is meant for Peter the Apostle.

The scenery we have passed through today has been a surprise to us. Range upon range of quite high mountains have been before us, behind us, or to the right of us nearly all the time, and every bend in the winding, expanding, and contracting river has given us a new and magnificent vista. The river banks, fringed with palms, acacias, and gum trees, form a bright contrast in colour to the black and grey volcanic, cone-shaped mountains beyond.

We have had some interesting talks already with the Vicomte de Reincourt and his mother, who, I find, are

Greeks. They are cultivated and intellectual people. I am getting from the Countess all the information I can about Greece and the Grecians of the present day, and it is a subject on which she waxes eloquent!

The sailors are having some songs and dancing all to themselves down on the lower deck. They are repeating the same measure over and over again with no variation — they have already done it over a hundred times, beating time with a tom-tom and clapping of hands, — I must really go and see them do it!

I found a double row of Nubians, with their shining, white teeth, sitting there and keeping up their monotonous refrain with great animation and obvious enjoyment. The dance was peculiar — jumping backwards and forwards with feet tight together. Miss Haggard attempted to imitate it and promptly fell down!

We reached Korosko at about tea-time, and our boat will be moored there for the night. This used to be the point of departure, from the earliest times, for merchants going to the Sudan, and there is a caravan route across to North Africa. Our dragoman persuaded us to climb Mount Korosko, which is close to the river banks, or rather, there is only a little Nubian village between the bank and it. The view on top is very comprehensive, and what a scene of dreary desolation the wide expanse of desert presents, studded in all directions with barren, volcanic hills and mountains, and never a blade of grass to be seen anywhere except on looking in the opposite direction towards the river! We saw clearly the caravan road at Khartum over which Gordon passed.

One of the ship boys brought some chameleons up to us which some one had just caught, and we have been playing with the beautiful little reptiles. I had no idea they were so large or that they had such big heads —

some that were shown me at the Chicago Exposition, caught in Florida, looked just like tiny lizards; these are six times as large, and rather lumbering in their movements. We have seen no crocodiles yet, though we are liable to run onto one at any moment from now forward.

March 8th

THIS morning I was awake in time to see the sunrise at Korosko from my stateroom window. Oh, the beautiful, soft glow, setting fire to the desert and changing it into molten gold! I wish I could have been standing at the top of the mountain instead of at my window! Last evening, when we were at the top, the sun aggravatingly refused to perform the setting act for us — maybe the audience was not large enough to make it worth while.

We stopped again at eight A.M. at Omâda and visited the temple, which is almost buried in the ever-shifting sand of the desert. We could barely crawl into the different sanctuaries, the space between the top of the entrance and what is now the floor of sand being only enough for a body *couchant* or " crouchant." It was nothing very remarkable after all. Since breakfast today we have not landed again, but we have passed several ruins which stood close to the river banks. First, the ruined castle of Garanok — a Byzantine structure. Later on we passed by a ruined fort on the top of a high cliff, named Kasr Ibrim, dating from Roman times. In the west slope of the Castle-hill are five memorial recesses of the Middle Empire; they are difficult of access, however, and tourists do not attempt them. Behind the fort you see other hills, crowned with the tombs of Shêkhs.

I am so glad that we came on this trip to the Second
Cataract, for I have to confess that, independently of
its great climax, Abou Simbel, the Nubian scenery, from
Shellâl onwards, has been much grander and much
more varied than that of Egypt proper as seen from the
Nile. The colouring is also more remarkable, for Nubia,
which means " Golden Land," is well named indeed.
I never saw anything so gorgeous as the avalanches of
sand between the black and purple granite cliffs and
mountains! We are to reach Abou Simbel at four this
afternoon, and we are wild with excitement at the anticipation of beholding this — one of the greatest sights
of the world.

March 8th
It is always a satisfaction to see, without disappointment, some famous thing that has been lauded to the
skies long and loud by all writers. This satisfaction we
have had. There is no disappointment in Abou Simbel.
It is truly one of the wonders of the world — this temple of giants hewn out of, into, and through the solid
rock! No matter how many pictures you may have seen
of the four seated Colossi, which form the façade, you
get a big surprise when you actually behold them — I
had almost said — in the flesh! These four colossal por-
trait-statues of the usual and inevitable Rameses, which
confront you as your boat turns a corner in the river, sit
sixty-five feet high, independent of their pedestals of
massive rock. When you are dealing with dimensions
like these; a nose three and a half feet long, a mouth
three feet wide, and so on, it seems a marvel that such
a face should possess sensitiveness or refinement, and
yet one of these Colossi — the best preserved one —
has precisely these qualities.

When you have gazed as long as you can at the remarkable exterior, more surprises await you in the interior. Eight huge figures of Rameses, four on each side, support the roof of the first large hall. These are thirty feet high, and represent Rameses impersonating Osiris, one of his favourite habits. There can have been no end to the self-adoration of that ancient and honourable person! He certainly was Rameses the Great, not to say Divine in his own estimation, and he was never tired of seeing his image multiplied, deified, colossified. Here in these caryatides, he not only supports the temple, but also the mountain out of which it is hewn. His beloved wife, Nefert-Ari, is continually represented in all the reliefs, as doing homage or worshipping him as a god, and the little quasi-lifesized figures of the wife, reaching barely up to the knees of the colossal Rameses, give a very significant symbol of the relative importance of the sexes in the estimation of these ancients!

We went through the eight chambers, studying carefully all the reliefs, and lingered in the inner sanctuary which was so constructed that it should be illuminated by the rays of the rising sun, so that the four figures in the recess — of Ptah, Amen, Ra, and Rameses deified, should stand out clearly to those within in spite of their long distance from the daylight. Of course I need hardly say that we were all of us up before sunrise this morning to see this phenomenon, several of our fellow passengers armed with both long exposure and short exposure cameras. It was worth while, however, to curtail our slumbers only to see the early morning glow light up and vitalize the four great colossi of Rameses on the *façade* of the rock temple.

We also took the opportunity to visit the smaller temple of Abou Simbel which Rameses condescendingly dedicated to his wife, Nefert-Ari. The cliff in which it is hewn is a little to the right of the Great Temple, and a huge avalanche of golden sand lies in between the two. That is the same sand which, but a few short years ago, enveloped the entire temple, and choked up the inside even to the Holy of Holies, and which daily, hourly encroaches and would swallow it up again but for the vigilance that is fighting it with shovels unceasingly.

Our boat has been moored here since four o'clock yesterday, and now we are starting again (it is ten A.M.). We have just turned the corner and seen the last of the mammoth statues in profile, leaving behind a pretty island of sand and an embankment bordered with delicate mimosa-acacias, laden at one and the same time with their pretty, round, feathery yellow blossoms and their curious, bead-like pods, like baby tamarinds. You know the saying *Vedi Napoli e poi mori*. I must paraphrase it with, " See Abou Simbel and then go home! " But we are not going home this minute. We are under way for Wâdi Halfah, the limit of our journey up the Nile, after which we turn back on our tracks.

[*Note by* H. M. R. " The *past* in temples and statues and tombs; the *present* in the exquisite Nile Valley, in the warm breezes, the cheering, God-given sunshine, the flowers, and all that Nature says of her obliviousness of time and decay and ruins and tombs, for she is her own, ever fresh and manifest Today. My heart belongs to *today*, I am sure. I do not think, excepting by reflection, I live much in the buried, or exhumed past. It is interesting, absorbing, and most stimulating intellectually, but I am not of it. I belong to the gods — of today. The *Sun* God especially and always first, for sunshine is to me the life-giving and soul-producing necessity of being. I wonder if I was originally a sun or fire worshipper! Perhaps in some other incarnation I was a Persian and a follower of Zoroaster. At any rate, I instinctively worship the Sun, or the creator back of it.

" And how I do revel in these climates and countries of warmth and of daily and hourly sunshine. Here it is not warm, but distinctly cool, even chilly mornings and evenings, on the river. An overcoat is almost always with me, on or off, as the case may be. In the direct rays of the sun there is heat, of course, but at this season a north-north-west wind is blowing for months at a time, with greater or lesser strength. It is always refreshing, never enervating. This climate of Egypt is a thing to be remembered — not especially at Cairo, but say at Assuan. At Cairo there seems to me a chilly feeling often. In Ceylon, in India and Egypt, they have the weather I like in the months say from November (in Egypt) December (Ceylon, India) to April."]

On the Nile, approaching the Second Cataract, S. S.
[" Prince Abbas," March 9th, 1904
THE scenery continues to be grand and of a beauty entirely its own on either side of the desert — vast, relentless, unconquerable! And out of its golden waves, standing up straight and black, great excrescences which look like pyramids artificially constructed, but which really are mountains, stripped to the bone or bed rock by the wind perpetually sweeping over the desert, and carrying away every particle of soil and sand which at some time formed a casing to their bare bones. The shapes of these rocks are not all pyramidal; there are other and most eccentric forms, some looking like great domes with huge knobs on top. Then there is always the exquisite green border of wheat, lupins, lentils, castor-

oil plants, or cotton, and a fringe of palm trees, interspersed with tamarisks and mimosas, by way of strong contrast. As I look over the broad expanse of desert and queer crags such a strong desire seizes me to wander out over it on a camel, without thought of the passage of time, that I think there must be a drop of Bedouin blood lurking about in my veins! Or it may be simply a microbe!

We are now in the Soudan, having just passed the boundary line, marked by an iron bar stuck into the top of a mound. Opposite is another Roman fort. The hour is twelve. We are to reach Wâdi Halfah at three P.M. — that being the extreme limit of travel on the Nile, which is not navigable, except by a small pleasure boat, beyond that point. We are to remain over night at Wâdi Halfah, and make an early excursion to the Second Cataract tomorrow morning, which will take five hours, two of which will be spent in a small sailboat, and the other three on donkeys. It will be too late to undertake this today, as it would be dark long before our return.

March 10th
ON OUR arrival at Wâdi Halfah yesterday we landed at once and strolled about the town after Harry had been to the telegraph office to dispatch a cable. It is a clean little town with not a great deal of character, because European influence is felt there very strongly. One good result, however, is that you are not surrounded and pestered for bakshish as you are everywhere else! It is a curious fact that the first crocodile we have seen this trip was lying at the corner of one of the streets, its monstrous old hulk stuffed with straw, and another small one was hanging up in a shop for sale! It is not at

all hot here, much to our surprise. We are fortunate in having a persistent north wind with us, which makes it very comfortable.

Not being satisfied that we had seen enough that was truly African in the town proper, Harry and I wandered off in the direction of the desert to a Soudanese village of the usual little square and oblong mud dwellings, which look so sad and dreary, and are only redeemed from unsightliness by a luxuriant grove of palm trees. Near it there was a pathetically poor native graveyard — not fenced in, simply an acre of desert, casually set apart for the dead, and most of the graves marked by just a jagged piece of stone of no particular shape, and by a crude trellis, moulded rudely out of dried mud. We also came upon a village, or camp, of Berberines, their cattle in shelters made entirely of sheaths of straw. That, at least, looked African enough to suit us! We have had a reinforcement of passengers. Thirteen new ones, just arrived by train from Khartum, came on board last night, and two of the original sixteen left us.

We rose at six this morning and took an early breakfast at 7 A.M. There was a splendid breeze, and our sail carried us along right briskly, and though we grounded twice on sand banks, we got off easily again with help from the oars. When we had sailed about two miles up the river we landed on the opposite bank and took to donkeys. Then came a canter over the desert, keeping the river always in sight, until, after a ride of an hour and a half, we reached the Rock of Abusir, which we mounted to get the most extensive view of the Second Cataract. There was no more of a real, bounding cataract to be seen at that point than at Shellâl, where the water is held up by the dam; but the river bed is even more curiously interesting with its smooth, black rocks and boulders, forming little islands round which the stream winds in and out. Interspersed with these black, smooth-stoned islands are varied stretches of sand-banks which, for some reason unknown, are white, forming a most vivid contrast both with the black islands and the sand of the desert beyond the banks, which is of a bright golden colour. Half a dozen natives were lying in wait for us to perform the feat of " shooting the rapids," not in boats but floating in inflated pigskins — the same kind that they carry water in. The rapids were not very violent, the water in the Nile being too low at this season for anything very exciting in that direction, but they performed their little trick very well and earned their bakshish.

After remaining on the top of the rock till we had taken it all in, and until our hats and every rag we had on was in danger of being blown off, so strong was the wind up there, our dragoman called to us to mount our steeds and take to the desert again. It was most exhilarating — that ride back — with the wind in our faces, and I really enjoyed it so much that three hours of it did not seem enough! I had a capital donkey this time, and when an Egyptian donkey is good, he is very, very good, and you can have just as good a gallop on him as on any horse. One of our party, Mrs. Findlay, was thrown by hers, but not hurt. He stumbled and fell, and she went over his head, but the sand was soft and she was fat, so it came out all right.

Of course I need hardly say that on our way back to the boats we had to stop and see a ruined temple! But six miles of desert without a ruin would be a rarity in this region! When we returned to the boats, the wind was against us, but the current was with us, so we dispensed both with sail and oars for the first mile and were towed along by six of our boatmen, who ran along the shore and pulled a rope to which our boat was tied, just as they did once on the Ganges. For the second mile we had to depend on the oars only, as we were in midstream. We reached the " Prince Abbas " in time for lunch and as hungry as hunters, and all of us agreed that the excursion had been delightful! We had the satisfaction of feeling, moreover, that we had done full justice to the Nile, and left nothing unseen which was supposed to be worth seeing. Nay, more, we had been told that the Second Cataract at this season was not worth the exertion of a five hours' excursion, yet we braced up and went. A few of our fellow passengers struck and would not attempt it.

After lunch, Harry, Mr. and Mrs. Mellor, and I sallied forth once more into the town to make a few Soudan purchases. None of us bought a stuffed crocodile, but we contented ourselves with some amber beads and silver amulets which we bought hot, as it were, from the hands of the maker. We started on our homeward journey down the Nile, at three P.M., reaching Abou Simbel again at seven. After dinner, when the dessert is brought in, it is the custom of our dragoman to walk into the dining room and announce the sight-seeing programme for the morrow. This evening he said, " Those who wish to see the Southern Cross will be called between three and four A.M. if they will give me the number of their staterooms. I gave my number, so I shall be there! As we leave Abou Simbel at 7 A.M. it is my intention to get up again at sunrise and take a last, loving look at those alluring Colossi over there in the Rock.

March 11th
WE WERE not called at three after all. It seems that the last quarter of the moon was shining so brightly that

the Southern Cross was not visible in the heavens, therefore the dragoman argued wisely that it was folly to disturb our slumbers for nothing. Harry and I got up at sunrise, however, and paid a last visit to the rock-temple, which looked stupendous in the early morning light. It was also good to be there *alone*, for we spent about twenty minutes with our stone giants both outside and inside the temple before even Mr. and Mrs. Mellor arrived on the scene, armed with a camera. Then I went back again to bed, our ship having started before seven, and having taken my last look at the point of Rameses' two-foot nose as we rounded the cliff. There were tears in my eyes at the thought that I might never see it again.

At ten o'clock we were landed at Fort Ibrim, the ancient Roman remains which we passed coming up the river. It is mentioned in the Bible, in 2 Kings, I am told, in connection with Tirshakah, the Ethiopian King, and worshipper of Amen. There was a certain patronizing air adopted by Rider Haggard and one or two others because the fort was " only Roman." There is nothing exciting in things A.D. to those who have been wallowing in the B.C. monuments! Yet there was within the fort the remains of a Byzantine chapel which interested me much because a fine, granite column, with the cross on it, had been thrown down right across the threshold of one of the entrances, so that no one could enter without trampling it under foot. We came upon a mummy-pit, where the common soldiers were buried one on top of the other. Rider Haggard insisted on crawling into it, and fishing out a lot of human bones and pieces of skulls and such unsavoury morsels. It is growing warmer as the day grows older. This morning it was quite cold, and the wind was chilly.

March 12th

WE ARRIVED at the end of our route today at one, that is, at Shellâl; but we shall spend the night on the boat, and take the train (one hour) that leaves for Assuan at 8.30 A.M. We have just made one more parting excursion to Philae, which seemed even more piteously under water than when we saw it eight days ago. We passed through Pharaoh's gate in a boat, and were only on *terra firma* in the Temple of Osiris and on the top of the pylon. It is much hotter here than at Wâdi Halfah, which is so much farther south. Our fellow passengers are already beginning to disperse in various directions. Some of them remain on board till tomorrow, like ourselves, and go to the Cataract Hotel to wait for the Tuesday boat for Cairo.

I have just bade adieu to my Greek friends, the Reincourts, with much regret. An intimate friend of theirs, who sat opposite us at table, the editor of a paper in Athens, named Lambrides, was an intimate friend of Mr. Anagnos in Boston.

We did stop at one more temple on our way this morning after all — the Temple of Dendur; but there was very little left of it to tell the tale. We saw a flight of huge pelicans. They were circling down by the water. Some natives shot one, and I saw the wretches hauling the beautiful white thing, all stained with blood, into their boat. Our ship is moored here, right at the elbow of Philae, which we now see by the light of the stars, and which will be our first vision when we rise tomorrow in the glow of the early sun. The more I see of the Island, the more sad I feel at that beautiful colonnade being submerged — the magnificent columns up to their chins in water — and to think what a lot of the Island as well as of the temple buildings lies *quite* submerged and out of sight.

Cataract Hotel, Assuan, March 13th, 1904
WE TOOK the 8.30 train up from Shellâl, and were in Assuan and enquiring for our letters at the post-office by 9.30. When we arrived at the Cataract Hotel we ran right into Boston in full force. There were Solomon Lincoln, Arthur and Frank Beebe, two daughters, Fred Stimson (J. S. of Dale) with wife and daughter, the Morrills, Dana Estes, and several others whom I meet frequently, but whose names I cannot recall. They all seemed glad to see us, and S. Lincoln and Harry went off for a stroll together after lunch. The weather is perfect, neither hot nor cold, full of sunshine and exhilaration. We look out on a very interesting bend of the Nile, where the river is studded with tiny islands and bold rocks. Right opposite is the Island of Elephantine and the famous old Nilometer, and on the opposite shore we see looming up the half-ruined tomb of a Shehk on the top of a high hill, and a liberal supply of ruined gateways and columns on banks of sand and granite boulders. The sand here is not so brightly golden as in Nubia, but it is good to look at, all the same.

March 14th
WE HAVE had a delightful day of *dolce far niente* — our last at Assuan. We have strolled about and enjoyed pleasant talks with our different Boston friends. The Princess Victoria Eugenia and Prince Henry of Battenberg, Princess Beatrice of Saxe Coburg, Prince Leopold, and a half a dozen other members of the royal family are stopping at this hotel. They take their meals in the public dining-room, and are waited on by the regular

Arab waiters just like us common folk. They are in Egypt on account of the delicate health of one of the boys, and Princess Beatrice and suite have been on a trip to the Red Sea from here over the desert on camels, camping out at night for the wonderful air, which is said to be so curative. They all seem to be enjoying it here up to the hilt. They like it because nobody stares at them or molests them in any way, and they feel free to go and do as they please, which I suppose is something of a novelty. Their names and the numbers of their rooms are stuck up on the blackboard in the office of the hotel, just like those of the rest of us, which, I confess, surprised me. However, as far as their appearance goes, no one would ever know them apart from the rest of the English and American guests at the hotel. They look " just as common "! I went up to Alice Longfellow's room this afternoon and sat with her for an hour or so — she is in bed, laid up with a sort of lumbago. We had many things to talk about, as I had not seen her for a long time. We set sail for Cairo tomorrow at noon.

On the Nile, S. S. " Amenartas," Mar. 15th, 1904
WE LEFT Assuan today at noon, with the greatest regret, and now our faces are turned toward Cairo. There are still one or two temples to be seen on our way down the Nile, which we did not stop at on our way up. This afternoon there was the temple at Kom Ombo. They used to worship the crocodile there, and, curiously enough, in poking around, I found in a small chamber the mummies of four crocodiles (for, no doubt you know, that the Egyptians were in the habit of embalming animals as well as ancestors). I have found no mention of these crocodile mummies in any of the books describing the temple, and I cannot think why, unless they have

quite recently been found in some crypt. The ruins of the temple are extremely picturesque. We anchor to-night at Edfu.

March 16th

THE programme for today was the Temple of Knum at Esneh, which they allowed us a half an hour to see this morning. It is also Ptolemaic, with Roman embellishments. The great Hall is reached by descending a long flight of steps, so that you receive the impression of going down into a cellar to see some magnificent columns and mural decorations.

The weather is much cooler today than it was yesterday. It was tremendously hot both when we left Assuan and on the river for several hours afterwards. It is wonderful, however, how much heat one can stand in this country without any feeling of lassitude on account of the extreme dryness of the atmosphere. It certainly is a heavenly climate except in summer. But it is so hard to realize that it is not summer now when one sees the tall lupins in blossom all along the river banks, and oleanders, hybiscus, and all sorts of flowering shrubs covered with blossoms in gardens, to say nothing of poppy fields, and the tall, waving, sugar-cane.

March 17th

THIS is our last day on the Nile, alas! We shall reach Assiut this evening — unless we ground on too many sand banks by the way. As our boat anchors there for the night we shall remain on board until eleven P.M., when it will be time to take the train for Cairo, where we expect to arrive at six A.M. tomorrow. We save a day and a half, in fact nearly two days, by taking the train at Assiut instead of continuing down the Nile to Cairo, and time is an object to us as we may have to sail from Alexandria next Wednesday or Thursday for Constantinople. If it were not for that we should have greatly preferred to remain on the boat. I love it and everything about it! The groups of Arabs squatting about the river banks near the wayside landing stations, the camels standing and lying about with their heads in the air and a sneering expression on their faces, the groups of natives offering chains made of mummy-beads, or B.C. beads, as I call them, and little amulets and clay images picked up in the dump heaps near the tomb excavations, or, I suspect, oftener stolen from tombs which *they* know about and the excavators don't, as yet! They are all natural thieves, and lying is to them as easy as breathing. Yet withal one cannot help liking them for their good humour, their great patience, untiring perseverance, and a certain gentleness which seems to be innate with those who are not brutal, as some of them are.

Then I like to look at these brown-skinned people, who cannot be associated with a black race, but who look only as if the sun had got into their blood. There are some fine, manly types among them, and they carry themselves superbly. I sometimes wonder what, in their hearts, they really think of us apart from the admitted and inevitable fact they regard us as ambulating money bags, to be robbed when possible. Something that Dr. Morrill told us may throw some light upon this. From living for several winters at Assuan he has become familiar with many of the street venders of scarabs and other antiquities (?) who, having discovered that he cannot be cheated, deal more frankly with him than with another. At the beginning of the season he noticed that one of these was loaded up with all sorts of trash — bogus scarabs, rusty nails, glass stoppers, rusty

CAIRO: View of City

tomato-can keys, and every sort of valueless junk. He said to him, " Abdullah, what are you doing with all that rubbish? " The answer was, " Damn fool tourist come soon, buy everything! " I fancy that is about the way they have sized us up! The boys pick up a handful of shapeless stones or pebbles by the wayside and pursue us with cries of " Antiker! antiker! " Still, I am sorry it is nearly over.

We only had a half an hour at Luxor yesterday, but, in spite of the broiling sun, Harry and I went to take a last, loving look at the temple, a few steps from the landing. Such a noble structure as it is, with its superb columns and its colossal statues of Rameses!

[*Note by* H. M. R. " Our journey down has had the pleasant incidents of travel — the visits to two or three temples we did not see on our way up the river; the chats with newly made friends, and the freedom and charm of river travel in this country. The days have been warmer a good deal than when we came up, and I suppose the ' season ' is drawing rapidly to a close. The hotels are sending off their guests, many every week, and have been for some days past, and people turn to Cairo *en route* for England very many of them, and a few linger awhile in Cairo and at Naples.

" The stars are out in their glory, and every evening we get fine sunset effects, and, as the afterglow continues, the palms on the banks of the river and the men on the shore, pumping the water from the river to irrigate the fields, just as they did it *thousands* of years ago. Occasionally you see oxen or a camel turning a wheel and drawing up the revolving buckets which empty themselves into long channels, which, when filled, are cut open, and irrigate the fields. This pumping from the river to the high banks and then sending the water over the fields is a most laborious process. Perhaps it may be described thus:

" Imagine three wells of ' the old oaken bucket ' kind, with a bucket at one end of a long pole, and a stone at the other end. These wells are arranged from the bank of the river to the river itself, in three steps, as it were; the lowest bucket takes from the river and is emptied into well No. 3, from which it is drawn by pole and bucket 2 to well No. 2; and then pole No. 2 draws it to the bank and empties it into long, trough-like cuts in the earth, channels, which conduct all over the fields.

" The men wear only a clout, and they hoist from the river some two or three tons of water a day. This is the way of it: from river to 3; from 3 to 2; from 2 to 1. It makes you ache to see it done all day and every day and all along the Nile. Sometimes a revolving wheel with continuous buckets is placed over the river, and a camel or oxen go round and round, drawing up the water. The oxen are often blindfolded to prevent their getting dizzy."]

Hotel d'Angleterre, Cairo, Mar. 18th, 1904
WE REACHED Cairo at about eight A.M., instead of six, as I thought, and found two connecting rooms ready for us at this comfortable hotel, which we like a great deal better than Shepheard's. We did not feel in the mood for any sight-seeing today, so we strolled about in the Muski, which is the chief thoroughfare of Cairo, and which strikes the most intensely Oriental key note in the city, with its bazaars, furnished with curiosities, precious stones, and wares from every country of the Orient.

They have a curious custom here of offering hospitality to their purchasers in the more important shops. We went into one to look at some embroideries and Nubian veils, and were at once invited to partake of Turkish coffee. When we declined, on the plea that we had just taken some after lunch, we were offered tea, Turkish Delight, cigarettes, and finally, in despair, perfumes — attar of roses, oil of sandal-wood, and Egyptian violets. The old Arab seemed quite distressed that we did not partake freely of his good things. I think the Muski is, on the whole, one of the most fascinating places I ever was in! I should like to have been there with Mrs. Hearst, who *buys* everything. The bargaining would have been truly exciting!

March 19*th*

THIS morning we started off on an excursion to the ancient city of Memphis, or all that is left of it from the inroads of the Nile. The ruins look dreary enough, and the principal mosque is scarcely more than a heap of stones, with fragments of Rameses lying about here and there. It is almost impossible to imagine how great a city it was because all the stones from the ruined buildings have been carried away to be utilized elsewhere. What remains is a squalid looking little place, the houses of which are of bricks, made of Nile mud and sundried. Near Memphis, in a palm grove, lies a colossal statue of the same old Rameses on a slight elevation, a curious and impressive sight. There was also another colossal statue of Rameses II, unfinished, concealed in a mud hut, where they have erected a platform above it that you may look down on it and examine the form and features.

The next on the programme was the Necropolis of Memphis, the extent of which was the only thing that made it possible to conceive the size and importance of the ancient city. We then explored three remarkable mausoleums, one of Mera, a gentleman farmer of 5000 years ago. To judge from the regal dimensions and decorations of the different chambers one must conclude that farming paid better 5000 years ago than it does in our own time! It was immensely interesting to follow the different incidents in the life of this ancient gentleman as recorded in the mural decorations of the different chambers. The tomb of Thi, royal counsellor B.C. 3500, was scarcely less interesting, but somewhat on the same lines as that of Mera. Then we visited the remarkable Serapeum or Apis mausoleum, where all the sacred bulls that lived in Memphis were interred. I shouldn't dare to say how many acres it covers. The part of it which is open to the public contains sixty-four vaults, excavated on either side of a gallery of enormous length, each one intended to receive a huge, granite sarcophagus. Twenty-four of the sarcophagi still remain in position, and they are immense. One of them, of polished, black granite, beautifully wrought, was simply magnificent.

After visiting the tombs we went to the house of Mariette, the famous excavator, and devoured there the contents of a well-supplied lunch basket, after which we mounted our fiery steeds again and rode for two hours more across the desert, bringing up at Gizeh, in front of the Sphinx, just as the sun was sinking. After riding on donkeys for three hours and a half it was grateful to throw oneself down on a sand bank in front of the ancient monster. I found him, her, or it, with a more benign expression than before. It seemed to say, " Well, after all, you are no greater fools than the rest of them! " Harry and I then discharged our donkeys and walked all around and about the Sphinx, finally mounting on its back and gathering a handful of petrified lentils of which the stone is full. Near the Sphinx I noticed part of an old Roman wall which had been entirely taken possession of by wild bees. It was literally honeycombed by them, there were millions of them!

But I haven't told you yet of the order of our own going. We drove to the station at ten A.M., took the train (one hour) to Bedreshen, there we hired donkeys and rode over dusty roads and through fields of lupins, Egyptian corn, and lentils, till we reached Memphis — a ride of an hour and a half. Then we visited the Colossi and the different tombs, after which came the long ride over the desert, which gave us near views of all the different sets of pyramids — Dashur, Sakkarah, and the Abusir. While we were dallying with the Sphinx, an insinuating Arab followed me about, whispering sweet words, " Try my camel, very good camel, better than donkey. Lady ride camel very nice ride camel." I felt that I wanted to experience every desert sensation so I yielded, and the next Harry saw of me was perched up on the back of the tall beast and relaxing to the wabbling motion, *en route* for the Mena House, where, on our way to the tram, we were to slake our desert thirst with lemon squashes. I did not find the camel as uncomfortable as I supposed. On level ground it is quite easy going, it was only on descending the somewhat steep slope from Gizeh to the Mena House that there came a little strain. I have now ridden on donkeys, camels, and — bicycles! We reached home in time to dress for dinner, I must confess however, in my secret soul, that I would rather have gone to bed!

[*Note by* H. M. R. " We wound up our day at the Sphinx — Dorie and I — by climbing on his back, joining hands, facing the setting sun, and asking him, her, it, if there were any news or any messages to be sent to Boston, and a *quick* answer would not only turn away wrath, but was absolutely necessary, as *our* time was limited, whatever his, hers, its might be. We feel now as if we had done our duty. What the Sphinx *told us* will forever remain a dead secret.

" I may mention, however, this fact, which like to the juror's question in the trial of Mr. Pickwick, may be *important*. Dorie descended from the Sphinx and immediately thereafter mounted into the saddle of a kneeling camel, on which she rode in triumphal state to the Mena House. I saw her talking to a venerable, turbaned Arab, and what the Sphinx had told us may have been translated by the Arab; then came the camel episode, and, like all other Egyptologists, I am brooding over the significance of the *hidden* meanings.

" You do laugh a little in Egypt over the tremendous importance attached to *everything* here, and to see how the Arabs play up to the wants of the tourists. One of them up the Nile tried to sell a *sardine box opener* as an antique, ' Very, vareeey, older, antiqua, gooder, chee-eeper — only ten seeleengs! ' When we were up the Nile, and they wanted me to buy some scarabei, made probably within a week as ' anteequaas,' I said, ' I don't *want* old things. I want *new* scarabs; the kind they make at Luxor. You know the man there, very good workman, sells *eight* for a piastre (5 cents) ! ' They used to *grin* at me. They are quick to respond, and one evening some of the new scarabs were *sent* for — these rascals are born actors, — and were offered as the *new* kind; you could not tell them from the ' antequaas ' these fellows were offering, and probably they were out of the same *bin*.

" I had a crowd around me one afternoon at Korosko

offering ' anteequaas.' I took one, looked at it, said
' Made at Luxor — you know man — good workman —
makes it so,' and I rolled imaginary mud, marked it,
and then I took the scarab offered me and *buried* it in
the dust, and then began to poke around and *found* it,
and yelled with joy, 'Anteeeequaa! ' They watched the
whole thing, and then joined in a chorus of laughter,
and escorted me to the boat.

" There is a constant succession of ' discoveries ' like
Mr. Pickwick's ' BILST — UM — PSHI — S.M. — ARK,'
over which the ignorant ponder and the wise men
smile, mingled with an immense amount of the real
thing, the value of which can hardly be overestimated as
a contribution to the knowledge of the world."]

March 20th

THIS morning I took for lying off as I was feeling a bit
stiff and tired after yesterday's exploits. We are affected
by the extreme sultriness of the weather. We spent the
afternoon in the Gizeh Museum, where everything has
acquired a new significance since our journey up the
Nile. I still think it a mistake that some of the hundreds
of mummies and sarcophagi, that are there in super-
fluity, were not left in the tombs where they belonged.
It would add so much to the interest of the tombs themselves, and give to these a significance which we have
to supply by imagination.

Late in the afternoon we went for a long drive in the
Shubra, which an enthusiastic writer about Egypt had
called the " Champs Elysées of Cairo." It was a great
disappointment, however, for all we found was an interminable avenue of acacias and banyans and an absolutely uninteresting country, and, instead of the vaunted
hundreds of equipages of the aristocracy of Cairo, we

only met one solitary carriage containing some much deceived tourists like ourselves. Tomorrow we are going to spend the day with the Reisners at their camp at Gizeh.

March 22nd

WE SPENT a delightful day with the Reisners yesterday. Their kindness and hospitality were unbounded. We were taken to see the more recent excavations, and it was astounding how much had been accomplished since we were there about a month ago. There are many disappointments, however, to the archeologist who undertakes such work here in Egypt, for it often happens that, after weeks of labour spent in digging out a fine tomb which promises everything, they find that it has already been rifled in the past, perhaps centuries ago, and all the treasures carried off, nothing being left but the bare walls, which, while the decorations of these are truly of much historic interest, they do not furnish material for one who, like Mrs. Hearst, is trying to furnish a museum with rare things. However, on the whole, Dr. Reisner has had good luck, both here and at the Necropolis at Gizeh, farther up the Nile, for he has found a number of tombs still sealed up and untouched — just as they were left.

Dr. R. took us for a walk across the rocky plateau on which his camp is built, and showed us a place where we looked out onto the boundless desert of huge sand-waves resembling a yellow sea in a storm. The colour of the desert here in lower Egypt does not compare with that of upper Egypt, or Nubia, however, and, on returning thence, one misses the wonderful golden hue of it at first. But you could never imagine how enchanting and varied the flowers of the desert are. The most delicate and exquisite little plants are to be found all over the sands — of brilliant yellow, purple, pink, and white, and, if you pull one up, you find that the roots extend several feet down into the sand, seeking the nearest thing to moisture on some buried stones. The sky was overcast and we had no sunset, neither could we see the pyramids by moonlight, but we had to bid them farewell as we walked past them on our way home by the light of a lantern carried by one of Dr. Reisner's Arabs, who took care that we did not fall into any of the burial pits laid open by his boss. The good doctor and his wife also accompanied us down as far as the tram, and we bade them good bye with true regret.

One grows more fond of the pyramids on a longer acquaintance. They never look the same twice over. They vary so with the light, and the denseness or rarity of the atmosphere. We noticed, moreover, this evening, that both the first and second pyramids are not built even, one side of the triangle being longer than either of the others.

This morning we went to see the fine old mosque of Sultan Hassan, after attending to a lot of necessary business at consulates, etc., incidental to our departure for Turkey on Thursday, so we were riding through the streets for several hours, and we lighted upon some characteristic scenes. There was a wedding procession, or rather the procession of the trousseau, for it consisted of the entire belongings of the bride — beds, chairs, tables, pots and pans, boxes of clothes, rugs and draperies, some of these carried on camels, some on donkeys. The personal valuables, in square cases covered over with purple velvet cloths, richly embroidered in gold, were carried on the heads of much " dressed up " Arabs. These were all going to be put into the house of the couple awaiting their coming.

At the same time, on the other side of the street, there

was a long procession of men chanting in a loud voice and playing on queer instruments. Then came a large, oblong case covered with a striped, camel's hair shawl in gay colours, in which was the body. It was a Mahommedan funeral, and our dragoman said it must be that of a rich man as all that noisy procession had to be paid. At another funeral that we saw was a man on a donkey carrying the body of a child in a small case, similar to the big one, in front of him, and several mourners following on donkeys. That was, I think, the queerest looking funeral procession we have seen!

In the afternoon we drove out again to see the tombs of the Kalifs, which are quite large structures — really mosque tombs, in a city by themselves with regular streets (but such dusty ones!) like any other Oriental cities. It differs from our idea of a cemetery in that there are no trees or flowers or grass, only roads and mausoleums. We entered only two of these, the oldest and finest, that of Kait Bey, and one quite modern one, of today, just to get the contrast, and I must confess that I found the latter very tawdry, though evidently nothing had been spared (except taste) to make it gorgeous and splendid.

After leaving this dusty city of the dead which, while one does not like to leave Cairo without having seen it, does not really fill one's soul, we went to a far more interesting place — to the great mosque of El-Azhar. This old mosque is also used for a university, where ten thousand Arabs are instructed daily in the Koran, its meaning and everything in connection with it, and nothing else except the pure Arabic which the study involves. It was a wonderful sight which met our eyes when we entered (with yellow, Turkish slippers, four sizes too large for us, drawn on over our harmless shoes). In the large, uncovered mosque-court, there were hundreds and hundreds of groups, consisting of youths of all ages from small children up, sitting on the pavement in groups of four or five, some squatting on small mats, and all of them reciting the Koran, either from books or metal sheets, with a page of it engraved thereon. They seemed to be reciting to each other, but I suppose that one of each group was a more advanced scholar than the others, and could correct their mistakes. While reciting they swayed to and fro with their bodies quite rhythmically, exactly as if they were riding camels. Wherever you looked you could see nothing but a multiplication of these groups, in every corner, in every recess of the inside as well as of the outside of the mosque — such a seething mass of young, Arab-scarab, harum-scarum humanity! It was all we could do to thread our way in between them under the guidance of the principal — a dignified old Arab, who escorted us. Some of the boys seemed in earnest and were prostrating themselves, but I am sorry to say that there were many more who were giggling, staring about, and making witty and, as I suppose, saucy remarks at our expense. There were also some few who shamelessly demanded bakshish of us — though not while the eye of the principal was on them! The sight interested us much, and I do wish we could have stayed till prayer time when a dead silence takes the place of all that racket. But no strangers are allowed then.

March 23rd
OUR last day in Cairo! We make an early start tomorrow, at 7.30, and must rise at five. We spent the morning in the Arab Museum, which does not compare with the Egyptian one — the Gizeh.

S. S. " Emperor Nicholas II," Mar. 24th, 1904

WE LEFT Cairo this morning at 7.30 and reached Alexandria after a comfortable journey of four hours. The country on which we looked out *en route* formed a strong contrast with that of Upper Egypt. Here were immense tracts of highly cultivated land, perfectly flat scenery, and no sand. High hedges of cactus standing up conspicuously in many places relieved the monotony of the regularly laid out fields of wheat, millet, lupins, white clover, etc. The only thing of special interest on the road was at Benha, about ten miles from Cairo, where we saw some curious mounds marking the site of the ancient city of Anthribis. I hope you know all about Anthribis — I don't!

We reached Alexandria at about 11.30, and were duly driven through the city on our way to the wharf, the docks being well filled with magnificent steamboats of almost every nationality. The town itself offers no particular attraction except that of cleanliness. It is all modern and commonplace — unthinkably so when you remember all that it was in ancient times. Nothing of interest remains now save Pompey's Pillar. The harbour is fine, however, and, as we steamed out of it, it was worth the price of admission to see the curious effect of the waters of the Nile flowing into the Mediterranean — the Nile water was of the brightest green, known as Nile green, and the sea water was of the most exquisite sky blue I ever saw, just touched here and there with an exquisite opalescence, the lines of the two being as sharply marked as if drawn with alternate green and blue colour by a painter. One gets this same effect on a smaller scale on Lake Geneva, where the temperature of the melting snow-streams, flowing into the lake, produces this difference of colour at certain points.

There was a strong wind yesterday, they tell us, and it was pretty uncomfortable at sea. Today also there is a good stiff breeze, but I think the tendency is for it to go down. We found the Vicomte de Reincourt on board, not as a passenger but to see off Mr. Lambrides, their Greek friend who sat opposite us at table on the " Prince Abbas." Mr. Lambrides and Mr. Nomico, who was quarantined with us at Moses' Well, are the only familiar faces on board, though the ship is quite full. By the way, they say that we have on board some of the officers of the Russian ship that the Japs blew up in the first *coup* of the present campaign. They are returning to Russia on parole.

I have never been on a boat where I feel as little in my element as on this one. None of the ship's servants understand a word of English, and their knowledge of the other languages which some of us speak is very limited. With the Greeks I can get along, as most of them speak some Italian or French, but the Russian contingent is hopeless! Still, I am already enrolled as interpreter general to a number of our fellow passengers. The languages which are spoken on deck by these are principally Greek, German, French, Persian, Arabic, Russian, Hungarian, Polish, Italian, and Spanish! Such a babel you never heard! But no one seems to understand the other fellow, apparently! The Russian hours for meals and the meals themselves are a bit queer. In the early morning — at any time between seven and nine — you can have coffee (served in a glass) and a biscuit, or bread and butter. At 11.30 you get a substantial luncheon; at five P.M. dinner, at half past eight they serve tea. At table all the plates for the full number of courses are placed before each person in a tall heap, the top one being removed at the finish of each course, so, as you eat down into the pile, you get the impression of consuming the crockery as well as the dinner. The table is furnished with a number of bottles of white and red wine — a Russian brand and very good — which is included in your meal, and there is a decanter of vodka also, from which you are expected to help yourself freely. I had the curiosity to taste this stuff, and I think it suggests a mixture of brandy, saki, and caraway seeds. So many people were taken with seasickness, and kept dropping away from table in twos and threes, that Harry and I and a half a dozen young men were all alone in the saloon by six o'clock.

March 25th

THE WIND has quite abated, and the sea has become quiet as it bade fair to do. It is now as smooth as a fish pond, yet our fellow passengers seem still to be laid low in large numbers. A few green and yellow looking faces have appeared from time to time, but quickly disappeared again. I can't for the life of me imagine how they can manage to be sick in weather like this! We land at Piraeus tomorrow morning at eight, and all passengers for Athens will be landed. We shall land also temporarily, as there is a train which runs up to Athens in a half an hour, and as our boat does not leave for Constantinople till twelve it will give us time to look around for an hour or two, and see how we like it.

This afternoon we approached Crete, or Candia, a lovely, curved chain of mountains — as it appeared to us at first. In an hour or so, as we came nearer, we could see that the island is broken up into three natural divisions by mountains. The Lenka, or White Mountains, were pointed out to us on the west, Mount Ida in the middle, and Dicte on the east. There was a slight haze which prevented us from distinguishing the snow on the

Lenka, which Mr. Lambrides assured me was there. Opposite Crete was the Island of Cassus, a rocky island, strongly contrasted to Crete. It is under the sway of Turkey, while Crete is ruled by Prince George, the second son of the King of Greece, though also nominally subject to Turkey. I suppose we shall be passing the islands of the archipelago at intervals until we reach the Piraeus tomorrow. I almost hate to go to bed for I so begrudge missing anything!

March 26th
WE DID not land as soon as we were promised. It was 10.30 before we steamed into the harbour at the Piraeus. The approach was simply enchanting. The beautiful Isles of Greece all along the route, with their soft, undulating mountains, were most alluring; the last one in sight being Aegina and Salamis. The lay of the land at the Piraeus is very attractive, the whole shore line being most interesting. Outside the promontory, close by the sea, was visible the tomb of Themistocles. There is nothing else of ancient interest at the Piraeus; it all looks very new and handsome, but here one also looks towards Athens, where the Acropolis looms up majestic from a distance, and, to the left of it, the Areopagus.

There was quite a familiar look about Athens as it appeared in the near distance — exactly like the pictures I have seen of it. We disembarked, being transferred to a small rowboat with an English, newly married couple named Pryse, who had arranged to join us in our excursion, and in less than eight minutes we were landed on *terra firma*. We walked a short distance to the station and steamed away to Athens in half an hour. Our way lay past the new Phaleron, a great watering place and summer resort of the Athenians, where there is a fine, large hotel. Arrived at the station we hired a carriage by the hour and drove first to the Toman Bank for letters, thence to the hotel restaurant Minerva for lunch, — a very good one, — and afterwards we drove about the city.

I am not going to attempt any description of Athens till we go there to stay, it would not be fair to do so after such a bird's-eye view of things, especially as there must inevitably be a shock at seeing for the first time a modern city, where one had pictured an ancient one with all its historic landmarks. Until one explores the Acropolis one cannot get any idea of the Athens one has read about and constructed in one's mind, and, although it stands up conspicuously as you drive over the Stadium, it looks from underneath only like an interesting, rugged old hill with some ruined Grecian columns on top. In other words, ancient Athens, or what remains of it, is not in evidence. One must go and seek out the old landmarks and piece things together all over again. The Athens that I have constructed for myself and visualized does not exist any more. What one sees in driving around casually is a clean, new, and attractive little town, with a fine palace and museum, regular streets, with houses of a yellowish white symmetrically arranged on either side, the Grecian style of architecture being suggested in all the more important buildings. The shops might be English, Italian, French, or what not. There are some hotels overlooking a neat little square, with a pretty garden of orange trees laden with their golden fruit. It is all very well, but " where is my Athens? " you say to yourself. I think we shall love to be there, all the same, when the time comes. I suppose, if the truth were told, Rome looks even less like Rome today than Athens does like Athens.

At the bank we saw one of the attendants in the real Greek dress, and I need hardly say that our eyes were riveted on him. It was difficult not to imagine that he was just off the stage, with his short, full, ballet skirt, which stuck out straight as does that of a whirling ballet-dancer, and long, flesh-coloured tights up to the middle of the hips where the skirt terminated. It certainly is not a manly dress! I should think, moreover, that his legs would be awfully cold with nothing but cotton tights to protect them, and at this season in Athens there is a " keen and eager air."

We had to take the one o'clock train from Athens back to the Piraeus, and by twenty minutes of two we were on board the " Emperor Nicholas " again, though we did not get under way till nearly three o'clock. On leaving the harbour we have, to the right and the left of us, a constant panorama of beautiful, mountainous islands, all and each one of which one would love to explore if there were only time. We have just passed the Island of Sunium, where the pillars of the ruined Temple of Athens greet us from the top of a high mound or cliff.

March 27th
WE WERE due at Smyrna this morning at nine, but we have been delayed so long at Clazomenae the new quarantine station, where the second deck passengers and their bedding and clothes are being conveyed in rowboats to be fumigated, that I don't see how we can get there till afternoon, especially as this harbour is at least twelve miles in extent. It is surprisingly beautiful! We are nearly surrounded by magnificent high mountains, and the colouring is fine.

Just as I predicted, we did not get up to Smyrna until afternoon — at two o'clock. It is a beautiful sight, with its gay-coloured houses built round the base and on the slopes of the mountains surrounding the bay. Mount Pagus is very prominent, with its fine, old, ruined fortress on top, and the whole effect is extremely attractive.

As soon as we had cast anchor, a whole fleet of tiny rowboats came up, and in a minute we were besieged and almost torn to pieces by their respective boatmen, each one wanting to get the job of landing us at the expense of the other. They fought and fisti-cuffed each other till it was dreadful to behold! We engaged a young man whose boat was below, who spoke English and offered his services as guide through the streets of Smyrna. The other boatmen tried to force us into their boats in turn and did all they could, short of throwing us into the water, to prevent us from reaching the one we had engaged. Meanwhile they brutally attacked our young man, and Harry, whose ire was roused, took the ring leader by the throat and held him fast till we were all safely seated. And all this fury and clamour was for the large price of a franc a head! Such a contrast with the quiet, decent behaviour of the Greeks at Piraeus. These men are brutes!

As the unsympathetic captain refused to give us any definite time to remain on shore, but would only answer the question as to how long the ship would remain at Smyrna with " Until we have landed our stuff," we did not dare to go sight-seeing, or attempt to go up Mount Pagus, but simply wandered about the Turkish, Armenian, and Greek bazaars, where it was gay and entertaining. We were shouted at in a perfect babel of languages by the different merchants to look at their gorgeous embroideries, bead-work, and silks, but as their chief aim seemed to be to find out how far they could cheat and make fools of us, rather than sell their goods, we purchased nothing. We were rowed back to the ship by a quarter to four and then, to our disgust, we remained in port till evening. It was aggravating to think how much more we might have seen of Smyrna if only the captain had been decently considerate. I hate what I have seen of the Russians! They are surly brutes!

In the night we are to stop at Mytilene or Lesbos for freight.

March 28th

WE ARE no longer in the Ægean Sea, but since breakfast-time we have entered the Dardanelles or Hellespont. At the entrance to the Hellespont we passed — in the distance — the Plains of Troy. Soon after we came up to the famous castle of the Dardanelles, erected by Mohammed II — surnamed " The Conqueror." The Asiatic side of the shore is richly wooded, and the mountains green and undulating, while on the European side the rocks and cliffs rise abruptly out of the sea, and are quite yellow and arid. The contrast is curious. We stopped again at Kilid Bahr, Key of the Sea, close by the castles, but only for about twenty minutes. Our way lay later by various spots of historic interest. On the Thracian side of the strait, opposite Nagara Point, is a strip of stony shore projecting from between two high cliffs, and this is where the European extremity of Xerxes' bridge was attached. This is also the part of the Dardanelles where Alexander, under Parmenio, crossed from Europe to Asia; it was here also that Leander used to swim across to visit Hero. You may remember that Byron performed the same feat, but he had to furnish the Hero in his own person by adding an *e*. The little " tekkeh " in which Byron lived is still to be seen. Beyond — on the Asiatic side — is a large white fort, Nagara Kalesi, and at the back of it the high mound Mal Tegseh, where Xerxes surveyed his army and fleet. This was the Acropolis of ancient Abydos, and the Hellespont at this point used to be called the "Straits of Abydos."

We shall soon come to Gallipoli and then out of the straits into the Sea of Marmora. We were due at Constantinople this afternoon, but, owing to the delay at the Clazomenae quarantine, and seeing that, in any case, we could not arrive till after sundown, when no one may land in Turkey, our captain has been saving coal by going at half speed. So we shall not reach our destination till tomorrow morning. What with the customs and other abominations our morning — if not our day — will be spoiled! The weather in these parts is bitterly cold. Somehow it comes upon us as a surprise, and, after our prolonged Oriental trip, it is hard to imagine ourselves in the land of snow again. Yet they tell us that in Constantinople spring is well advanced. It is true we may be feeling the cold more because it is overcast, and very windy. Harry does not like it, though, and more than once has threatened to go back to Cairo and wait there till it is warmer. He won't do it though!

Constantinople, Pera Palace Hotel. Mar. 29th, 1904
OUR SHIP anchored at Constantinople at midnight, so we missed the approach by the Golden Horn, which is supposed to be an impressive sight. I can well imagine it, too, for here at anchor, *in* the Golden Horn, Constantinople presents a most imposing spectacle. As seen from the water-way, it impresses one as the most magnificent of cities — really and truly grandiose, built up, as it is, all in terraces on seven high hills, so that the gorgeously handsome mosques, with their graceful, tall minarets, stand out in startlingly clear relief, instead of being con-

cealed amongst other buildings as in cities built on level
ground, like Cairo. We shall see that fascinating approach, however, when we leave for Piraeus again, as
we have to go out the way we came in.

We were promised the most wonderful blue sky here,
but alas! it is overcast still, and bitterly cold.

We were met on board by one of Cook's agents who
took us and our friends, the Pryses, in tow, and procured
for us an excellent guide when we reached the custom
house, where our luggage, or some of it, was examined as
a mere matter of formality. Our guide who, I think,
must be half Armenian and half English, speaks English
almost like a native. We succeeded with difficulty in
getting a couple of victorias to drive us to our hotel, because the German giant tourist ship, the " Kurfürst,"
has just arrived with 815 tourists on board, who have to
be put through the sights of Constantinople in two days.
The streets were simply blocked with their carriages, and
we had to take to bye-streets and go by a roundabout
route — a serious matter in Constantinople, where the
roads are shockingly bad directly you get off the principal thoroughfares, and none too good even on these. I
was greatly surprised at finding such narrow and unim-
portant looking streets in the business portion of the
city, and also where the principal hotels are. As you see
the city rising so proudly from that beautiful water-
way, the Golden Horn, you expect something quite different. We congratulated ourselves that the 815 tourists board and bunk on their ship, for otherwise we
should not have been able to get shelter in any of the
hotels. As it is we are very comfortably disposed of here
in two rooms on the fifth floor with a magnificent view
of everything. We get the whole sweep of the Pera,
which is the modern, European side of Constantinople,

and also across the Golden Horn to Stamboul, where the old city walls are in evidence with all the finest mosques, the Turkish bazaars, the Sultans' tombs, and the Seraglio. It is reached from the Pera side by two bridges, one old the other new.

One of the first things that one observes on driving through the city is the remarkable number of large dogs in evidence on all sides. They are to be seen everywhere in groups of from five to eight, curled up on the sidewalk, under the curb stone, in the road asleep, and huddled up together for warmth. The breed is a sort of mongrel collie, of all colours from white to black, and some of them very shaggy. These dogs are not owned by any one. They live on the streets and feed on what they pick up. There must be a rich harvest for these scavengers, I should think, for they are all fat and generally seem thoroughly gorged. The guide says they keep strictly to their own beat, and do not allow any other dogs from another district or street to encroach on their domain.

After we had unpacked, and refreshed ourselves with a *déjeuner à la fourchette* at eleven, we and the Pryses started off in two victorias, which we have had to hire by the day while we are here, to see some of the wonders of the city. We drove down hill and up hill and down again, over the new bridge, across to Stamboul, and visited the three most beautiful and representative mosques. First, the Geni Valideh Mosque, built by the mother of Sultan Abdul Aziz. Its peculiar feature is that the walls of the interior are entirely covered with superb Persian tiles. There was a service going on, part of which we witnessed from the women's gallery, through Arabian fretwork screens, to reach which we had to climb up a number of steep, stone passages. The next on the

Constantinople: Shipping in Harbor

programme was the famous Saint Sophia, once a Christian church, now altered over with its face to Mecca, and all the crosses scraped off. It is one of the most splendidly impressive mosques I have seen, and the beauty and splendour of it grow on one every minute. The wonderful curves of the galleries, the fine pillars and arches, the rich mosaic ceilings, and the exquisite prayer rugs — such rugs! All make you look and look again, and stay and stay to look some more. We noticed two huge, white pillars encircled with brass bands near the Holy of Holies, and I asked our guide what they were made of, as I could not make them seem like either marble or alabaster. He answered, " Those are candles which are burnt only at the Ramazan."

When we had been almost forcibly dragged from Saint Sophia, we went to the Ahmed Mosque, famed for being the only one with six minarets. I did not enthuse over the interior, though the exterior is most imposing. I found the decorations somewhat tawdry and the columns too heavy. We then visited several tombs of the Sultans, which are decidedly queer and very unlike any other tombs. Imagine a square or octagonal chamber with from twenty-five to fifty tombs shaped like the ordinary raised mounds in our cemeteries, these being of children of the royal household; and a few others six times as big for the Sultan and a few wives — the Sultan's being the biggest of all. One cannot tell whether the mound-like tomb is of stone or wood or what, as it is entirely covered with embroidered velvet of black and silver or purple and gold. Over this hang costly cashmere scarves of all kinds and colours. The children's tombs are not covered with velvet, but only with striped cashmere.

After visiting several of these family chambers we

refused to see any more, as they were all alike. I am
ashamed to tell you how many things we saw today! It
seems so like cramming! We went to the Hippodrome,
where there were two fine obelisks — one from Egypt,
then to a little museum where specimens of every one of
the old Turkish costumes were shown, draped on
painted figures. Then to the Mosque of the Sacred Pigeons, where, as at the Piazza San Marco, in Venice,
thousands of these birds congregate in the courtyard to
be fed by strangers and the people. Then we went to see
the Serasheriate, or War Office. After that we struck,
and said we wanted to go home!

March 30th

THIS has been a most interesting if not quite as full a
day as yesterday. We spent most of the morning in and
about the old Seraglio and its grounds, most of the buildings on which are the remains of the palaces of former
Sultans. It has a peculiar interest by being so thoroughly
Turkish in character, from the Imperial Gate, Bab-i-
Humayun, outside which the heads of decapitated of-
fenders used to be exposed in niches, to the buildings
where the ladies of the Hareem were lodged, and the
gardens where they played about. The position of Seraglio Point in the landscape is something incomparable!
From it you look up the Bosphorus and towards the
Giant's Mountain, which not only commands a magnificent view of the Black Sea and Bosphorus, but has also
a good share of tradition attached to it.

For instance, it is told that Joshua, the son of Nun,
after settling the Jews in Canaan came to live on the
Bosphorus. He was of such enormous proportions that
he used to amuse himself with standing astride the
straits while ships passed under him. He also used to sit

on the top of the mountain at eventide and bathe his feet
in the waters below — which speaks better for his size
than for the height of the mountain! Yet I assure you
that the mountain looms up very majestic, and is an impressive feature in the land- and sea-scape, regardless
of its tradition. There is also a small mosque and a tomb
on its summit where, it is said, Amycus, King of the
Bebryces, was interred. I suppose that there was no
room for Joshua himself to be buried there, for his remains, or a part of him, are believed to be in the tomb
on Yosha Dagh, or " Joshua's Mountain."

We went into the Alai Kiosk, opposite the entrance
to the Sublime Porte, which is the place where the Sultans used to view the processions of the Esmafs, or trade
guilds, of Constantinople. Near the point, in among the
trees, stands the Column of Theodosius, as they call it,
but I don't think they feel quite sure about it. In the
Court of the Janissaries is the Orta Kapon, where there
are double gates, which, with the room to the right,
formed the chamber where, in the olden times, those
who had lost the favour of the Sultan were executed as
they left the palace. It was by the Orta Kapon that we
entered to see the Treasury, one of the great sights of
Constantinople, which no one may miss who can possibly find a way to get there.

We were fortunate in accomplishing this without any
trouble, thanks to the alertness of our Anglo-Armenian
guide, who, as he was conducting us to the Ottoman Museum this morning, which is very near the old Seraglio,
suddenly found out that a party of people from the
" Kurfürst," armed with the special permit to see
everything obtained from the palace by the " personally
conducting " agent, were just about to enter the Treasury, so he quickly turned our horses' heads about and we

fell in with the procession, which, I am happy to say, did not embrace the entire 815 passengers of the " Kurfürst," but only about fifty of them. I need hardly say that we did not fall in behind but in front, and it looked very much, to an impartial witness, as if we led the procession! I don't know who they thought we were, but certain of the " personally conducted-s " appealed to us for information on various subjects from time to time, as if they thought we had the inside track. One of them actually came up to us and said that some of the officers in charge of the palace (which we visited later) would like to be invited to the ball tonight on board the " Kurfürst," and could we manage to bring it about. We teased Mrs. Pryse about this, because, as she is young and very pretty, we declared that the palace officers wanted to go to the ball because they had cast their eyes on her and supposed her to be one of the " personally conducted " who would be there.

But now for the Treasury. We saw there such wonders of wealth and splendour as can only be imagined in connection with enchanted palaces, and where every step of the way, at every corner, at every individual case of valuables, stood an officer on guard. As we entered, these, fifty or sixty of them, were all ranged at the entrance to receive us. First we were ushered into one of the reception rooms, and there we were served with rose-leaf jelly, which is put in a glass of water and eaten with a spoon, after which you drink the water, unless you prefer to stir it up and make just a drink of it. Then all the chambers and galleries were opened to us. Just to give you some little idea of the kind of things we saw — there was a large throne of beaten gold and inlaid work, set with thousands of precious stones, which used to belong to the Shah of Persia, Ismael, but was

captured in 1514 A.D. by Sultan Selim I. A divan of Turkish inlaid work encrusted with pearls, rubies, and every
kind of gem, over which there hangs an emerald as big
as the palm of your hand. A mirror and toilet table entirely inlaid with flat diamonds; a huge, golden tankard
studded with over 2000 diamonds. Armour, swords, dag-
gers, and shields — all one mass of gems, pearls as big
as pigeon's eggs, rubies as big as door handles. There is
also a collection of the state robes of the Sultans — one
blaze of jewels, and of such wonderful old brocades and
stuffs! Jeweled aigrettes with centres of either enormous diamonds, pearls, emeralds, or rubies, mostly uncut, as seems to have been the custom in the East. In the
belt of one of the Sultans, I forget whether it was a
Mustapha, a Mahmoud, Suliman, Abdu Ahmed, Ibra-
him, or who, there was a knife, the handle of which was
of solid emerald; other knives were of jade, wonderfully
studded with gems. It would be impossible to give any
idea of the hundreds of cups and saucers, plates,
bowls, candlesticks, etc. of jade, onyx, and carnelian,
set with jewels. And, to top off, there were, in one
of the glass cabinets, all huddled up together, dozens
and dozens of long necklaces of large rose pearls, turquoises, and all the aforesaid precious stones, and
three large basins one filled with rough pearls of all
colours and dimensions, another with rubies, and the
other with emeralds, which had been collected during
the reign of the different Sultans and not made use of
— any one of them worth a Jew's ransom!

It was a grand sight, and I am sure it was very good
of those Sultans to spend such fortunes in collecting
these things for us to feast our eyes on, that being apparently the only use they are ever put to at present! We
passed out by an avenue of cypress trees (which seem to

be one of the features of Turkey) across the court to
the Gate of Felicity, where there were certain buildings
only shown to privileged visitors, to wit, the Throne
Room, or Hall of the Divan, built by Suliman, and decorated with five arabesques and *faience*, and the library
where there is a fine collection of illuminated manu-
scripts in Persian, Turkish, Arabic and Greek.

After we had done the Treasury and thoroughly explored the old Seraglio and all that appertains to it,
we took to our carriages and followed the procession
once more to the magnificent palace of the father of the
present Sultan, which stands in a fine garden, entered
by lordly gates which are oppressively ornate. One of
the garden gates opens out on a level with the water-
way, and it is there that the Sultan received illustrious
guests who arrived in ships. We went all over the interior of the palace, even into the Sultan's bathroom. It
was all very gorgeous, but some of the rooms were too
suggestive of the Continental Hotel in Paris for my
taste! I wonder why they don't turn at least a part of
it into a hotel. It would be just the thing to do, for none
of the royal family lives in it now, and it is the custom
for every Sultan to build his own palace and his own
mosque and promptly abandon that of his predecessor.
This monster palace is only used very semi-occasionally
for some big function, where princes from other countries are entertained.

After that we returned to our hotel, chuckling at having seen the show of shows at so small a cost, for you
must know that while it is quite practicable to get a
permit to see the Treasury, etc., it costs not less than
twenty pounds to do so, all of which goes in fees to the
fifty or sixty guards who have to turn out for the occasion. That being so, it becomes expedient either to make

up or join a party of people and divide the cost. As you already know, we did the latter — it was a case of accidental selection!

This afternoon we drove over to Stamboul again to the great Bazaar, where we had to get out and walk through an intricate series of passages lined with stalls of merchants of rugs, embroideries, jewels, curiosities, and ancient arms. The passages are all covered with stone vaulting, decorated in high colours. A large part of it was destroyed by the earthquake of 1894, and has since been restored. Of course, as we walked through, there were the usual supplications to " buy of me, not of him, he is one rascal," " and you are another! " thought we, and we bought of nayther!

March 31st
WE SPENT the greater part of the morning in the Ottoman Museum, or Imperial Museum of Antiquities, which are housed in two buildings which face each other. One of these, the Chinili Kiosk, or Faience Kiosk, so named from the interior decorations, was finished under Mohammed II in 1466, and is a very interesting building. It contains many fine specimens of Greco-Roman sculpture and reliefs, and one room is devoted to Dr. Schliemann's collections from Troy. In the opposite building there were some perfectly magnificent sarcophagi, some of great age, and we found ourselves at home once more in the B.C. centuries. But what a refreshment it was to feast on this beautiful Greco-Roman art after being steeped in the barbaric Indian and crude, stiff, conventional Egyptian product! There was the so-called " Alexander " sarcophagus of Pentelic marble, found at Sidon and in an almost perfect state of preservation, which was one of the most exquisitely beautiful

works of art I have ever seen. Then we took a look at
the Fountain of Ahmed, and the Basilica cistern — the
latter curiously situated on the Place of Saint Sophia.
You enter from the courtyard of a Turkish house, and
descend a number of stone steps, when suddenly you
find yourself in a large chamber with 336 fine stone
columns, about 40 feet high. The floor of this chamber
is covered with water, which keeps bubbling up from
underneath.

The weather still continues unfriendly. We have
hardly seen a bit of blue sky since we have been here.
It is regular, old-fashioned London weather. Poor Harry
has fallen victim to one of his bad Boston colds, with
loss of taste and smell, and no wonder, after jumping
from an Egyptian climate to this! We expected to find
Spring much more advanced here than it is. Many of
the trees are quite bare still, others dressed in tassels
and fringes, and a few willows and small shrubs in green
frocks. The almond trees are in blossom, and, curiously
enough, in the plastering of all the walls about the city,
there is quite a rank growth already of nettles, tansy,
thistles, and weeds of various sorts, and occasionally
one sees a wallflower in full blossom. This seems incongruous, but so it is! I should not like to live here for any
length of time. It is not a sympathetic city. No city is
where there are no temptations to walk about; where
all the distances are great; where everything is up and
down hill, and where everybody lies, but without the
humour and good nature of the Arabs! After one has
seen the sights one has no further use for Constantinople, and certainly one has none for the Turks. Still, we
would not have missed seeing it, even though we might
not care to return here.

March 31st (Evening)

THIS afternoon we made an excursion to Scutari, which lies on the Asia Minor side of the way. It is called a suburb of Constantinople, but, as you see it from the water, it looks like a very large and important city on its own account. It is built on the site of the ancient town of Chrysopolis, and it has much historic interest attached to it. Chryses, son of Agamemnon, was buried there; Xenophon stayed there for seven days on re-treating with the survivors of the " Ten Thousand." Constantine the Great here gained the victory over Licinius, which made him sole ruler of the Roman Em-pire, and we all remember the modern Scutari in con-nection with the Crimean War in 1854. It was chiefly to visit the cemetery, where the thousands of English soldiers who were sacrificed in that war were buried, that we made the excursion; for Scutari offers no special attractions in itself, except Mount Bulgurtu, which rises 850 feet above the sea, and which we were to have mounted for the sake of the superb view of the city, the Bosphorus, the Sea of Marmora, the Valleys of Thrace, and the mountains and valleys of Central Asia Minor. The clouds became so thick, however, that our guide said it would be of no use to go up.

The boat which took us to Scutari landed us there in twenty minutes from Galata Bridge. We took carriages, and were joggled over roads the like of which I have never seen. Why the victorias were not shattered to atoms, or why we were not spilt out again and again, passes my understanding! At the top of the first and very long and steep hill, we stopped at a stuffy little mosque where there was a service of howling dervishes going on, which the Pryses were keen to witness, as they

did not do so when they were in Cairo. It was in some
ways different from the service we saw in Cairo, and,
if anything, more peculiar and queer. It was not conducted in so orderly a way — it was less of a function,
and it seemed to come more from the heart.

The dervishes threw themselves into it with an ear-
nestness and an exaltation which were astounding. When,
at the early part of the service, the Precentor, as we
should call him, chanted from the sacred book, at certain passages they wept, grovelled in the dust, beat their
breasts, sobbed, howled, and groaned. When the time
came for the various throat and chest noises with swaying of the body, several of them were seized with violent
convulsions and could hardly be held. Meanwhile, one
solitary dervish, who kept his overcoat on, took it into
his head to whirl instead of expressing himself in the
other way, and you can imagine nothing more sublimely
ridiculous than to see this serious and intelligent looking person calmly spinning round and round for fifteen
minutes at least, while the groanings, snortings, and convulsions were going on around him!

Towards the latter end of the service (if there ever
is an end, which I doubt), fathers brought their little sick
children into the midst to be healed by the blessing and
laying on of hands of the chief, and they also brought
garments and cloths belonging to the sick ones who
could not be moved for him to touch and blow into. To
see great, strong, burly men kiss the arm and nestle with
their heads close up to the chief to get just a little spark
of holiness from him — peradventure — was really
touching. Our guide tells that at another convent of
howling dervishes here, near Pera, at the close of the
performance the children of the neighbourhood are
made to lie on the floor, when the head dervish walks

CONSTANTINOPLE: Mosque of Hagia Sophia

over their bodies, which is supposed to give them immunity from all the ills of the flesh. This order is of the whirling dervishes, however, and, by the way, I understand that their gyrating dance is meant to represent the planetary system revolving round the sun. It is supposed by some to be a survival of Hindu mysteries.

When we left the poor little half-ruined dome where the dervishes held their service, we mounted farther up the terribly indented hill, passing miles of Turkish cemetery. This one at Scutari is the largest in Constantinople, being the most used of all on account of the Moslem preference for being buried on the side of the water nearest the holy cities of Mecca and Medina. It looks very untidy and tumble-down-y with its thousands of curious long, almost sword-shaped tombstones, all awry, interspersed with avenues and groves of funereal cypress trees.

What a contrast was presented by the English cemetery higher up, where the English soldiers lie! So combed and brushed and so well cared for, and with English lawn daisies all over the mounds. I gathered some of these and a sprig of rosemary in bloom.

Tomorrow we are going to see the Selamik, or Sultan's Procession to the Mosque, which takes place every Friday at noon. It is easy to obtain cards of admission to the visitors' or ambassadors' pavilions in the palace grounds through our Consul or Ambassador, but our guide advises us not to do it, as he says in case of rain you have to stand out in the wet in your best bib and tucker and get soaked through, for you may not put up an umbrella. He says we can see it all just as well from our carriages, where we can remain snugly till the moment arrives, and then mount on the box. Moreover, he says it will surely rain tomorrow.

April 1st

YES, it did rain, it poured! Harry declined to go to the Selamik, and he was right. These things at best are nearly always disappointing. Either you don't see well, or you don't know who anybody is that you do see, and, if you do happen to know who it is that you see, he looks so much like any other common fellow that it doesn't matter!

Of course there were the troops massed round the gates in their gay uniforms, which were wet through, and their movements were of more or less interest. The hour of worship was announced by the muezzin from the minaret of the Hamidied Mosque, at the gates of the grounds of the Yildiz Palace, where the Sultan goes to worship. His coming was announced by a great fanfare of trumpets, and the Turkish national hymn was played. Then came his body guard, and the Sultan himself in a smart victoria, but nothing extraordinary! He had on only the usual red fez, and might have been any common Abdul or Ahmed. After his devotions he drives back to the palace, followed on foot by his high officials, but we did not care to wait three quarters of an hour while he prayed, so we drove off, feeling that we should prefer having some salame better than any more Selamik.

The Pryses and I agreed to go to a famous Turkish restaurant, where Mr. Nomico had told us we must not fail to try some of the real Turkish dishes, cooked in the very best style. As Harry, who loathes messes, and is not gastronomically enterprising, was absent, it seemed a good opportunity to be initiated in foodlings *à la Turque*. So we went to the Tocatlian, and got our dragoman to order for us some representative dishes. Mrs. Pryse and I found them all delicious except the pillou, which we considered rather tame after the succulent dish our own cook prepares at home. But the joke was that Mr. Pryse, who never touches anything with oil in it, had to abstain from nearly all the good things because they were prepared almost uniformly with oil. There were mussels stuffed with heaven knows what all; and rice; and another strange mixture of rice and things, wrapped up in small cabbage leaves and braised; another nameless concoction likewise wrapped up in vine leaves and pickled. Delicious artichokes *en brochette*, with little pieces of meat between; pillou; and some little squares of lamb broiled on a skewer. This last dish saved Mr. Pryse's life, for there was no oil in it! I found Harry very lonesome and forlorn on our return, and, as there was no temptation to go out again in the rain, I made a merit of staying in and devoting myself to him. Mr. Nomico sent me four boxes of delicious Turkish Rahat Locoum or Turkish Delight, filled with nuts. I shall make myself ill with it, but no matter — it is worth it!

April 2nd
IT IS still raining very hard, and blowing too, so it is useless to attempt any sight-seeing today. All we have left to do are some water excursions, which really are the most fascinating of all the things to be done from Constantinople. We want to go up the Golden Horn, or Bay of Constantinople, to the " Sweet Waters of Europe " in the Valley of the river Kedar. We also want to go up the Bosphorus to the Black Sea. But what is the good in such weather?

April 3rd

THIS morning, behold, the sun was shining when I drew the curtains! Our spirits went up accordingly, and visions of the Bosphorus rose up smiling before our mind's eyes. But by the time we had finished breakfast the clouds were in possession again, and a sharp hailstorm was coming down, so we stayed at home. Towards noon, however, the sun made a second attempt to take charge, and this time succeeded, so we took an early lunch, and drove down to the wharf to catch the half past one boat that leaves the Galata Bridge daily for the mouth of the Black Sea.

The trip was delightful, and so interesting! The lay of the land on both sides of the Bosphorus presents fine scenic effects, as it winds about most fascinatingly, the Asiatic side being grander than that of the European side. We stopped at a number of way-stations, but only one of them was on the Asia side. It was curious to have the ship zig-zagging between Asia Minor and Europe, which, when you are on the Bosphorus, are only eight minutes distance from each other, because one always thinks of Europe and Asia as being oceans apart. Soon after we left the Bay of Constantinople we had a splendid view of Brusa and Mount Olympus, with its two peaks covered with snow. It is a beautiful mountain! A great many people make an excursion to Brusa and ascend Mount Olympus, which is over 7000 feet high, but we had such a splendid view of it that I am satisfied not to go, as it would take three days to do it easily.

We passed the Cheragan Palace, where Sultan Murad, who disappeared mysteriously some time ago, is said to be secretly confined. The people here tell it under their breath! The present Sultan must be desperately afraid of his life to judge by the way he safeguards himself! When he goes to ride in his own park he does so only on a road defended by two high walls. We passed a number of his palaces and those of his daughters and brothers, also that of the Khedivial mother at Bebek.

Near an Albanian village is what they call the " Devil's Current." The water here becomes wild and whirlpooly, and for a long distance takes on the aspect of rapids. It was interesting to go into the current and to see several small boats with seven powerful oars pulling against it. One of the finest bits was where the Castle of Europe, a magnificent old castle which might be in Wales or Scotland, looms up with its massive, turreted towers and walls, and the Castle of Asia on the other side of the water. We went close by the former, the latter we saw from the opposite bank. Architecturally it is quite different from the other, its towers being square, while those of the Castle of Europe are round, but they are both magnificent piles and very imposing. We also passed quite close to the Giant's Mountain that I told you about in my last.

On our return, I was again, and more than ever impressed with the grandeur and magnificence of Constantinople as it is seen from the water. Its extent is something fabulous, so much so that it surprises one just as much after one has seen it again and again as it does at first, perhaps even more, for one cannot take in the vastness at first. I am more than ever convinced that the best of Constantinople is to be seen from its waterways, and that a closer inspection results in disappointment — I mean, of course, as a city and independent of its historic interest or the beauty of some particular landmarks.

April 4th

I HAVE just returned from an all day outing with the Pryses. Harry thought it would be more prudent to stay housed today, in spite of the sunshine, as he wants to get rid of his cold, and he knew there would be of necessity more or less exposure in following our programme for the day. In the morning we drove to the wonderful old walls, known as the Theodosian Walls, which cross from Zedi Kouleh on the Sea of Marmora to Aivan Serai on the Golden Horn, a tremendously long stretch. There are ninety-six towers at distances, I should say, of about a hundred yards, forming part of the walls, which are very massive, although in parts they have succumbed to earthquake. It was a long and painful drive along the road parallel with its walls, the roughest road I have ever been jolted along — if possible worse than that at Scutari.

We first got out at Zedi Kouleh (The Seven Towers), a Turkish fortress built by Mohammed II, situated about a quarter of a mile from the junction of the land and sea walls. We went over the fortress into some of the dungeons, and into the gruesome chamber where thousands and tens of thousands of enemies were executed, and their heads and bodies thrown from a trap door in the floor, down a deep well into the sea. The guard opened the trap door for us, and we looked down into the narrow well to which there seemed to be no end. The ambassadors of nations at war with Turkey were always confined in that fortress during hostilities. The view from the top, over the Sea of Marmora, is beautiful.

We then visited the Kahringeh Mosque, which used to be a Greek church. Its actual interest consists principally in the fine and curious mosaics in the outer and inner narthex, representing the patriarchal ancestors of Jesus, according to the different gospels of Luke and Matthew, representations of Christ's works of healing and incidents connected with the Virgin Mary. There is nothing beautiful about the mosque itself, but it is historically interesting in that it is the Church of the Monastery of the Chora, and that Saint Mark's in Venice, built at the same period, was modelled after it — a fact one would never suspect if one were not told so!

We lunched at a Turkish restaurant on good, queer messes, and then we went on a pretty excursion up the Golden Horn, to the " Sweet Waters of Europe." We did it in a large and beautifully fitted canoe, called " caique," rowed by two Turks. It was very comfortable and felt like a gondola, but it was not covered at all, so we had the full force of the cold wind blowing up the Horn from the Black Sea.

We are to leave Constantinople tomorrow by the Khedivial steamer for Athens at 3 P.M. It is our intention in the morning, before starting, to ascend the Galata Tower for the wonderful view. It is a very fine and picturesque structure, and is now used as a fire-signal station, it is named the Tower of Christ, or Tower of the Cross. I don't exactly know how many hundred steps we shall have to climb! I strongly suspect that Harry will not join us — he has rather struck on sight-seeing.

Khedivial S. S. " Ed Kahira," Apr. 5th, 1904

WE CARRIED out our purpose of mounting the Galata Tower this morning before sailing away from Constantinople, and I was right in predicting that Harry would not have the enterprise to mount the 200 steps. The view we got from the top was quite worth the exertion.

It not only commanded the whole of Constantinople, which includes Pera, Galata, and Stamboul, but all its outlying stations on both sides of the Golden Horn and the Bosphorus, Scutari being the largest and most prominent of these. We also had a view of the Sea of Marmora, with its beautiful array of mountains, islands, and a splendid view of Brusa and Mount Olympus.

We walked home up the curious and quaint " step street," one of several in Constantinople. The Pryses, like myself, like to walk once in a while instead of riding everywhere. In one street we counted twenty-one dogs within a radius of fifty feet, lying curled up on the road and what in civilized places would be the pavement! These all-pervading dogs will always remain in my mind as a characteristic feature of Constantinople. They own the streets just as the pigeons own the interior of the mosques and towers, some of which a stranger might well mistake for guano factories!

We bade adieu to our cockney-Armenian guide, and were safely on board this good ship by 3 P.M. It seems to be a fairly comfortable boat, and much more sympathetic than the Russian boat. Many of the servants are either Italians or Greeks, and nearly all of them understand Italian. Mount Olympus stayed with us for more than an hour after we were under way, and most regretfully we bade farewell to its beautiful, rounded peaks covered with snow.

April 6th

THIS morning we reached Mytilene, with its beautiful castle of the middle ages planted on top of a green hill, and its two ancient harbours — the town nestling under, and on the slopes of the mountains, surrounded by groves of olive trees. It is a most attractive and lovely place — a place where one would gladly linger more than an hour, which is the time of waiting allotted to the ship. Still, we are only too glad to get such a good look at it, for, on the journey from Smyrna, we anchored there in the dead of the night and saw nothing of it.

Opposite Mytilene is the coast of Asia Minor, with Mount Ida, of which Homer sang, rising majestic above the rest of the fine mountain range, with the plains of Troy beneath. Just behind these mountains of Asia Minor are a number of ancient cities cited in the Bible, the names of which I dare not attempt to spell, with the exception of Philadelphia. In the harbour there was a large, Turkish gunboat, and the Austrian gunboat just coming in. The numerous salutes from ship to ship, as well as from the Castle were quite exciting. We are now under way again for Smyrna. We are already in the Gulf of Smyrna, and I suppose we shall be there by three o'clock.

We were glad to get a second look at Smyrna with its boasted Ionian sky. It looked very attractive as we approached — lying at the foot of Mount Pagus and at the head of the gulf, backed up and surrounded with magnificent mountains, the old Turkish fort Sandjak Kaleh standing up to the right of the city on a high, green hill, much as the Castle did at Mytilene. As we were to remain in port from two to three hours, we landed, drove about the town and walked about the bazaars. We found it much warmer than in Constantinople, to Harry's great delight. The pepper trees and many others were in full leaf. We noticed a tree of the acacia family without any leaves as yet, but literally covered with brilliant purple blossoms something like wistaria, but growing not in sprays but in little bunches right out of the stems. A friendly Turk gave Mrs. P.

and me a branch of it. The captain tells us he will land us at Piraeus tomorrow at about noon.

Hotel d'Angleterre, Athens, Apr. 7th, 1904

WE REACHED our destination today after a perfect orgy of beautiful island scenery in the Ægean archipelago. Nothing could be more lovely than the approach to Athens, for you see Athens, the very best of it, perfectly from Piraeus. The harbour with its near and distant mountains, tier upon tier all around it and in every direction, presented a dream of loveliness. So much for the glamour of sunshine! It seemed four times as splendid and captivating today as when we landed here before, the brilliant blue of sky and sea only broken by the many tinted hills and mountains, some of them slashed and tipped with snow.

Instead of waiting for the train, we drove all the way from Piraeus to Athens with our hand baggage. It took barely three quarters of an hour. I cannot tell you what a restful sensation it gives one to be here in a civilized European city after our long dealing with Hindus, Arabs, and Turks! And to be in a place where you can actually walk about the streets without being either mobbed or poisoned with dirt is, for a change, bliss untold! We like this hotel very much, and our rooms look out on a charming square, where there is an open-air café like those in Italy, and a beautiful garden of orange trees laden with fruit.

After our much-needed lunch (for we were famished when we arrived), Harry went to the bank for letters which were awaiting us in generous measure. After that, Harry and I went for a stroll, through the orange garden, up some steps, and along a beautiful avenue, bordered with pepper trees, coming out squarely in front

ATHENS: With View of Mount Lycabettus

of the Temple of Jupiter, where we walked about and sat about undisturbed for a long time amongst those majestic columns, looking out towards the glorious mountains and the sea. To the right loomed up the Acropolis, to the left there was the Stadium. We left by the Gate of Hadrian, and then we rambled about the streets for a while.

The inscriptions on the shops are unreadable, the Greek characters being altogether too much for me. The only familiar sign being " Five o'clock Tea " over a café — an English oasis in a Greek desert! We entered in and had some. Then back to the hotel to dress for dinner. The Pryses are here with us, but we agreed not to go sight-seeing together on this our first day here.

I could not help thinking today, as we were strolling about between the columns of the Zeus Olympian, as the Jupiter Temple is more frequently called, how one finds almost everywhere something incongruous! There was a young man taking a lesson on a bicycle in the court of the Temple. It didn't look classic!

April 8th

What a heavenly day we have had! I have found *my* Athens! The sun was shining radiantly, so after breakfast Harry and I went to the Acropolis to spend the morning and revel in being quite by ourselves, and without a guide. We drove up the hill as far as the plateau of the Propylaea, not that it was in the least necessary, for it is an easy walk from our hotel, but riding in foreign cities is a *culte* with Harry!

We mounted the marble steps to the Propylaea with its six great Doric columns — raised on four steps — of Pentelic marble, and behind these the remains of the vestibule, the roof of which was held up by massive and more delicately shaped Ionic columns. The surrounding sward, strewn with huge blocks of marble fallen from what was once the ceiling above. Inside the gate stands a votive altar to Athena, the Healer, built in the same period, which was likewise the time that the mystic temple at Eleusis was built. In the open space between the Propylaea and the Parthenon stood once upon a time the colossal bronze statue of Athena, made by Phidias, which was carried off to Constantinople and destroyed there in a riot. Alas! There are all too many of these " used to be-s " in all ruins! Places where not a trace of the interesting object is left that once was! We must too often content ourselves with treading the soil where wonders were. That, however, is only partly true of the Acropolis, for enough yet remains to enable one to reconstruct much of its past splendour in one's mind.

The Parthenon! On crossing the Acropolis Hill, there it stood facing us in all its majesty. No one could exaggerate the exquisite harmony of this beautiful creation. While, of course, in its day the crowning charm of the Parthenon was the sculpture with which it was decorated, and of which little or nothing remains, yet the mere bare columns, marking as they do its beauteous proportions, made a profound impression. As we were roaming about on its marble pavements, and in and out between its columns, I began to reflect on the rapture excited in us by what our vision embraced. Was it the effect produced by the columns themselves, or by what one saw from the columns — that vast, enchanting, all-embracing view of the archipelago?

Anything more heavenly than the sight of the soft, undulating mountains in the very near distance, as they appear through the spaces, as a glorious picture of Almighty creation framed in the delicately curved columns of marble, cannot be conceived. But, truly, I am more than convinced that it is the wondrous — the unique combination of natural and artistic beauty that holds one so strangely enthralled, rather than the architectural idea alone. What a noble crown to the city must the Acropolis have been in the days of its living splendour! Wherever you stand, whether looking out to sea, towards Salamis, Ægina, and the numberless other islands, towards Phalerum and the Piraeus, or in the direction of Marathon or Eleusis, a panorama greets you which cannot be surpassed! Then the air — the clear, bright atmosphere and the deep azure of the sky, complete the spell.

As we wandered about in the Parthenon I gathered many kinds of exquisite flowers which were growing bravely in the cracks of the classic marble pavement, winking at its antiquity. The whole Acropolis is covered with pretty wild flowers, amongst which are little tiny poppies of a deep red. But, of course, no one but a crank like myself would talk wild flowers in connection with the Acropolis! One has comparatively little to say of the other interesting ruins and landmarks of the Acropolis because the Parthenon overshadows all else, but there is the Erechtheum, the Temple of Rome and Augustus, also that of Nike Apteros. Of the Temple of Athena nothing now remains but the mere foundation of stones and *débris*. From the Belvedere there is a marvelously comprehensive view which includes the city itself.

One interesting landmark in evidence from the first plateau of the Acropolis is the Areopagus, or Mars' Hill, where Paul preached. Lower down from the other side you get a good look into the Odeum of Herodes, a very interesting and picturesque ruin. There are, no doubt, other things to be explored which we have not caught onto yet, but give us time! In any case we had a pretty full morning, and we, ourselves, were almost too full for utterance! It was a strange effect to hear from the Acropolis the bells of every church in Athens — and heaven only knows how many there are of them — inviting to Good Friday services, which apparently never cease from early morning till midnight.

In the afternoon we ascended Mount Lycabettus, which stands up so straight and tall that as you approach Athens by the sea it is the first thing that strikes your eye as a prominent feature, even before the Acropolis. It was quite a climb up there, the little, zigzag paths being at times very steep and rough. At the summit is the quaint little church of Saint George, open to all, always — to believers and unbelievers alike. We met numbers of people on the mountain, some going up others coming down from worship, and they looked very picturesque winding about on the slopes.

We entered the little tiny chapel, filled in every inch with quaint icons against which devout women and men kissed and rubbed with their faces. A kindly looking Greek priest sat there and welcomed everybody. To us each he gave a spray of orange blossom or some other flower, and saluted us with great cordiality. The Greeks seem delighted to have strangers take an interest in their doings, whether religious or otherwise. The wild flowers on Mount Lycabettus were very interesting to me; there were so many kinds that were quite new. And, then, it was a perfect joy to see, in some of the little, public-square gardens, the acacias abloom, with their long sprays of yellow, rosette-like blossoms, a perfect blaze of colour, and near them great trees of marguerites, which, under cultivation, seem to grow to great

perfection here. The roses are also abloom in great profusion — some with sprays of tiny, little yellow blossoms, no bigger than a three-penny piece, others white
and climbing, like the Japanese rambler. You see them
everywhere, popping up over walks and fences. It does
seem early for roses, doesn't it? Especially as the
weather is far from warm.

Tonight there are to be great goings-on — Holy Friday processions from all the principal churches. Con-
stitution Square, on which our windows look, is all
illuminated with arches of electric light, presenting a
most brilliant appearance. As there can be no better
place than this to see the show, instead of walking the
streets, we shall take up our position on our balcony,
where we have invited the Pryses to join us. All over
the streets yesterday and today they were selling thousands of long, slender candles, of the dip variety, for
the holy-week celebrations. We have been told so much
about the wonders of holy week in Athens, as celebrated
by the Greek Church, that we feel ourselves fortunate
to be here at this time.

April 9th

IT WAS really most interesting and exciting what we saw
from our balcony last night. A seething mass of people,
each person bearing a lighted candle, thus adding to
the already daylight illumination. These were walking
about, waiting for the various religious processions to
come out of the churches, which it is the custom for
them to do at the end of a short service inside. These
various processions kept arriving on the square in grand
array, some accompanied by a male choir, and others
by a band of music. The procession from the Cathedral
was the finest, so I will describe that as being typical.

After the band came priests bearing large gold and silver icons, in the form of banners, some of them framed in cloth of gold and rich embroidery; then came one bearing a large, black cross of ebony with the image of Christ in silver or gold on it, and, last of all, a sort of bier, borne by dignitaries of the church, and surrounded by people of distinction, such as the King's ministers, etc. This bier had nothing on it but a magnificent cloth, all embroidered in gold, on which some flowers were strewn, possibly meant to represent the grave cloth of Christ, or the body itself. At the head of this bier stood the Metropolitan, or head of the church, bearing a large, sacred book, bound in what looked like massive silver icons, from which he chanted and declaimed. He was gorgeously robed, and except for the tall, embroidered, and bejeweled Greek cap, looked something like a pope in full uniform. They stopped almost under our balcony, so that we saw everything, and there they went through a funeral service, after which the procession moved on. It was a wonderful sight, that great mass of people with their candles, crossing themselves during the service many times in succession. The lamp posts were all draped in black.

There were four or five such services and processions on the Square during the evening from other churches, but they differed from each other only in degrees of splendour, and not in kind. It seems that here in Athens most of the great church functions take place in the open air, preceded by a short church service inside. This certainly gives a finer opportunity for the people at large to come into touch with the church, and has the effect of *diffusing* holiness, so to speak. By the way, one of the things played by the cathedral band was Elsa's Dream. But Wagner has become such a classic in these days of

Debussy and Fauré that it did not jar one bit to hear him in Athens. Tomorrow night there is to be the most impressive of all the services, in front of the Cathedral itself, in celebration of the Resurrection. We shall be there!

We spent the morning in the National Museum of Antiquities, the celebrities being the Hermes of Andros, very beautiful and admirably preserved. But it does not impress me as much as the pictures of the Hermes of Praxiteles, the original of which we shall see at Olympia. There is quite an array of the other Hermeses, all of them interesting. Then there is the magnificent Apollo, as they at present call it, which was recently found by a fisherman in the sea. It was under dispute at first, however, whether it was not meant for Hermes. We did not have time to examine closely Schliemann's Mycenae collection — that must be for some other day. It was interesting to see so many things that had been dug out of places where we had been, or where we are going.

In the afternoon we paid a visit to the Theseum, which lies at the foot of the Acropolis. It is one of the best preserved of all the temples which remain to us, but somehow it failed to fill my soul, or even to give me a thrill. I don't know whether this was because there is a building in Liverpool which looks just like it, or because there is no beautiful vista from it as there is from the Parthenon. We then walked up the hill on the other side of the Acropolis from where we were before, passing some ancient Roman remains of which only the foundations are left, and also what is supposed to be part of ancient Agora; they are not sure about it, however, and for my part, I can only vouch for the fact that it is ruins! From there we passed on to the Odeum of

Herodes, which we examined more closely than we had done before. It must have been a fine theatre in its day.

April 10th

THE OPEN-AIR service last night took place slightly under difficulties, for when we sallied forth at eleven P.M. it came on to rain a little — not violently, but just enough to make one uncomfortable. Nobody seemed to mind, however, and the proceedings went on as usual. In the middle of the square where the Cathedral stands was erected for the occasion a large wooden platform with a wooden fence round three sides of it, leaving room for a number of strangers to stand and see the ceremony at close quarters. In any other place this privilege would have been *for sale,* but not in Athens. Here all is courtesy and consideration for the people who pay them the compliment to visit them. For instance, Harry and I were first invited to ascend to the second story of a building overlooking the Square — by a total stranger, the owner of the shop underneath. We went up, but did not like it there, so we came back to the street, where, while struggling to disentangle ourselves from the crowd and get somewhere — anywhere — with a whole skin, a young man accosted us and undertook to escort us to the strangers' gallery on the platform. This was no easy matter! But the extraordinary part of it is that when, after many tribulations, he landed us safely on the platform, while I was fumbling for a five drachma note to reward him for his zeal and politeness, the youth had disappeared, and we could find no trace of him then nor afterwards. It really staggered us after a sojourn in India and Egypt to find any one who would render a service to strangers without expecting to be paid for it! We stood outside the inner platform enclosure, close up to the fence, where we could see everything. The enclosure was carpeted with fine rugs, and in the centre was a small altar table covered with a handsome brocaded cloth, embroidered and fringed with gold. On this were two large, tall candelabra, each containing about a dozen tall candles not yet lighted, and that was all the furnishing. A few officials were there on guard, and doing the honours to some of the *élite* who were arriving and taking up their positions near us on the platform.

Meanwhile a service was going on in the Cathedral at which the Crown Prince and Prince George were assisting. At about a quarter after midnight, the doors of the church were thrown open, there was a fanfare of trumpets, and out came the grand procession of church and other dignitaries, the banner-icons, the princes and people of the Court, headed by the richly robed Metropolitan, and mounted the platform. The princes were in full uniform and had on all their stars and decorations. They are fine-looking, manly men — both of them, but especially the Crown Prince, who has authority in his glance. They stood at the left of the Metropolitan, who took up his stand in front of the altar table as soon as he had given light from his holy candle for the altar illumination. After this the light was passed around, and all the people lifted their candles which, till then, they had held in their hands. Meanwhile it continued to rain gently, but there they all stood in their gorgeous robes and other stage properties. Nobody seemed to mind it, even the candles did not — they only blinked a little from time to time, except once when Prince George's went out and the Crown Prince gave him a light. Then came a service chanted by the Metropolitan, who frequently held the sacred book aloft and waved it with dramatic effect. The princes seemed

very devout and crossed themselves religiously every
other minute; so did everyone else. It was really very
solemn and impressive.

At last the service ended — the boy choir sang
" Christ is Risen." It rang forth joyously from mouth
to mouth, and everybody kissed or shook hands with
his neighbour. The procession returned to the church,
the princes and courtiers took to their carriages, and the
crowd dispersed. We followed the procession into
the Cathedral, into which the crowd was also pouring,
for there was to be another service lasting till four in
the morning. The poor, tired Metropolitan evidently
was going to make a night of it! " We won't go home
until morning " was in the very air, but no one sang it.
Inside, the Cathedral was simply packed with people —
all of them still holding on to their lighted candles at
the cost of setting fire to each other's back hair, and
spilling wax and tallow over their best frocks. There was,
however, a narrow space left down the middle where a
priest held up a silver icon with, I think, the Ascension
embossed on it for the people to kiss. This they did in
a steady stream, passing out of the church afterwards.
First, on approaching the icon, each one bowed low and
crossed himself, then kissed the icon reverently, laying
their faces against it with ardour, and then kissing the
hand of the priest.

There was something to me very touching about it
all. The people all seemed so sincere and earnest! Meanwhile, antiphonal chanting was going on vigorously by
the choir, and the Metropolitan from his perch took part
in the service from time to time. We left as soon as we
had taken in the gist of it all, as we did not think it
necessary to wait till all Athens had kissed the sacred
icon.

Today it is not as bright and beautiful an Easter Sunday as one could wish. It is somewhat overcast and quite chilly. But there have been great doings all day. Easter lambs are being roasted, barbecue fashion, in the streets; there is feasting, and there are flowers everywhere. The great headquarters for feasting and revelry are the barracks. It is the custom of the King and the Queen to visit all of these in succession, and for the King to have his health drunk, and to drink with his soldiers, tasting their food also. Citizens and strangers take carriages and drive from barrack to barrack in the hopes of catching up with the King and the Queen, and getting a good look at them as they get in and out of their carriage. We did likewise and satisfied our curiosity to the full. The King has a nice face, but the Queen is very plain and faded, and quite without any presence, dignity, or style. She looks like a kindly but commonplace woman.

The last place the King visited this morning was the officers' quarters, and when the royal party had driven away, on observing that some people were going in and out of the quarters, we went in too, to see the feastings and hear the festive singing and shouting. In the officers' quarters, however, there was nothing of the kind going on. We found ourselves at the door of a nicely fitted up library, at one end of which was a table spread with confectures, bottles of cordial and wines. About a dozen or more officers and a few other distinguished-looking men were there drinking to each other. Seeing this, we retired at once, but as we were making for the hall the Colonel of the regiment caught sight of us, and insisted on our going in with him. He was so charming that we could not resist him, and he spoke very good French. He persuaded Harry to take a glass of cordial, and when

I declined it he brought me a glass of champagne, saying that I really must not refuse to drink with them. So we stayed and conversed with the jolly Colonel as though we were old friends. He asked to be allowed to introduce the Mayor of Athens to us, and brought up forthwith a very distinguished-looking person with a fine face whom I had noticed on the platform doing the honours of the Resurrection service last night. He spoke nothing but Greek, unfortunately, so the Colonel had to interpret in French.

I must say, I think these Greeks are very courteous to strangers. I have never known anything like it elsewhere. It may be that Harry's Loyal Legion button, which he always wears when he is travelling, had something to do with the particular attention shown to us. When we bade them good-bye the Colonel handed each of us a bright-red Easter egg, saying, " It is always our custom to lay an egg in the hand of one who is amiable enough to visit us."

In the afternoon there was a Greek dance performed by the King's Guard in the palace grounds, right in front of the Palace. Of course we went to it. It was a strange sight to see from forty to fifty men in the starched and fluted petticoats sticking out like those of ballet girls, forming a ring and taking hold of hands while they danced round and round like a pack of overgrown children. During the dance they sang their own music — a wild sort of chant in a minor key, not unlike what they sing in their churches. There were distinct evidences in their voices that the King's Guard had dined!

While all this was going on, the King's carriage drove up to the palace door, and his Royal Highness and the missus mounted and started off to do more barracks. We also went again to the barracks, and saw a lot more dancing similar to that of the King's Guards, only the costumes varied a little, and a piper piped instead of the singing. When this began to grow monotonous — for they seemed inclined to keep it up forever — we left and drove down to the Cathedral, where the grand service was going on as it had been, no doubt, since yesterday, and as I should not be surprised if it still is!

Just now, as I was writing, I heard the sound of muffled drums and a funeral march, so I went out to the balcony to see what a Greek military funeral was like. What was my surprise to see a soldier bearing the lid of the coffin upright in his hands in the rear of the band, and then the rest of the coffin carried by bearers with the body exposed to the gaze of the passers by. There was really nothing unpleasant about it, for it was almost covered with flowers up to the chest, only it seemed such a strange custom. This is not peculiar to military funerals — the usage here is always to carry the corpse through the streets exposed in that way.

Well! it certainly has been a full day this Easter Sunday! You may have already gathered that we love Athens and should be well content to settle down here for a long time. 'Tis a winsome place — take it for all in all!

April 11th

We spent this morning at the Acropolis again, exploring some of the ruins below, which we had not visited before. We roamed about in the Theatre of Dionysius, where some interesting sculptures are still in a good state of preservation. We sat in one of the marble chairs where the 500 B.C. *élite* used to sit and listen to the plays of Æschylus, Sophocles, and Euripides. I cannot believe, though, that it ever held 30,000 spectators, as report has it. It is considerably larger, however, than the other theatre under the shade of the Acropolis — that of Herodes Attikus, which, though it was built nearly seven centuries later, is not nearly so well preserved in the interior. We spent an hour or so round about the Parthenon, the charm of which does not grow less from familiarity.

To close one's eyes from the glare of the sun and open them again on those splendid Doric columns which bar off into sections the grand ranges of Hymettus and Pentelicus, is a sensation to be remembered! It seems to me that no one could be dead to the impression produced by this classic art standing proudly in the face of such natural beauty. In me every fibre responds keenly to the wonder of it — the joy of it. Of course we did not confine ourselves to the Parthenon, but wandered off to the Erechtheum, the Temple of Nike Apteros (Wingless Victory), and the Propylaea. The day was heavenly, and there was real warmth in the air — the first we have felt since we left the Orient.

On our return to the hotel we found a charming letter from Mr. Lambrides, that lawyer of Athens, whom we met with the Reincourts on the Nile. It was to invite us to the Royal Theatre tonight to hear a concert of ancient Hellenic music. He little knew how much in my line that is, and how greatly interested I shall be to hear it.

April 12th

THE CONCERT last night proved to be quite an occasion, and all the royal family were present, occupying two boxes. There was a mixed chorus and a small orchestra of strings and wood-wind. The solos were sung by a baritone and tenor in the chorus, without coming forward to the front. The quality of the songs surprised me, they were so unlike what I should have expected from Greek music. It was a combination of archaic simplicity and wild flights of Orientalism. After phrases, *à la* early Haydn, there occasionally came a progression which quite out-Loefflered Loeffler! How I wish I could get hold of some of the tunes and study them out a bit! Mr. Lambrides has promised to find out from the conductor whether they are to be found. He tells me that until last night none of these songs were known to the Grecians of today, and that they had for the first time been unearthed and collected by the conductor of the concert.

This has been a general holiday to celebrate the independence of Greece. The real anniversary was last Thursday, but as that was Annunciation Day, it was celebrated today instead. The King and the Queen, accompanied by all the royal family and household, went to a special service at the Cathedral this morning. All the troops and bands were out, and there was a grand procession which again we saw finely from our balcony. Afterwards we went to the Cathedral to see what was going on there, arriving just about in time to see the royal *cortége* come out and take to their carriages. Again we experienced Athenian courtesy at the hands of one of the King's officers, who placed us on the steps of the Cathedral right in between the guard, so that we were quite close to their Royal Highnesses and saw everything.

In the afternoon we went to explore some of the ruins which lie around the base of the Acropolis — some Roman and Grecian market places (agoras), the Tower of the Winds, and the Pnyx. Then we went to the Areopagus (Mars Hill), climbed up, wandered all over it, and sat in contemplation on the precise spot where Paul preached to the Athenians. By the time we descended, we felt as much at home on the Areopagus as we do on the rocks at Ingonish! After that we mounted the steps of the Acropolis and sat for a half an hour under the shadow of the Parthenon, looking down on four different rings of dancers, who were celebrating their independence in the usual way by taking hold of hands and going round and round, occasionally kicking up their legs — to the music of fife and drum. The whole of the Acropolis was just swarming with people. All Athens seemed to be having their holiday there, taking in the gorgeous vistas of sea and mountain, drinking in the delicious air, and gathering wild flowers. The presence of such a swarming humanity did not add to the attraction of the ruins, but it was so good to see them all flocking there as in the old days, and caring to be there rather than elsewhere, — enjoying innocent drinks of pink and yellow lemonade, and eating cakes and oranges from the little stalls planted all over the plateaux for the occasion, with their bright, yellow wares showing up amidst the thick growth of grey-green aloes and straggling cactus. We found some English acquaintances there, the Pantons and the Thompsons, and we sat and chatted with them till it was time to go home.

April 13th
WE SPENT this morning in the National Museum, and examined the Mycenae Collection at leisure, which we did not have time for when we were there before. We also had a chance to go over the sculptures again. I am bound to confess that I expected to find a great many more of the important specimens of Greek art here than

there are. I should have thought that Athens would be headquarters for it, but in point of fact they have been practically divided up between all the great museums of the world, and Athens has retained only what one would call a small collection of things in a good state of preservation together, with a large amount of broken stuff, much of it too much damaged for one to recognize what it is intended to represent.

This afternoon we went for a walk the length of Amalia Avenue, through the gardens, bringing up at the Stadium, which lies at the farther side of the Ilissus — a river bed with about ten quarts of water in it! The Stadium lies in a hollow formed by three hills — spurs of Hymettus. It was used as a running place even before Lycurgus levelled the place and set a wall round it for spectators, B.C. 331. About five centuries later Herodes Atticus fitted the slopes with marble seats, which duly fell into decay, and recently — in 1896 — a Greek gentleman, named Averoff, of a public-spirited turn of mind, is having the whole thing reproduced in marble in the hopes of resuscitating the ancient games of Greece. It is a perfectly huge place, shaped like a long and narrow horseshoe. It seats 6500 people. The view of the mountains and sea from the top seats is something magnificent, and I should think that to sit up there through any entertainment, whether interesting or otherwise, and drink in such superb air with your lungs and such a view with your eyes, would in itself be worth the entire price of admission.

We were invited to go up on the roof of our hotel tonight to see the Acropolis illuminated. It was one glow and glare, first of red limelight, then of green. Rockets and Roman candles were let off galore. It looked as if the Parthenon was on fire, and it sounded as if the

Acropolis was being bombarded. The illumination should
have been last night as a climax to the celebration of
independence, I think, and I don't know why it was put
off till tonight.

It was very warm today, almost like Summer, and I
saw a fig tree in a garden with fruit on it already two
thirds of its natural size in maturity. I can't make out
this climate at all!

April 14th

THIS morning we went Acropolising again for about
the last time before leaving, as we go on our wanderings
again on Saturday. Our main object in going there this
morning was to explore the museum which was built up
there to receive the antiquities found on the spot, and
which was closed on every other occasion when we were
there, it being holiday time. It is a museum of fragments, one may say, there being few if any unmutilated
works. In Room 1, for instance, you are told in the cata-
logue that No.-? is a colossal group of two lions attacking a bull, but all you see is a bull prone on his stomach,
and some sections of lion's paws on his back, the tails
of the two lions reposing sweetly in two glass cases below. Again, in " Heracles fighting Triton," you see part
of Heracles, but no Triton, while in " Zeus slaying Ty-
phon," the three-headed monster is all there — in fragments — with a complaisant smile on all his three heads,
but no sign of any Zeus! However, in this cradle of ruins
one has grown so accustomed to supplying with one's
imagination heads, arms, and legs to most of the statues
that when a whole one turns up one feels almost ag-
grieved, as when some one insists on informing one about
something that one knows already!

After we had done the Museum, we wandered and sat

ACRO-CORINTH: An Outdoor Native Stove

about the Parthenon, moving from one point to another to take one last, long, loving look at all our favourite landmarks. On looking towards the Hill of the Muses, on the top of which stands the fragment of the monument erected by Philopappos to his grandpa, we were reminded that we had not yet ascended it, nor yet explored the rock chambers known as the " Prison of Socrates," which lie at the foot of the hill. So this afternoon we wended our way thither. The monument itself is scarcely worth the climb, there is so very little left of it, and it really looks much better as seen from the Acropolis than near to. But the view on top of the hill was splendidly comprehensive and quite worth while. We also climbed up the Hill of the Nymphs, which lies on the opposite side of the main road, and mounted the Observatory, which has been placed on top, to see the sunset, which, by the way, we could have seen just as well on the Hill of the Muses. On our way down we took in the prison of Socrates without lingering there; there is, in fact, little to be seen but three chambers hollowed out in the rock and protected by iron gratings — they are interesting chiefly by association.

I think now that we have explored Athens pretty thoroughly. Nevertheless, we would gladly stay longer just to loaf about in this sympathetic environment if we could spare the time, for we have grown to love it and to feel very much at home in it. The only drawback has been the difficulty in understanding and making ourselves understood, for the Athenians in general do not seem to be linguists, and you may accost a dozen people on the street to ask the way, giving them a choice of French, English, German, or Italian, without finding one who can answer your question. It is the same in many of the shops. Add to this the inability to read the signs or

names of the streets, which are all written in Greek characters, and you get a very blind, deaf, and dumb sensation! Harry, as a classic scholar in the days of yore, has
the advantage of me, for he can spell the names out if
you give him time. Meanwhile, I have grown so accustomed of late to using French, German, and Italian in-
terchangeably that I declare I am hardly aware, most
of the time, which of the three I am speaking.

April 15th

OUR LAST day in Athens! We leave tomorrow at noon
for Corinth, that much be-earthquaked town. We went
to the King's garden, adjoining the Palace, where strangers are allowed to walk on certain days — this being
one of them. It is a beauteous garden of many fine
avenues, orange groves and lovely flowers everywhere;
we came also on a fine, old, tesselated pavement. As we
stood outside, looking through one of the gates, trying
to make out a building unfamiliar to us, we heard quick
footsteps on the gravel walk, which proved to be of the
King himself, who, accompanied by a few of his suite,
was taking an evening walk in his garden. Salutes were
exchanged as they passed, and then, fearing that we
might be encroaching on his recreation hour, we turned
and made for the gate by which we had entered the Palace garden. We soon became aware of hurried footsteps
behind us, and, seeking to efface ourselves, entered a
bye path in a shrubbery. The footsteps continued to follow in our wake, however, and soon we were arrested
by, " I hope you like my garden," in a very courteous
tone. We responded naturally, and there ensued a very
pleasant conversation, in which the King displayed a
simple, unaffected, and human disposition. He was interested in what we had to tell him of our country, asked

how long we had been in Athens and how we were impressed with what we had seen, and, in his turn, told us with pride of the growth of the city during the last few years. He then pointed out to us certain features of his garden, commenting on the " late Spring " (which to me had appeared so advanced!). And so we chatted away about this and that with the same freedom from restraint that we would have felt with any one — not a royal personage in full uniform! He speaks English admirably — with a slight foreign accent, and we found his personality most engaging. It was a pleasant episode and a fitting climax to the courtesies received here.

On our return to the hotel the porter told us that Colonel somebody with an unpronounceable name had called to enquire if we were still here. Evidently the one who was so nice to us at the barracks on Sunday, and with whom I drank champagne. I am afraid we are leaving Athens just too soon. Evidently Colonel Blank wants to pay us some attention, and, who knows, perhaps the Queen might call on us and bid us to tea at the Palace!

Tonight there will be performed Sophocles' play of " Ajax " at the Municipal theatre, and we mean to go.

April 16th

WE DID not go to see " Ajax " after all, as we could not get good seats. Mr. and Mrs. Lambrides called to see us before dinner and we had a very pleasant chat. Mrs. L. seems a very sweet woman. They told us that the Vicomte and Comtesse de Reincourt will return today, having completed their journeyings. Certainly we are leaving Athens a week too soon! It would have been pleasant to see something of them on their native heath, and I am sure that Mme. de Reincourt would have been glad to see us again. However, leave we must! Our trunks have already been taken away, and we are to bid good bye to these pleasant rooms in an hour from now. We shall be in Corinth this afternoon at three.

Corinth, Hotel des Etrangers, April 16*th,* 1904
HERE we are in Corinth, and, if we walk a little way up the road, in sight of Parnassus and Helicon! We arrived at 3 P.M. Our dragoman put us into a carriage as soon as we had seen our rooms, and we were driven to the canal which is quite something out of the common. It is three miles long, and a mile of it is cut through the solid rock of the isthmus to a depth of more than 200 feet, the bridge that spans it being high enough to allow any kind of ship to pass under it.

The position of Corinth is altogether enchanting. The little town is built on a curve which embraces part of the gulf, and is rich in superb mountain views, snow peaks and slopes being frequent in the landscape. It is only a little bit of a town — scarcely more than an overgrown village now, earthquakes being responsible for its present modest appearance, the whole town having been destroyed in 1858. We shall visit ancient Corinth — what remains of it — tomorrow morning, and after that we are to ascend the Acro-Corinth on mules. From its summit one is promised a view of the whole of the Peloponnesus, and, on a clear day, Athens, Ægina, and Salamis can be seen. We are to get up at six, and start on the excursion soon after seven. The Pryses, who are travelling with us and sharing the cost of the courier, do not like the prospect of such an early start, but we don't mind!

Our journey from Athens this morning was full of interest and brimming over with beauty. Our way lay partly through mountain ranges and partly on a ridge

curving round the shore. For a long stretch of many
miles, after we had passed the bay of Salamis, there was
a fine road beneath us suggestive of the Cornice Road
at Nice. Our way lay by Eleusis — such an indescribably lovely spot! Never did Nature evolve a more exquisite composition of mountain and island scenery. It
is simply heavenly! We had a look at the ruins and the
Albanian village that Eleusis has now become; also of
the " Sacred Way," but there is little or nothing to be
seen of the objects associated with the " mysteries " or
of the coming of Demeter, so I think we were wise in not
making a separate excursion to Eleusis from Athens.
We saw the best of it today — the bay and its unsur-
passingly beautiful surroundings.

We passed Megara, Ægina, and Salamis, and went close
up to Mount Pentelicus. On the shores of Eleusis were
large groves of olive trees and something which looked
like Scotch heather, not yet abloom, and yellow gorse
in full flower, growing out of the rocky mounds. Picture
to yourselves also miles of vineyards just beginning to
grow, and fields of wheat interspersed with deep-red
poppies and a dark-blue flower — not unlike the English
cornflower, and having in the distance the same effect.

On our return to the inn our courier had five o'clock
tea ready for us. Later on, Harry and I went for a stroll
on the beach lining a vast stretch of curving and winding shore. We were repaid by a wonderful sunset and
afterglow. I can never forget that luminous sky beyond
the mountain peaks in contrast to the bright-blue waters
of the Gulf — its waters transparent and clear as crystal. We found, on walking back through some of the
streets of Corinth, that it was more of a town than it
had at first appeared to us. The streets are wide and well
laid out, and there is a little common, well covered with

pine trees. As we gazed across the sea toward those grand mountains we could not help deploring that inevitable feature of travel — constantly having to run away from some heavenly spot instead of staying long enough to drink in all of its beauty. We should love to remain awhile in Corinth, but alas, we must move on tomorrow!

April 17th

OUR EXCURSION today was very delightful. First we drove to the base of Acro-Corinth, where a bunch of mules awaited us (ordered beforehand by our courier) with the most remarkable trappings I had ever seen. We had to sit on one side of the animal, with both feet hanging over and passed through a loop of rope for support, the position being precisely the same as that of the chairs put for children on donkeys, only there was no chair or anything half as comfortable and secure. We had to provide both support and equilibrium with our own backbones. Indeed, I would far rather have walked, for, although the mountain is nearly 2000 feet in height, the road rough and steep in places, it would really have been far less fatiguing to do it on our own two feet than to suffer the jiggling and jolting on the backs of our quadrupeds in such an unwonted and uncomfortable position — with no reins and nothing to hold on to. When, however, in something less than two hours, the summit was reached, we soon forgot all physical discomfort in the glory of the scene.

From our perch we could take in comprehensively the lay of both land and sea of the whole of Greece as one could do from no other point. The country was spread out before us like a map — the Gulf of Corinth to the west, the Saronic Gulf to the east, the canal connecting the two, the little town of Lepanto nestling at the base of the hills, Loutraki across the bay at the foot of Mount Geraneia, old Corinth at the foot of Acro-Corinth, and the few remaining Doric columns of the Temple standing out in bold relief. We tarried there on the top quite a while noting the positions of the big mountains to the south of the Corinthian Gulf — Kileyne, with its snow cap, Phouka and Chelmos, and, to the north, Chiona and Vardousa, Parnassus and Helicon. We could also get a look back at Salamis and Ægina, but there was a little haze that prevented us from seeing Athens itself, though they say that on a very clear day you can actually see the Acropolis and the King's Palace. It is hard to believe!

The wonderful outlook over the Peloponnesus, however, was not all there was for us to take in after our climb. There were the walls of an immense fortress which showed evidence of the different hands into which it had fallen. On the Hellenic foundations are Frankish, Venetian, and Turkish masonry, and the remains of Byzantine churches, Turkish mosques and cisterns. The foundations of the Temple of Aphrodite are also still to be seen.

On descending we visited the famous fountain of Pirene, where Bellerophon caught Pegasus. It is situated on a plateau very near the summit. We descended into it, but we had to fight our way among the swarms of wild bees which had taken possession of the old masonry and renewed it after their own fashion. On reaching the foot of the mountain again, we visited the Temple and went over the excavations of old Corinth which have been carried on for some years by Americans, chiefly in the neighbourhood of the Agora market. The thing of most interest to be seen there is the well-house of Pirene.

Diogenes was visited by Alexander here 323 B.C., and there are many historical facts connected with it which make one want to see it, but when one gets there it is only to realize its utter desolation. It is now merely the *site* of all those happenings, nothing more. If money enough is found to continue the excavations much more will be unearthed that will stimulate the imagination than is now to be seen.

It was once a very large and important city, extending all the way, and covering all the ground between it and modern Corinth. Otherwise, as one notes the modest dimensions of the latter and the small number of inhabitants (only about 4000), there seems to be hardly a *raison d'être* for the Apostle Paul to have lived and preached his famous gospels here. His church, built on the site of the one he preached in, is round the corner from the hotel where we stayed. If, however, Paul selected Corinth as an abiding place on account of its heavenly situation, I certainly approve his taste! It is also hard to think of a Julius Caesar in connection with mild little Corinth, and yet he gave it a new lease of life which lasted a long time after his death.

We have enjoyed Corinth and its surroundings up to the hilt, and were sorry to leave it today. Amongst other things I delighted in the wild flowers, which are exquisite. On Acro-Corinth today I counted fourteen varieties I had never met with before, and I was excited in recognizing that interesting plant called " Mother of Thousands," of which I have such a number in Boston in my windows — growing wild and almost rank all over the place; but at Corinth, instead of multiplying itself in so many tiny plants, its energy goes into a tall, handsome blossom. As our carriage drove along the road several friendly women and children threw in large bunches of wild gladiolas of a delicate purple colour, and only one of them — a child — waited for a " thank you " in substance.

We left for Patras at three, and the journey along the shores of the Gulf, with the ranges of snow mountains on the other side of the way, were indescribably beautiful. The azure-blue water, calm as that of a lake, the lovely modelling of the soft hills of island and shore, backed up with rugged rocks and cliffs and the more distant mountain ranges, tier upon tier beyond, were a constant feast for the eye. Greece is indeed an enchanting country. It is all beautiful from end to end!

We learned this evening, to our consternation, that the North German Lloyd steamer, which was to have conveyed us to Brindisi on Tuesday, is so crowded that they have to put first-class passengers in the second-class cabins, and four in a cabin at that, separating the women from their husbands in order to pack the people closer! Of course, neither we nor the Pryses are going to subject ourselves to any such discomfort if we can help it, so the question arises what other boat, if any, can we take. Cook's agent tells us that a German boat will come this way tomorrow from Alexandria, going direct to Brindisi instead of stopping at Corfu, and that the chances are we can get good accommodations on her. That would mean giving up our excursion to Olympia tomorrow, which we should be sorry to do, but needs must when the devil drives! The agent is to let us know tomorrow morning what our fate is to be. As he thinks the boat will not leave Patras till the middle of the day, we can take it easy and poke round Patras a little before starting.

S. S. Urano (Austrian Lloyd), April 18th, 1904
WE DID not have the breathing space we expected this morning, for the Austrian Lloyd steamer, on which

Cook's agent was to try to get us a stateroom, steamed up the Gulf of Patras between seven and eight A.M. Soon after we were awake we received word that a cabin had been secured for us, and that the boat would start at 11 A.M. So we dressed and packed and went down to breakfast. While we were calmly discussing it, in came our carrier to inform us that as there happened to be no freight to discharge or take on, our boat, the " Urano," would start at once, so we were hustled on board, bag and baggage, scarcely being allowed time to say good bye to the Pryses, who had no idea we were to part in such a hurry; for, after going to Olympia together, we were to have taken the steamer together on Tuesday — they, continuing on to Trieste, we, stopping at Brindisi.

However, there seemed to be nothing else for us to do but what we did, and we are consoling ourselves with the thought that we shall have a little more time in Naples in exchange for a sight of the wondrous Hermes of Praxiteles, and the remains of the Stadium, where the Olympic games took place, and where the length of the course is said to have been determined by Heracles pacing out 600 feet. After all there is not much to see in Olympia! It is chiefly made up of associations, and you may just as well supply with your imagination the whole outfit as have it crutched up by the sight of a few broken columns and steps! Then, as to the Hermes, one can study that excellently well from the photographs, which represent it to perfection. In fact we have already done so in Athens. So, the grapes are sour, and we don't care for them!

They have made us very comfortable on this boat, and we feel already quite at home on her. They have given us each a cabin to ourselves, for there are scarcely a dozen passengers owing to the fact that the advent of

NAPLES: View of City and Bay

this boat was not generally known at Patras. The Captain is an Italian, so my long imprisoned tongue is unloosed. At table I talk German on my left, French opposite, and Italian in the middle and at the head.

The sea is a dream of calmness and azure. We have passed out of the Gulf of Patras, which is all beauty, like the rest of Greece, into the Ionian Sea, and are now dallying with the Ionian Islands. We have passed Cephalonia, the little village of Samos, Ithaka and Leukas, and I am ready to endorse them as first-class islands. We are now close by some wonderful cliffs and split rocks. The colouring is superb — bright reds and yellows, grey, green, and white. Now we are going into the open for a while till we strike the Straits of Otranto, which lead into the Adriatic, and tomorrow morning we shall land at Brindisi, on the heel of Italy.

Naples, Hotel Santa Lucia, April 20th, 1904
OUR BOAT reached Brindisi earlier than we thought yesterday morning, and we found that we could get through the customs and catch the 10.45 train to Naples. It was an accommodation train and stopped at every station, but it certainly accommodated us in getting us to Naples at a quarter to ten P.M. The journey was most interesting. First, there were many miles of broad, flat country — a true picture of fertility. Long stretches of olive groves, fig trees, and every sort of blossoming fruit tree — a beautiful sight to behold. As soon as we passed Taranto, the beautiful, undulating hills, covered with richest verdure, and wonderful wild flowers and flowering shrubs, began to come on the scene, and after that there was a gradual *crescendo* till all Nature broke out into grand mountains, smiling valleys, wonderful gorges and ravines.

There was the Valley of Basento, the gorge of the

river Platano, and any number of fascinating mountain streams. Then there were those queer, picturesque Italian towns built on the top of high hills, any number of them. It was all so different from what we had been seeing elsewhere that the novelty excited us immensely. Harry was in a state of wild elation. Italy seems to get into his blood and warm the cockles of his heart as no other country does. I tell him he is an Italian born in America by mistake. But it is lovely to be here. I feel the sunny influence myself. This is a charming hotel and we are going to like it very much.

April 21*st*

YESTERDAY, our first day in Naples, passed most delightfully, the more so that we did not attempt to do anything in particular. We just drove about and strolled about to get our bearings and a first general impression of the Naples of today as against the one in my memory of nearly half a century ago. I found everything almost unrecognizable except the bay, Vesuvius, and the islands. Even the very gardens on the water's edge, where we used to walk in the evening, are no more, but have given place to the Villa Nuova, entirely changing the lay of the land — nay more, as the bay itself has been filled in to make room for more streets and houses! Most of the old streets are demolished, and fine, broad, clean roads and thoroughfares have taken their place. It is a handsome and attractive city now, but the dear, old, dirty, smelly Naples, which I used to love, is no more. It is evident that I shall have to make its acquaintance all over again! Even the San Carlo Theatre, whither our footsteps naturally led us, did not seem the same because of the Galleria Umberto II, which shuts it into a narrow space. We saw that there was to be a performance of Verdi's " Ballo in Maschera " in the evening, and as I had not heard it but once since I played in it myself, I was keen to go, and to have Harry see an opera in which I had sung over two hundred times.

It was really quite startling to find — in the midst of so many radical changes — that the old man in the ticket office was actually the same one who was there when I sang at the San Carlo, and that he remembered perfectly my singing the solos of the " Sonnambula " and " Lucia." It really pleased me to feel that I had not completely lost my identity, although I frankly own that it seemed to me as if he were talking of something that had happened in a pre-existence!

As for the performance in the evening I cannot say very much for it. The women were both inferior. They neither sang nor acted well. The tenor had a good voice and presence, and the baritone was a very good dramatic artist. The chorus was both flat and perfunctory, but the orchestra was fine, and the conductor excellent — he just held up the performance with his baton! Of course that cannot be counted as a representative San Carlo performance, because the real season is over and the best singers have ended their engagements and gone their ways. We were glad they did not interrupt the opera in the middle for the ballet, as they used to do, but gave it afterwards instead. We stayed for a little bit of it, as I wanted Harry to get an idea of the gorgeous setting of a San Carlo ballet, and we found that quite up to the mark. It was past midnight when we left the theatre. I found no difference in the auditorium. It looked just as it had in the old days, but it smelt musty. Was it, perchance, the effect of decayed Art?

We spent this morning in the National Museum, where we feasted on masterpieces until long past lunch time. It is indeed replete with rich treasures, especially in sculpture, what with the beautiful works of art found at Pompeii and Herculanium, the Farnese collection and others, one feels that a month of continuous study would hardly suffice to get an adequate idea of it all. After reaching the point where we could look no more, we went to a restaurant to get some ballast, and thence to the Botanical Gardens, in which we were disappointed.

Lastly we drove to the bank for letters and, to our great joy we found one from Rosamond [1] which we had been anxiously awaiting in Athens, to tell us when we may expect to meet her in Rome. We are so delighted that she has decided to join us there, for I know how much she has, for years and years, longed to see Rome, without any prospect of getting there. The fact that she will spend a dozen days with us, away from all her usual cares and responsibilities, will afford us a great deal more of her company than we could ever hope to enjoy in London. And now, with our only reason for going to London removed, we can, with an easy conscience, take a steamer for home from Naples on May 11. This will be a pleasant variation from our Atlantic crossings, and give us a chance to take a look at the Azores. Tomorrow we intend to visit Pompeii.

April 22nd

OH! BLUE sky of Naples, where art thou! It is raining hard, so no Pompeii for us today. Instead, we spent the morning in the aquarium, contemplating that wondrous submarine world. It was of thrilling interest to us both. What countless shapes of extraordinary living things! What rare and ingenious pieces of mechanism! What radiant colours, what beauty, and what ugliness! I had

[1] Mrs. Rogers' sister.

never before happened to see an octopus — that fiend among fish. I never want to see another!

Later when the clouds dispersed, we rode out to Posilipo and beyond to the extreme point. It was delightful, and upon that fine, new road we had immunity from dust. The Bay from there looks its very best towards evening when we saw it, and the dark clouds settling over Capri, without obscuring it, made it only the more interesting. We passed miles and miles of terraced vineyards, trained in espalier mode (which seems the Italian way), and large fruit orchards, filled with fig, almond, peach, and other fruit trees, and there were ripe nespole (a sort of medlar) hanging in the boughs, and oranges and lemons galore, olive groves also, and such flower gardens! It really does my heart good to see how happy Harry is here. He enjoys every minute up to the hilt!

April 23rd

ANOTHER overcast day with frequent showers, so again Pompeii was out of the question. Now we must put our excursion off till Monday, our last day here, because Sunday, being free to the public, is a bad day for Pompeii, many of the most interesting houses being closed. Let us hope that it will be fine on Monday! In the afternoon we took the cable car up to Saint Elmo. There we could spend our time profitably in spite of showers, for there was the interesting Chiesa di St. Martino, with its enormous collection of pictures, some of them very fine, also the Museum and the Belvedere, which afforded a magnificent outlook over the whole Bay and " fixings." Oh! but the Bay of Naples *is* beautiful! We went to the Royal Palace in town this morning, to get a permit to go over the Palazzo Reale at Capo-di-Monte tomorrow, so that a walk over the Royal Gardens is our programme for tomorrow, weather permitting. It is very hard for us to have to reckon with the weather now, after such a long obliviousness to rain or cloud!

April 24th

THE WEATHER was bright this morning, but by the time we got up to the top of Capo-di-Monte it was quite overcast again, and a black, threatening thunder cloud scowled at us. We were under shelter in the Palace however, so we didn't mind. It is a very regal, dignified, and gorgeous place both in the exterior and interior. We were taken through miles of picture gallery, where some few masterpieces were interspersed with inferior modern stuff, the only interest in the pictures being their subjects. But the custodian insisted on our seeing them all whether we would or no! The ball room is magnificent, and the collections of china and armour were fine. There was one room — a boudoir — the walls and ceiling of which were entirely of Capo-di-Monte china. I could hardly believe my eyes! When we came out of the Palace it was pouring rain, so we made our way home instead of going to see some of the churches, which we should otherwise have done.

April 25th

A REALLY fine day at last! Old Vesuvius presents a cloudless top, the sure sign of good weather here, so we went to Pompeii, and spent the day in that silent city. A large number of tourists were at the station bound for the same goal, but we only saw small groups of people here and there, for the city is large and a crowd would not make much impression. Of course there is four times as much of it as there was when I was there before, and many interesting streets, houses, and baths have been excavated since then.

It is a wonderful place, and has the same indescribable charm that I felt at the Acropolis, and for the same reason — that is, the glorious situation, the unrivalled outlook. When we mounted the raised platform of the Forum we had such a magnificent view of the Apennines! And what a noble range it is! Vesuvius was particularly interesting today. There was no wind, so the smoke and steam from the crater went up straight into the air, forming the regulation mushroom shape which the pictures affect, and the beauteous blue Bay was spread out before us in peaceful mood, looking as if it could not harm a baby. It was a strange sensation to be walking through those silent streets, where the only sounds were those of one's own footsteps, where the roads all paved, were of immaculate cleanliness. One could not help varying the saying " only man is vile " to " where man is not, all is pure and sweet." The dear little maidenhair ferns seemed to feel this as they poked their graceful drooping sprays out of the crevices of the pavements and walls.

In the train, on our way back, we fell in with some quondam travelling companions, the Camerons, who seem to be following in our tracks. They likewise are going to Rome, though they do not leave Naples till Thursday, whereas we, alas! must go tomorrow in order to be on hand to welcome sister Rosie, who will arrive on Wednesday.

There are to be great doings here April 27th — a grand review of warships in honour of President Loubet, who is coming. Ten of the ships are in the harbour already, and still they keep arriving. The officers are doubtless being entertained royally by the Neapolitans, and wine is flowing like water. It is a pity we cannot stay for the jinks, but I believe we are going to run right into some big church celebrations in Rome this week, which must make up for our loss here.

Rome, Hotel d'Europe, April 26th, 1904

OUR JOURNEY from Naples to Rome was delightful. Such a wealth of gorgeous scenery as we had with us the whole of the way! From Capua on we were passing through range upon range of wooded mountains, I think they must have been the Sabines — a spur of the Apennines, and farther on the Apennines themselves. Then every now and then we came upon some of those queer and picturesque little townships which lie either nestling in the arms of the mountains, or seem to be climbing up their sides to reach the top if they can. There were ruins of fine old castles, too, looking much like some of those on the Rhine. A few miles from Rome are long stretches of the ancient walls, and the Aqueduct of Claudius, which usher in the great historic city most harmoniously.

As we drove from the station to the hotel, we found that there was a grand illumination. The streets were thronged with people. Of course we took it to be in our honour (!), but we learned that also President Loubet had something to do with the festivities, this being his last day in Rome before leaving for Naples, where the great review of warships is to take place on the 29th. As soon as we had put ourselves outside of some supper we sallied forth into the crowded streets to see the fun. The Corso Umberto I was one blaze of light, and every balcony and window was hung either with pieces of French tapestry or some other handsome drapery. The French flag was conspicuous everywhere, and the Marseillaise was played by street bands, sung and shouted in drunken snatches all over the place.

We were pushed along by the seething masses of humanity as far as the Piazza Colonna, where the wonderful Antonina Column was illuminated with red light, and looked superb. We managed to elbow our way back to the hotel by eleven o'clock, as we were too tired to make a night of it like the good Romans, numbers of whom had brought with them their sleeping babes and two- or three-year-old children — dropping with drowse, in order that no member of the family should have to stay at home to mind the baby. How these Italians do love excitement and a show or a noise of any kind! I must confess I was surprised a little though, at such a fuss being made here over President Loubet. I should have thought that his attitude towards the Church of Rome would render him anything but an object of enthusiasm within walking distance of the Vatican. However, I dare say that thousands of the people didn't know what it was all about — they only knew that there was to be an illumination and larks!

April 27th

WE WERE sorry to see an overcast sky this morning, for I should have liked Rosie to be introduced to the city as seen under a real Italian sky. However, when she drove to the door of the hotel we provided considerable sunshine between us, for you can well imagine what a joy it was to meet again after a separation of seven years — the longest ever! We thought she looked remarkably well, and has changed very little except that her hair is nearly white. We made her take a hearty breakfast forthwith, for she was famished, and then, as it was raining like fun, we concluded that we would not go out till afternoon.

The weather cleared in the middle of the day, and so

we hired a large, comfortable carriage and drove about
for three hours, getting a splendid birdseye view of many
of the streets, notable monuments, and churches. We
drove first to the Capitol, about which we prowled, examining the statues of Rienzi, Marcus Aurelius (which
used to stand in the Forum), and the Castor and Pollux
at the head of the imposing flight of steps. Then we
passed through the narrow street where one gets a grand
view of the Forum, the Palatine, Caesar's Palace and
the Colosseum. What a promise of delights to come it
was to take this preparatory view of these noble ruins,
which at once appeal to the imagination and conjure up
all sorts of memories of ancient history! Rosie and I
were full of wild excitement and Harry was in the
seventh heaven at his personally conducted party being
such a success, to say nothing of his own enthusiasm on
revisiting these familiar scenes. Then we went to see all
that remains of the Tarpeian Rock, and we were more
interested in the fine old garden of the German Embassy,
from which it is viewed, than in the " Traitor's Leap "
itself. We also went into three or four interesting
churches, though not into any of the very celebrated
ones — you see, we mean to work up to a climax!

April 28th
A RAINY day greeted us this morning, so we wisely decided to spend the morning in the Capitoline Museum.
We drove to the Capitol, and knew nothing more of
weather till we had to leave for lunch. I don't know when
I have been more filled with glorious impressions and
ideals than today in the midst of the numberless masterpieces gathered together there. Could one ever forget
the Venus of Praxiteles in its overwhelming grace and
exquisiteness! To behold that and the Dying Gladiator

ROME: Ruins of the Ancient Forum

is alone worth a pilgrimage to Rome. But really great statues in this museum are as thick as blackberries, and I must say I have never been in any gallery where works of art were arranged to better advantage or with finer discretion.

In the afternoon the rain abated, and we wended our way to Saint Peter's. What a marvel it is! How impressive, how noble its *entourage* — the broad space encircled with colonnades of massive columns, the magnificent approach, are a fitting prelude to the glorious solemnity within. We were simply overwhelmed. To-morrow we shall return to explore the Vatican, for we remained in Saint Peter's the entire afternoon, and there was no time for anything else.

April 29th

WE SPENT the morning in the Vatican, as we had planned. The first thing we did was to take a number of rosaries and medallions, which we purchased near Saint Peter's yesterday, to be blessed by the Pope, so as to make happy some of our Catholic maids and friends at home. Then we ascended the Scala Regia, passing the Swiss Guards in their gaudy uniforms of yellow and red, stopping to gaze at Bernini's equestrian statue of Constantine the Great, until we reached the room where the permits are issued, thence proceeding to the Scala Regia, and beyond to the Raphael rooms, where a feast of frescoes awaited us, such as we never dreamed of.

In fact the splendour of the Vatican, in all its parts, simply takes one's breath away. Wherever one's gaze happens to fall are great works of art, rich decorations, grandeur, magnificence. Yet it never palls on one. It is all too well, too artistically arranged for that. But what ought one to expect when such Titans in art as Raphael and Michaelangelo, plus Giulio Romano, Perugino, Botticelli, Roselli, and that ilk, had a hand in it! The Sistine Chapel alone would be enough to glorify the Vatican as a cradle of Art! It is a fit place indeed for cardinals and bishops to receive the pallium, and for popes to preside in. I was tremendously impressed by the grand fresco — Michaelangelo's " Last Judgment." Even at first glance, and before I had made out anything of the conception in detail, the whole gist of the picture came to me with tremendous force. The mere outlines are in themselves so expressive that one *feels* the pathos of it before one knows why. We must return to it again tomorrow; once is not enough! No, nor twice, nor indeed twenty times!

In the afternoon we went to the Colosseum, which came upon me in its rugged immensity with almost as startling an effect as if I had never seen a picture of it or heard it described. We wandered about its ruined arches and colonnades — stood before the dungeons where the victims were stowed till they were brought out to be torn to pieces by wild beasts. It brought some of the scenes of " Quo Vadis " before me with great vividness, for here was the actual background of the picture in this amphitheatre of Imperial Rome. After we had taken in also the remains close by, the Arch of Constantine, the Temples of Venus and Rome, and the Titus Baths, built on the site of Nero's house, we went to the famous church San Pietro in Vinculi, to take a look at the original Moses, by Michaelangelo. How full of treasures Rome is! How can we ever hope to see them all!

April 30th

WE SPENT this morning again in the Vatican, making at once for the Sistine Chapel, where we lingered long, making a careful study of the frescoes. Then we went through the Raphael gallery again, and finally mounted up one flight higher to the picture gallery, which is full of old masters — Murillo, Guido, Perugino, Correggio, Leonardo da Vinci, Veronese, Titian, Guercino, Ribera — all so plentifully and so nobly represented. There also is the last picture painted by Raphael — for the Cardinal Giulio dei Medici, the " Transfiguration," a picture not to be forgotten when once seen.

After lunch we went to a number of fine churches, amongst others Santa Maria Maggiore, Santa Maria in Trastevere. It quite takes one's breath away to see so many magnificent churches in one city. The splendour of it all is overwhelming! We then told our coachman to take us for a drive on the Pincio, where a good military band was playing, and where " the quality " and all the grand equipages were in evidence. It is an adorable park, and the view from it, overlooking Rome and the surrounding hills, is superb. I hope we may have time to visit some of the famous villas in the Pincian Gardens before we leave Rome. But there is so much to be done that something must needs be left undone.

May 1st

A LOVELY May Day! And such a full one that I hardly know where to begin. Rosie was very keen to attend high mass in Saint Peter's, so we took an early breakfast and commenced with that. The service was rather long, and we had to stand through the whole of it, but there is a great deal to hold the attention in the celebration of high mass in a church like Saint Peter's — the " stage properties," so to speak, fill the eye, and the constant action makes it as entertaining as a play — in a foreign language. I was disappointed in the choir and the choice of music. I expected to hear Gregorian chants,

Palestrina, and that sort, as I understood that the present Pope had tabooed all modern stuff and operatic music. But alas!, though it was ecclesiastic in character, it was not good of its kind.

After that, having learned that a sermon was being delivered by one who was considered the greatest preacher in Rome, we joined the eager crowd of listeners. We did not stay long, however, as our Latin equipment did not suffice to enable us to follow his inspired utterances! I could not help wondering how many of the Roman citizens understood what he was saying any better than we did. And why a living faith should be preached in a dead language? Of course the Latin service has become more or less easy for all good Catholics to follow, but a sermon is quite another matter.

Later on we drove to the Capitol, and spent some time in the Hall of the Conservators, surrounded by superb statuary, pictures, and antiquities found recently under fields about Rome. The interior of the building is majestic — a dignified and fitting home for Justice. Our next step was to take one more look at the Venus of Praxiteles and the Dying Gladiator in the Capitoline Museum, and then we started on such a round of general explorations as would seem impossible to be accomplished in less than a couple of days. But we were fortunate in having a good coachman who knew his Rome thoroughly, and who laid out our road so wisely that we were enabled to get over an enormous deal of ground in a limited time.

First we went to the Piazza del Quirinale to see the superb colossal statues of Castor and Pollux standing by their horses — by Phidias and Praxiteles. Then we managed to gain admission to the Quirinal Palace (although unprovided with the necessary permit) by the

judicious use of the coin of the realm. And what a palace
it is! Such splendour and grandeur as I had not dreamed
of. As I went through room after room hung with the
most superb Gobelin tapestries, I was thinking what a
feast they would have been to any collector. But there
were other treasures besides tapestries — pictures and
vases, regal decorations and furnishings which pass description. This palace was for a long time the seat of the
Conclave and the summer residence of the Popes, but
now the building is used as the residence of the Italian
Court.

After that we took a look at the following places: the
Porticus of Octavia, erected by Augustus Caesar, 33 B.C.,
in honour of his sister Octavia, wife of Mark Antony;
the houses of Rienzi and of Michaelangelo; the Temple
of Hercules; the Tiberine Island, where the Temple of
Æsculapius used to stand; the remains of the old Ghetto,
a large part of which is now occupied by a fine, large
synagogue; then through the Appian Way, teeming
with its memories of Peter and Paul, to the place where
Paul was buried with Timothy, and over which now
stands a wonderful church, second only to Saint Peter's
in magnitude and magnificence. It is called St. Paul's
Beyond the Walls.

We then visited the English cemetery, where Shelley's
grave is — such a heavenly spot as it is! And also Keats'
grave, which is in the old part of the cemetery, where
is also the Pyramid of Caius Cestus. It is a fine little
pyramid, but looks something of a toy after the monsters
of Gizeh! There were so many interesting things pointed
out to us there on the Appian Way, and we had a near
view of the old walls and aqueducts of Claudius, and
the Gate of St. Paul, which used to be called Ostiense.
In fact it seemed to me that there was almost as much

that is thrilling to be seen outside the walls as inside Rome.

Then we drove back to the city, passed the new quay of the Tiber, and brought up at the Pantheon, which is truly a marvel. While it is really a monument of ancient Rome, it is in such a perfect state of preservation that it seems to bring the ancient city to life again. It is used now as the mausoleum for the graves of the Italian kings, and Victor Emmanuel's grave stands opposite to Raphael's tomb. We wound up with the Pantheon, and, as we mounted the carriage again, we implored our driver in a feeble voice to take us home!

May 3rd

SIGHT-SEEING in Rome is hard work! We spent yesterday morning in the Vatican Museum of Statues — another revelation of great things. Amongst others the Apollo Belvedere, the Laocoön of Praxiteles, and the Wrestlers of Canova, all of which are memorable sights. It was literally a morning spent with the gods! We were also conducted by an obliging official to a glass door overlooking the private garden and windows of the Pope's apartment, where there was a superb view of the Sabine mountains, the city, and its surroundings.

In the afternoon we just walked about the streets of Rome for the purpose of familiarizing ourselves with some of the many fine columns, fountains, and palaces we had visited before. The Trajan Column and the Forum demand more than one visit, and though we have driven by many times on our rounds, that is hardly enough. The same may be said of the Fountain of Trevi, which is really a very unusual conception.

This morning we drove to the Villa Borghese through its delightful park or garden, now annexed or about to be annexed to the Pincian Gardens. The Villa now is just a museum and nothing else. Frank Beebe told us on no account to miss it, and spoke as if it was the only-*only!* To be candid, however, I found the collection, both of statuary and paintings, a sort of anti-climax after what we had already seen. There were pictures of Titian, Correggio, Perugino, Domenichino, and others — old masters galore, but somehow they did not impress me, with few exceptions, as the best examples of these. What did interest me very much, however, was the rest of our morning's exploits. We went to two remarkable churches — the Santa Maria Della Vittoria and the Santa Maria degli Angeli — a magnificent church which occupies the Pinacotheca, or the great hall of the Baths of Diocletian, altered by Michaelangelo for the purposes of Christian worship. There is also the tomb of Salvator Rosa.

The most unique thing we saw this morning was the Capuccini in the Piazza Barberini. Not the church itself in particular, although it contains the splendid picture of the Archangel Michael by Guido, which we are all so familiar with from its numerous reproductions, but because of the four low, vaulted chambers under the church which form the cemetery of the convent. The walls and ceilings are covered with the skulls and bones of the defunct monks, and in each vault are whole skeletons of some of the principals, dressed in their moks, robes and cauls, either standing in niches or reclining — a gruesome sight! If I thought that my bones were to be exhibited to the eyes of survivors in such a guise it would add to death a horror where there was none before! The skulls and detached bones are all arranged in the most artistic — I had almost said beautiful — designs, and even the candelabra and hanging lanterns are made of bones selected from various appropriate parts of the holy fathers' anatomy. When a monk dies he is first buried in these vaults under some earth brought from Jerusalem, which is very dry and causes the flesh to become rapidly desiccated. They put him in the oldest grave, from which the bones of the last occupant are then removed and placed on exhibition in the vaults with the rest of them. What a strange idea, isn't it?

I don't think I have told you of all the churches we have visited — there are so many of them. But I should not have omitted the Basilica of St. John Lateran, which is famous. The site alone would make it so, for it has such a history. It was originally the house of the senator Plautius Lateranus, who was put to death by Nero. Then it passed into the hands of the family of Marcus Aurelius, who was born near the palace, and after that Constantine gave it to the Bishops of Rome for an Episcopal residence. Later Constantine founded the Basilica, and helped to dig the foundations with his own hands. It has always been regarded as the most important of all the Christian churches in Rome, and the Chapter still takes precedence over Saint Peter's. When a new Pope is elected the ceremony takes place there.

Close by is a small chapel built for the preservation of the Sacred Steps, which, according to tradition, were used by Christ in ascending to Pilate's Pratorium in Jerusalem whence they were brought by the mother of Constantine, Saint Helena. Pious Catholics ascend them on their knees, no easy task, as it is quite a high flight, at the top of which is the Holy of Holies, where the Pope alone officiates, as a rule. We saw a number of good people ascending — an extremely slow process. And one rheumatic old man was having a pathetically hard time!

Rosie seems to be enjoying her visit to Rome up to

the hilt, and is revelling in all the churches and galleries to her heart's content. We are going back to Naples next Saturday, a few days sooner than we intended, in order to give her an opportunity to see it again after so many years. We have really seen an enormous deal of Rome in a short time. Although, of course, we have by no means exhausted it, yet we should not be able to take in much more without a plethora, unless we were making a prolonged stay and could afford to take our sight-seeing in a leisurely way from now forward.

There are yet many villas and palaces to be seen. Of the latter, we have so far only been to the Palazzo Mattei, the Quirinal, and the Doric — from outside, also the Barbarini and the Farnesi. We intend to make an excursion to Hadrian's Villa, which comprises such a number of different things that the wonder is how any one could be expected to see it all in one day.

May 5th
WE HAVE had our delayed excursion to Tivoli and Hadrian's Villa at last! We were greeted this morning by a heavenly day, with plenty of light clouds to screen us from the glare, and a delightful breeze which saved us from the dragged feeling one always has on walking over grounds and ruins in sultry weather. We took the train to Tivoli after breakfast, hired a comfortable carriage, and drove to the " sights."

First there was the charming old Villa d'Este, and a prolonged ramble over its splendid, old-fashioned garden, rich in fine vistas. We looked towards Soracte, the Alban Hills, and the little town on top of a high hill was pointed out to us as the place from which the Sabine women were raped. I should have said that before visiting the Villa d'Este we drove around the ridge of the glen, and got a splendid view of the waterfalls. These are really artificial, being the result of two tunnels bored through Mount Catillo by Gregory XVI in consequence of a great flood which caused much damage. The town is now protected from inundations by this outlet, provided for the waters of the Anio when swelled by rains, and the result is two really fine waterfalls, one of which falls into the valley from a height of 500 feet. There are a number of smaller falls which greatly add to the beauty of the scene, with their gush and liveliness.

We did not descend to the Grotto of the Sibyl because we had reason to think that it would not be time well spent, but we went to see the fullest view of the falls from the grounds of Villa or Hotel Gregoriana, which answered every purpose. There were also some quaint ruins in sight near the falls — the Temple of Vesta, or Hercules Satanus, it has not been decided which by the authorities, so, perhaps it is just as well that it should go by the more popular name, the Temple of the Sibyl.

Whenever a circular edifice is found with Corinthian columns they always begin by calling it a Temple of Vesta! Having been told by a very nice guide (who spoke the purest of Italian by the way,) that we should get a really good lunch at the Hotel Regina, we proceeded thither, before attacking Hadrian's Villa, which we knew would be a long session, and therefore we reserved it for the last. With renewed strength and vigor we repaired thither after a satisfactory meal, with our purist guide, who proved very intelligent, and conducted us over the intricate ways of the Hadrian grounds as expeditiously as possible. There is so much to be seen there that this was very desirable.

Why it should be called a " villa " passes my understanding — it resembles more our idea of a University enclosure had the Romans been given to universities as we understand them. There is a Greek theatre, a Hall of Philosophers, a temple — the Serapeon of Canapus, a Basilica, a large, oblong portico with a double colonnade, an open court used for gymnastic sports with a plunge bath in the middle and a peristyle. Then there is the Imperial Palace, the Imperial Baths, or bathing establishment as it should be called, I think, and a little circular building called the Nympheum.

Most of these buildings are not too far gone to be still interesting and suggestive ruins. Of course all the statues have been removed to the Vatican and other galleries, but some good mosaic pavements are still shown, particularly in the hospital wards, for there was also a hospital in Hadrian's Villa! Apart from the ruins there is a splendid outlook over the Campagna — particularly at the end of the portico, or Stoa Pacile. It was a delightful ramble over the ruins, which have an altogether undiluted, ancient Roman atmosphere. It seems a funny way to put it, but I should say that here at Tivoli one gets an impression of concentrated essence of Rome! I think Tivoli would be a charming place to spend a week in if one only could spare the time — the air being most bracing and exhilarating, and the surrounding country, including a fairly near view of the Sabine and Alban hills, being most attractive. It was a most successful excursion, and the three of us enjoyed it immensely. We reached our hotel in time for dinner.

May 6th

OUR LAST day in Rome! We spent it in going over the old ground to impress the picture of ancient Rome on our minds. First we drove round the Fountain of Trevi, in which Harry threw a coin the night before his departure from Rome twenty-eight years ago, which, according to common superstition, ensures a return to the sacred city at some future time. It is really a magnificent fountain of noble design, well worth looking at many times. Then we went to take leave of Trajan's Column, and descended into the little Forum in which it stands, examining the odds and ends of columns and statuary which constitute the ruins; thence to the picture gallery of Saint Lucca, to complete the purchase of a picture which Harry had taken a fancy to, and for which he had negotiated the day before; afterwards to the Cloaca Maxima, which name suggests something more dignified than a " chief sewer." We took a last look at the Tiber near the new quay, the broken bridge, the Temple of Vesta, the house of Cola di Rienzi, and the church of Saint Cecilia, winding up at the Roman Forum, where we lingered a long time, locating thoroughly all the famous old landmarks of " the heart of Ancient Rome."

Then, hungry and exhausted we betook ourselves to a famous restaurant hard by on the Palatine, which has appropriated to itself the old Palace of Constantine for carrying on its benevolent functions of feeding hungry tourists. There we sat for over half an hour, refreshing ourselves with meat and drink and a splendid view of the old Circus Maximus. After lunch we went to the Monastery of the Knights of Malta, on the Palatine, where we looked at the Dome of Saint Peter's, first through a hole in the garden gate and afterwards from a fine avenue of trees, whence one gets also an extensive view over the Campagna. After this very full day we dined at the Café Colonna, and then home to bed.

Hotel Santa Lucia, Naples, May 7th, 1904
WE LEFT Rome for Naples at 1.50 P.M., and reached Naples at 7.30 P.M. in time for dinner. We have charm-

ing rooms looking out on the quay and with a fine view of old Vesuvius. Rosie is delighted to have a chance to see Naples as it is today. It was on her account that we left Rome three days earlier than we intended, in order to give her this opportunity.

May 8th

WE SPENT this morning in the Museum, pointing out our favourites to Rosie, and, after lunching at a restaurant in the Gallery Principe Umberto I, we went to Posilipo, thence to Pozzuoli, a charming drive, including a most interesting outlook over the Bay and islands at " Bella Vista," and some " sights." First there was the Salfatara Amphitheatre and Serapeum, but really we have been so glutted with ruins lately that these did not hold us spellbound. What was much more thrilling was a ramble over the extinct crater of Solfatara, where the ground is hot under one's feet and seems as if it might crack, gape open, and swallow one up at any moment; where sulphuric fumes assail one's nostrils, where one comes every now and then to a large hole in the ground with boiling lava bubbling up and forming a kind of lava whirlpool.

But what makes one really marvel the most in this hell-gate-like enclosure is the sight of the exquisite wild flowers which flourish there. Two kinds of beautiful and most uncommon orchids I gathered there, besides a very handsome variety of bell-heather, wild roses, and all sorts of other beautiful blooming plants and shrubs. It was a veritable garden, such as might allure lovers of flowers to the sulphurous depths which it seems to cover.

We then drove to the Grotto del Cane, which is so charged with warm, carbonic-acid gas that no creature could live in it for many minutes. Nero, it is said, used to amuse himself by throwing his slaves into it for the pleasure of seeing them die. Some rather interesting experiments are shown there with the gas, beyond the usual one of holding a dog in the fumes till it is overcome. The animal recovers quickly, however, as soon as he is set free again, otherwise the experiment would not be tolerated. We took the train from Pozzuoli home, for the sake of variety, and came out at La Torretta — its terminus. Naples is one of the places which, to be thoroughly enjoyed, demands that you should take many excursions like these, for its surroundings are altogether enchanting.

May 10th

THIS afternoon Harry took Rosie to Capo-di-Monte and the San Martino, while I remained at home to dispatch some correspondence and pack for our journey tomorrow. Yesterday there was not much to record. Rosie and I went into one or two churches — amongst others the S. Francesco da Paula, which looks like the Pantheon inside, and the rest of the time we simply strolled about the streets and gardens. We are all three of us sorry that it is our last day here. Our little Italian episode has been a very sweet one!

May 11th

OUR SHIP, the " Canopic," was quoted to sail today at 3 P.M., but she did not move off, really, till five. Rosie, whose train for Rome and Bologna was to leave at 2.55, came to see us on board. We left the hotel early to give her time for it. She had never seen one of the big liners, so she wanted to, and the size of the " Canopic " quite took her breath away. After she had taken a good survey of our stateroom, etc., we put her into her omnibus on the wharf, and sent her, in charge of the hotel porter, to the station. We bade each other adieu in the happy conviction that her visit with us had been a perfect success, and that the recollection of it would be a joy both to her and to us for many a day!

The weather is lovely and we are making a favourable start.

S. S. " Canopic," May 12th, 1904

WE SIGHTED Sardinia this morning early, and have had it with us, sometimes in the rear, sometimes in the distance, all day. It is now late in the afternoon, but some of its outlying rocks and islands are still very distinct and *seem* very near. If Sardinia were not in the way we should see Corsica, so says the captain.

May 13th

YESTERDAY was also fine. The captain says the Algerian coast was dimly visible. Too dimly for my vision. This morning's sunlight revealed to us beautiful Sierra Nevadas, and their exquisite outlines, slightly veiled in a light haze, remained in sight throughout the day. Our latest excitement was the famous Rock of Gibraltar, which we approached a little before sundown. We went so near that we had a good look at it in detail, fortress and all. It really is a wonder, and you really must hold your breath when you first contemplate its perpendicularities!

May 15th

SINCE we passed the shores of Gibraltar, which we must have left behind us in the night, there has been no more land in sight, only sea and sky, but at least smooth sea, although the sky has been somewhat overcast today. The next and last land we sight will be the Azores, before reaching Boston Light.

May 17th

YESTERDAY we had another beautiful day, and somewhat cooler. Towards evening the wind rose, there was more motion, and some of the passengers were laid low. A hard storm came up in the night, and today has been still active. In fact we are having a taste of good, old-fashioned, nasty Atlantic weather! We sighted the Azores — Punta Delgarda Light — this evening at eight. A typhoon struck us later. We are to lie off tonight and start tomorrow at 10 A.M., so we shall have a chance to go ashore if we choose to get up early, and we *shall* choose if the weather be fair. The captain says it will be.

May 18th

PUNTA DELGARDA was a pretty sight this morning. A peaceful, quiet-looking, pink-and-white little town, lying in the curve of the harbour at the foot of rolling and cone-shaped hills, cultivated up to their summits, with some shapely mountains in the near distance, here and there a windmill, and a large number of very decorative trees of the cryptomeria family. We landed in row-boats, seven of us in a boat, for we were joined by a few of our fellow travellers. We strolled about the streets, which surprised us by their extreme and un-Portuguese neatness and cleanliness. We noticed several houses, the entire faces of which were done in pretty blue-and-white, glazed tiles. The other unusual thing we saw was a little cart drawn by a big, black sheep, who seemed to take to his harness quite kindly. It is a friendly little town, and the air is delicious.

There is a charming square, or common, planted with queer trees, on one side of which is the Cathedral and the Hospital. We visited the Fortress, an interesting old place, built of the volcanic rock which is in evidence

The Azores: The Harbor of Fayal

everywhere, and with which the very streets are paved. All sorts of flowers were growing about it, looking as though they had come up of themselves — nasturtiums, wandering Jew, and candytuft filled the moat, and the walls were well decorated with maidenhair fern and the usual flowers that grow out of old plaster and stone. The general effect of the town would be Spanish except for the fact that it is so clean and sweet. There was a church on a square, close to the wharf, the *façade* of which was most queer and attractive — Moorish in style, but the inside was ugly and belied the outside.

We ended up our outing with a walk over the beautiful old Borge Garden, which is well worth exploring. It is full of the most beautiful trees and palms of every kind. Camellia trees of great size, and all kinds of flowers which with us would not be abloom till July or August. Salvia, for instance. The garden was full of birds, wild canaries bursting their throats with song, and many other strange varieties. It was hard to tear oneself away from all these green, blooming, and chirping things, but we had to be back on board for breakfast at 9.30. We started soon after ten, and the pretty little island was soon behind us.

May 19*th*

LAST night we passed Fayal and the beautiful and symmetrical Mount Pico. This morning I spent in conversation with some American missionaries from India, who told me many interesting things about Indian customs that I did not know. The weather is overcast today, but the sea is quiet.

May 21*st*

YESTERDAY was a fine day, but an uneventful one. Today the weather is ugly; it rains, and the sea is kicking up quite a good deal. Withal it is unpleasantly warm and sticky.

May 22nd

THIS morning the fog horn sounded for the first time. The fog is not very thick or alarming, though, I suppose we must be off the Banks. Much indignation is felt by the passengers that we are not to land till two days later than due. We *should* be in Boston Monday the 23rd. We shall not be, so the captain says, till Wednesday the 25th.

May 24th

WE HAVE just taken the pilot on board, and if all goes well we are to land tonight. Yesterday it was foggy all day, also this morning the fog was still lurking, but now it is clear again, I am thankful to say.

So this ends our journeyings! We have been away from home about eleven months. It would seem almost impossible to have visited all four quarters of the globe and to have seen so much in less than one year! Will everything seem tame to us for a time? I think not. There will be such sweet compensations — the reunion with family and friends, and, after that, our beloved Ingonish to look forward to.

INDEX TO JOURNAL–LETTERS